Southern Transformation: Searching for educational success in South Auckland

Southern Transformation:
Searching for educational success in South Auckland

Bernardine Vester

VICTORIA UNIVERSITY PRESS

TE WHARE WĀNANGA O TE ŪPOKO O TE IKA A MĀUI
VICTORIA
UNIVERSITY OF WELLINGTON

VICTORIA UNIVERSITY PRESS
Victoria University of Wellington
PO Box 600 Wellington
vup.victoria.ac.nz

First published 2016

National Library of New Zealand Cataloguing-in-Publication Data:
Vester, Bernardine.
Southern transformation : searching for educational success in South Auckland / Bernardine Vester.
Includes bibliographic references.
ISBN 978-1-77656-096-7
1. Educational equalization—New Zealand—South Auckland.
2. Educational planning—New Zealand—South Auckland.
I. Title.
379.260932—dc 23

Printed by Ligare

Contents

Though wonderful to watch, transformation from larva to pupa or from pupa to butterfly is not a particularly pleasant process for the subject involved. There comes for every caterpillar a difficult moment when he begins to feel pervaded by an odd sense of discomfort. It is a tight feeling—here about the neck and elsewhere, and then an unbearable itch. Of course he has moulted a few times before, but *that* is nothing in comparison to the tickle and urge that he feels now. He must shed that tight dry skin, or die.

—Vladimir Nabokov

Foreword

by Gary Hawke

Southern Transformation is a compelling account of how educational issues appear on the ground and the challenges involved in any attempt to resolve major social issues.

In 1996 I chaired the Advisory Council on Quality of Education at the Education Review Office (ERO) when, under the leadership of Judith Aitken, we published what was characterised as a highly critical review of the quality of education provided by schools in Māngere and Ōtara. The topic had been a concern for as long as I could remember and there had been no signs of improvement. The ERO review was widely condemned but there was a positive reaction: the Ministry of Education's consequent intervention, 'Strengthening Education in Māngere and Ōtara', encouraged schools not to wait passively for the ministry to act, but to take initiative and define with ministry staff reasonable expectations for the improvement of their students' educational outcomes. They did.

While one sometimes still hears about the 'destructive' ERO report, after about 15 years I was present when educationists in Māngere and Ōtara acknowledged that it had created a positive outcome. Now, the challenge does not need to come from outside. *Southern Transformation* leaves no doubt that effective demand for better education is endogenous.

Whenever I hear it argued that there is an obvious way to secure an improved policy outcome, I ask whether what is obvious will not already have occurred to those responsible for the policy implementation. It usually has. By carefully considering the constraints that have prevented its adoption, one can promote the change that secures *most* of the desired outcome without incurring unintended and unwanted side effects. The core of policy development is through selection of feasible alternatives rather than assertion of a desirable outcome.

Furthermore, any significant policy intervention will have multiple objectives. Thus the introduction of National Standards intended to ensure that parents would not be fobbed off with generalities about performance at 'more or less the expected level', and even more, that parents would not be given inconsistent messages by successive teachers, especially at the major transition points in a school career. However the prime purpose of National Standards was always as a diagnostic tool, not as a signalling device. The teaching task did not end with a judgement of achievement; rather the judgement should initiate inquiry into what next steps would best promote the individual student's learning and what was needed for the teacher to be able to stimulate those next steps. There were other objectives such as the creation of data that permitted analysis of where resources (primarily teachers' time and energy) would have most impact on student learning. But it is through facilitating diagnosis by teachers that National Standards have most impacted student achievement, especially for Māori and Pasifika students. Something regarded as needed for at least 40 years has begun to be realised. It is by identifying students at risk of not achieving and responding to that risk that National Standards have been most fruitful.

The skills of teachers are not apparent to all whānau or education commentators. Mastery of the syllabus is important, but even more so are reliable judgements about the core competencies of the New Zealand curriculum—thinking, using language, symbols and texts, managing the self, relating to others, and participating and contributing. These are not qualities that can be directly assessed in schools, but they should be the basis for informing whānau about student progress and for self-evaluation of teaching and school management.

At an even deeper level, community values are important. New Zealand has a strong tradition of 'equal' access to public resources. Once we go beyond public rhetoric, it is obvious that what is important is that everybody who satisfies specified eligibility conditions has access to a public service. The goal of a quality education for every student requires professional judgement about different treatments for individual students. What should be equalised is opportunity to learn.

Reconciling expert knowledge and community aspirations poses issues far beyond education, and this is clearest in the education sector. Parents and whānau on the one hand, and teachers on the other, are each the best source of some relevant knowledge, but we need mutual respect for when the other party is better informed. We learnt in the 1980s that if 'community development' is allowed to become a synonym for political activism, it will be ineffective.

Southern Transformation tells us about the knowledge located in the communities of South Auckland. When that knowledge is combined with teachers' expertise, and with equal expertise in the design and management of public policy, we can be confident that we will build on what has been achieved in the last 20 years.

Preface

Because I work in South Auckland, I must first say who I am and where I have come from. My mihi is European. I am a daughter of the post-war baby boom. My father was an assisted immigrant who arrived here by ship in 1952 with £20 and two suitcases and was assigned to work in the dairy factory at Waharoa. It was his gateway to Kiwidom. My mother arrived here on a 'bride flight' a few months later. My first language is Dutch, my schooling was in the South Waikato rural town of Putaruru, my university education (in language, literature and linguistics) was at Waikato University, and my early married years were also in small Waikato towns. When my husband was appointed to Tereora College on Rarotonga, my two-year stint in the Cook Islands formed my understanding of culture and context. I'm an educator by profession. When I was elected vice-president of the New Zealand Post Primary Teachers' Association (PPTA), I became versed in the big picture of educational reform and the alliances and feuds, relationships and subtleties of the education sector. I was later appointed to lead a Manukau City Council-owned charitable trust for education called COMET, and I quickly discovered I needed to learn how to connect what I already knew about the education system to something somewhat alien to most educators: the twin local government agendas of community development and economic development.

Community development is a big idea. Tweak the synapses of community development activists and you will spark off issues like poverty and inequality, youth unemployment and job creation, healthy homes and affordable housing, healthy children and active lifestyles, student achievement and lifelong learning, environmental sustainability and climate change, and spiritual health. These topics shape the ecosystem of communities; their social, economic, cultural and environmental wellbeing. They often surface as separate problems, connected to education but apart from it. Policy writers often call them 'wicked' problems, because they are horribly complex and have resisted solutions[1]—problems like youth unemployment, family violence, debt or the diabetes epidemic. From the mid-1970s councils were encouraged by legislation to provide community development functions.[2] I soon met the Manukau City Council's force of community development workers, became aware of the role of 'community houses', and learnt about community development services. In my new position, I found that community development is a philosophy, a way of thinking about how communities make decisions regarding their futures. I discovered that while education and community development ought to go together, in real life they rarely connect. I uncovered local stories that illustrated how the public policy which shapes these two sectors fails to deliver transformation—or any kind of community empowerment.

Economic development is a second big idea. The conversation revolves around infrastructure, investment and skills. As a teacher, I never had any connection to the economic aspirations of the communities I taught in. How could I have prepared students for a world of work that I knew so little about? I discovered that 'logistics' was a major employer in the area. I hadn't realised that it applied to a whole industry that included Auckland Airport, freight companies and warehouses, the language of supply chains and 'just-in-time delivery', a science of materials-handling which included forklifts and fancy trucks operating in a competitive world full of new technologies. In Manukau City, the connection between skills and jobs was of enormous concern to city leaders and the council's economic development experts. I came to see why. For businesses to compete effectively in the global market they need access to skilled labour and schooling that delivers it. So what was the role of the council in growing the talent pool?

Over the dozen years I led Manukau City Council's purpose-built education trust, I worked with people who, though *not* part of the education milieu, worried about system underperformance. They proposed all sorts of fanciful solutions, as people who don't actually have to make things work on the ground will do. At the same time, it was frustrating to recognise that viewpoints from the world outside schools bounced right off education's defences. These learning fortresses sat high above their communities, the people inside often paternalistic and professionally isolated. It was as if schools stood apart and education's problems could be solved without referring to *place*. Public schools are supposed to be part of a network of learning institutions, like Russian dolls nesting inside each other, serving a neighbourhood, a suburb, a city, a nation. But the education system does not operate like this.

The case for a supercity was at least partially built on the observation that social change in Auckland could not be driven from Wellington.[3] To reconstruct Auckland without bridging its chasms of ethnicity and social class would be a colossal waste of time. It is no surprise, then, that transformation in South Auckland became one of the top priorities in the adoption of the new city's first ten-year plan. Government agencies, too, added South Auckland as a priority area.

However, the *how* of transforming South Auckland hasn't been agreed on—or delivered. There is no discernible theory of change or any system-wide direction of travel.

A city leader tells me that three things matter for Auckland's economic future: modern infrastructure, investment and talent. This book is about the last item in that equation— talent—and in particular how public policy-making has contributed to underperformance and widening disparities in Auckland's south. Education needs the big ideas of community development and economic development to play its part in transformation. This book suggests a leap into *place-based* innovation, alongside policy settings that empower communities to work alongside and with the schools and learning institutions that serve them.

Part 1:
The Southern Skills Narrative

1
Looking for results that matter
Introducing South Auckland

In 1984 New Zealand was going broke. Outgoing prime minister Robert Muldoon passed on a financial drama to the newly elected Labour government, led by David Lange. The crisis tipped the post-war social democratic consensus on its head and Chicago school economics arrived on its coat-tails. Given Lange's electoral support base in the Māngere electorate, it is ironic that economic upheaval hit the poor and the unqualified in South Auckland hardest. The calamitous closing of the old railway workshops in Ōtāhuhu and the AFFCO freezing works at Southdown; the reorganisation of the electricity and telecommunications industries; the reorganisation of social systems and the introduction of markets for schools; and the benefit cuts of 1991—these disruptions form the background to Manukau's story.

Stories about communities mostly focus on their leaders and people, not the structures that make them tick. Local government in South Auckland shaped its communities. In Sir Barry Curtis, Manukau had a mayor who was competent and powerful, if a little eccentric. His chief executive, Colin Dale, brought with him a strong community development philosophy. In dealing with the disastrous consequences of government policies in the 1980s on Manukau, both believed it had to be within the power of local government to mitigate social calamity and to stimulate new economic opportunity. Following a savage Education Review Office (ERO) report on schooling in Māngere and Ōtara in 1996, education suddenly became, like the canary in the coalmine, a tangible symptom of communities in crisis. Schools are central to the wellbeing of suburbs. Good schools attract families, businesses and jobs. The problems of schools bounded right across into a local economy already reeling from reform. Education was undermining the city's economic development agenda. The council could not stay on the sidelines.

Sir Barry Curtis called the education leaders of his city together. By one verbal account, the mayor was totally taken aback by the enormity of professional concerns expressed at that meeting. Principals were bitter about the ERO report on their patch and ferocious in defence of their schools. They pleaded for support, mostly in the form of 'more resources'—the government had withdrawn and left a vacuum, whereas the council's interest promised help. Yet pouring resources into schools was not what the mayor could do. Sir Barry, Colin Dale and Dr Jack MacDonald of the Manukau Institute of Technology pulled together a working party to develop an education strategy that would sit alongside the city's Economic Development Strategy and Employment Strategy.

With a government uninterested in deep engagement with the council and indifferent to the mayor's interest, what could a local education strategy look like? It says much about the quality of the people involved that the idea did not head into the too-hard basket. Instead, the working party prepared two simple recommendations for the council. Firstly, establish a stand-alone charitable trust (later called the City of Manukau Education Trust, or COMET). And secondly, give the trust a brief for drawing things together.[1] The net effect was to create an experimental mechanism for city engagement in education. That's how I became involved.

Governments spend a lot of money on education because it powers social change and economic development.[2] Education can be linked to higher wages, lower unemployment, reduced crime and imprisonment rates, longer life expectancy and better health, and a properly functioning democracy.[3] Professor John Hattie told the 2003 Knowledge Wave conference that New Zealand could become the global flagship for schooling.[4] If we want our best and brightest to stay here, the professor advised, to bring expatriates home and to improve the standard of living of all New Zealanders, we could do no better than invest in our schooling system. Success for all in education would be a coup that would add immensely to our economic standing and international reputation.

Except for a worrying hiccup. It turns out that our education system's gloss in the global league is fading. Andreas Schleicher, the 'world's schoolmaster',[5] special advisor on education policy to the OECD's secretary-general, and director of the OECD Programme for International Student Assessment (PISA), pointed out on his 2013 visit to the country that New Zealand's education system has plateaued rather than improved. Despite a history of producing top-notch achievers and well-rounded people with skills and personal attributes that make Kiwis highly sought-after employees around the world, we have the second highest level of relative educational disparity in the OECD. Students from high-income households are nearly three times more likely to achieve university entrance than students from low-income households. The basic minimum qualification you need to operate in the knowledge economies of the globe, NCEA Level 2, is a challenge for too many students in low-income communities. In round figures, out of the three-quarters of a million young New Zealanders in schools, about 100,000 of them won't reach their potential. Disadvantage accumulates like dust-blobs in forgotten corners. Auckland's southern suburbs have become disconnected from the economic wealth of the city as a whole.

We've known about these social and educational disparities for some time. Underperformance has become a convenient rationale for all the major education policy shifts in New Zealand over the last quarter century. Having devolved the governance and administration of schools in 1989, governments one after the other overhauled the qualifications system, redesigned the curriculum, turned teacher education and early childhood services into a market too, and rejigged post-compulsory education and training. Employment task forces critically examined youth [un]employment and were appalled by the wastage. 'Jobs Jolt' initiatives and other investments were designed to do something about it. In a drive for Better Public Services, policymakers have sharpened system 'targets', as though they might, of themselves, deliver the magic punch for a turnaround in educational success—especially in South Auckland.

But applying generic policies to place-based problems hasn't delivered change. Giving *all* schools a funding boost or a staffing boost might look electorally appealing on the surface, but it doesn't close the gaps; it never has done. Despite every effort from those working in poor schools and low socio-economic communities to make policy initiatives, flagship programmes and market systems transformative, they have regularly fallen short of being so by the limitations of scope placed upon them, and often by the lack of a sufficient link to any bold, ongoing strategy that is relevant to *place*. We search for effective interventions as if there were a single cure yet to be discovered. With a touch of cynicism, eminent educator Dr Stuart Middleton told me when I arrived here: 'The road to educational nirvana is paved with pilot programmes in South Auckland.' The remedy for educational underperformance has too often been pinned down to one or two pills that schools could take, as though the ills of education could be solved by education policy alone.

Where is South Auckland? It doesn't exist on a map. When people talk about 'South Auckland' they are really talking about the suburbs of Ōtara, Papatoetoe, Ōtāhuhu, Māngere, Manurewa and Papakura. These are no minor specks. Each may be larger than provincial cities like Nelson or Hastings or Palmerston North. Somehow, South Auckland exhibits an amoeba-like geography that is as much about income, class and ethnicity as it is about place. While the name 'South Auckland' carries only symbolic value, it is a space with real and rising political clout. A good voter turnout here delivered Helen Clark three terms of office. It put the supercity's first mayor in his chair. City-making, as

Aucklanders are learning, is about being liveable—and liveability is bound up in economic and social wellbeing. Education has an important part to play in that.

So now, over half a dozen years into the new Auckland, city leaders and national politicians alike cast about for the solutions to under-achievement in South Auckland. They leap at the idea of transforming the place into a vibrant, socially dynamic, economically healthy and culturally cohesive essence. If only we could 'fix' South Auckland, the whole of Aotearoa would be a richer and more comfortable place to live in. Fixes involve a complex wish list, mostly beginning with the assumption of a single set of social and economic aspirations and national initiatives that are supposed to flow down to local circumstances. Unfortunately, solutions imposed on the *symptoms* of social inequalities, like struggling schools and children who fail to learn, rarely have the results that their backers hope.

Once a month, on Tuesdays, the Ōtara Music Arts Centre (OMAC) hosts a community forum. It's community development in action. Many connections are made here. Today, the chairs are arranged in a large circle in the community hall, with several tiers of ragged circle behind. Somewhere between the front and the back is the demarcation between participant and observer. Here, people from community-based organisations and agencies work the network, make presentations or discuss significant local issues. Everyone hopes for the nugget of opportunity, the 'Eureka' discovery that somehow from the relationships in the room new possibilities for Ōtara will emerge. There's never a shortage of characters. From the impassioned ex-prisoner to the perpetual comedian, there's an endearing but loony looseness to these proceedings.

Sometimes, though, the monthly meeting has a less attractive side. I recall some of the hundred faces in the room on my first time there. Tony, then the Manukau City Council's community advisor, facilitated the meeting. Bill and his diabetes support team is there in the front row; Jim, representing some now-extinct Ōtara trust; Lusi, reliably there for the Ōtara Tongan Wardens; Mereana, from the Māori Wardens; Yvonne from Ōtara Neighbourhood Support; Gray, representing himself. There are bound to be people from the Cook Island, Samoan and Niuean network, the Ōtara Mainstreet Association, South Seas Healthcare, the Citizens Advice Bureau, the Community Law Centre, the Budgeting Service, churches and youth groups and community safety teams, political aspirants and local identities, and even the Inland Revenue Department (IRD) on its community outreach—if you want to know what is going on in Ōtara, you should be here. I'm new today. I feel pretty conspicuous because my sponsor, Olivia, carefully seats us in the front row. Olivia stands up to present me in my new role as manager of an education trust hosted at the Manukau Institute of Technology campus next door.

The flavour of what happens next remains with me. Three or four speakers stand up and begin hectoring Olivia and the audience. *How come this woman is here? When did the council decide to make this appointment to the trust? Why were Ōtara people not informed about the opportunity to be appointed to this role?*

It's what I represent that they are talking about. I'm a blonde who has suddenly turned up southside, and I'm being introduced as part of an ongoing parade of middle-class faces that arrive, get well paid to do something in the community, and leave. Our investment in Ōtara appears slight. We don't live here or educate our children here. We don't shop here, or go to church here. We get paid well to advise or counsel or facilitate, support or manage; rarely to empower. Our relationships are superficial. Our clothes and our cars and even our language are different. We're professional. We pretend that we are part of the community, but really we are tea-bag dippers, rarely steeping in the politics and personalities of the place, staying only one or two years. The pilots and programmes we lead get covered over like moss over damp pavers, leaving barely visible traces. We don't 'do' transformation, because the urge for change is too slow for our careers. How dare we imagine that we can change things!

My face feels hot and flushed. The tirade is not long, but the community anger behind it is clear enough. I've been other places where good manners come second to point-scoring. But here the tart message is: we, the Ōtara community, are looking for results that matter—but the mahi, the work, must involve us.

Just as South Auckland is not named on the map, nor is Manukau City. It's a hollowed form of its former status, now just a high-rise secondary centre called Wiri. In January 2000 it had a beating heart. A welcome letter invited me into the Manukau City Council team. I was told 'someone' needed to make education work in Manukau. It was an unreasonably tall order for a someone with no phone, no desk and no bank account. Many educational issues lay waiting for me to discover and address. The whole school-to-work connection seemed broken. Truancy was endemic. Literacy was an issue, including adult and workplace literacy. The digital revolution was underway, but not here. Early childhood education was suffering from market failure. Adult education was frozen in a time-warp of the 70s. Young people were pouring out of Manukau's schools, but didn't have the skills to meet labour market needs. Where did this litany of problems even begin? Schools were bemused and suspicious about local government interest in them and principals non-committal about getting involved in yet another 'initiative' being run by people who didn't know about *their* schools—as though principals owned them. I was floored. It was all very well for the Manukau City Council to establish a trust for education, but that in itself wasn't *doing* something. My trustees could define the kinds of things a council-owned charitable trust should do: to advocate, lead, facilitate, co-ordinate. But these words would not be enough. The trust needed to secure ongoing political commitment from the council and the community for its work, and to build credibility for engagement with principals and school trustees. What could a trust do with a workforce of one?

I started my own picture of the learning landscape in this patch of Auckland. No one else had one. It was complicated. I could observe educational markets—the early childhood market (approaching 1300 services across Auckland), the rivalrous schools market (around 520 schools, 132 of them in Manukau), uncountable private training enterprises and a dotted arc of industry training organisations. Crown-owned tertiary education institutions were in a market too, pulling education's strings through their faculties of education, their social services training and their links to research and evaluation services. A support services market contained myriad not-for-profits, 'initiatives' and entities orbiting the formal institutions. And then there were inward-looking closed networks: teachers' and principals' associations and subject associations and school trustee networks and unions. There were thousands more people to 'engage with' about learning in the south. Local government had a broad reach into learning through public libraries, museums, galleries, theatres and cultural services. It partnered with schools to run walking buses and Travelwise programmes; it led community development networks, and ran sport and recreation and leisure services. Add the community sector: it includes iwi networks, some actively engaged in educational initiatives and organisations for literacy, workers, refugees, migrants, community education and parent education services. Youth organisations, churches, marae, philanthropists and planners filled the learning spaces in between. All of these were 'stakeholders' in the discussion about education in South Auckland. Mapping them all was exhausting, and never finished. How could anyone turn this big basket of incredible resources for learning into a cohesive effort to make a difference?

Collaborative project work seemed the obvious answer. Where to begin? In project after project, our trust showed it was doing something valuable by drawing in new resources to the poorest communities and involving them in collaborative project design. We set up a pilot partnership for intergenerational literacy which over the next ten years gained international attention for its outcomes. A highly successful youth transitions initiative involved multiple partners and over four years successfully placed over a thousand young people in positive post-school destinations.

Projects build partnerships, engage politicians, demonstrate action and show off outcomes. Successful projects are terribly seductive for their 'owners' and shareholders. The City of Manukau Education Trust was getting kudos for its work. Central government policymakers watched from the sidelines. Yet we were slowly being sucked into becoming a service provider in a crowded and competitive provider market. Were projects the tools for social transformation?

Something was missing in the landscape, but I couldn't quite put my finger on it. To get schools and educational services to work together, to connect them to the big ideas of community and economic development, there needed to be something in between. An international visitor pointed out the missing part: South Auckland needed an intermediary.

How do intermediary organisations work in other contexts and places? I researched their various forms—in the fields of youth connection,[6] workforce development[7] and social investment[8]—as loose regional or sectoral networks, not-for-profit organisations, network-owned companies or public-private partnerships. Intermediary work was full of dense definitions. A *project-focused intermediary* joins up two partners—a learning institution and a business, for example, in a 'school–business partnership'. We facilitated some of that. A *system-focused intermediary* facilitates complex networks with multiple actors. We co-ordinated some of these. In travels and internet explorations I discovered many other intermediary organisations operating in cities all around the world, powerful in their effects, yet often invisible. The evaluative literature about them shows how critical they are to creating results that matter.[9] It was easy to work out that the strength of an intermediary for education and skills in Manukau lies not just in partnership-building, but in being a shape-shifter, a prime mover to new interactions. So what could a system-focused intermediary achieve in Manukau?

Towards a theory of transformation

Education in South Auckland is quicksilver—you see plainly what it is, but you only have to touch it to know that it is something else. The tidal wave of public sector reforms in the 1980s washed educational governance by hierarchy away. Hierarchy had manifest disadvantages: it was too top-down, too inflexible, too slow and too 'captured'. Whatever the original intent of the New Zealand reforms (were they a right-wing plot? an opportunistic take-over? a mistake?),[10] schools and early childhood services were soon governed by the market, and in South Auckland the market was inadequate to the task. Self-management in education was supposed to empower consumers (parents) and offer choice. It took years for the idea to crystallise: reform was making no difference at all to the pattern of problems that triggered it—and might even be making problems worse. I met many educators, principals and sector professionals in our poorest communities who were world leaders in schooling improvement, who cared passionately about the places that they worked in, and who knew how to make a difference in their schools, and did. But it seemed that failing communities and failing schools were always together. New ways of educating did not deliver social or economic transformation.

I'm reminded of the now-apocryphal story from American scientist and philosopher Loren Eiseley, of the thousands of starfish expiring on the windblown beach, and a young boy hurling them back into the surging sea one by one. Shouts a passerby: 'Isn't all of this effort rather pointless? What difference does it make?' In the biting onshore wind, the boy stoops to pick up the next starfish. 'I made a difference to that one,' he replies, flinging it into the tide. Yet when is the starfish project ever done? The power to impact the lives of others is present everywhere. Many schools, learning institutions and projects do make a measurable difference. But the starfish on the beach, waiting to be picked up, are limitless.

Reform is a small word—it suggests a do-up, a makeover, a public policy version of TV's *The Block*. Transformation is an enormous one. Transformation is more than a change in appearance. It's so messy, unsettling, out-of-line, unpredictable, disruptive and even unimaginable that it cuts to the core of our understanding of what was there before. And it's a word city officials bandy about, looking for a 'southern transformation'.

Catchphrases accompany the political intention of transformation. Auckland ought to be, and is, concerned with building, attracting and retaining skills. It's a key economic driver. So when the mayor of the brand-new supercity calls for a comprehensive initiative to address the social challenges of the city's south, who imagines the outcome? In reality, transformation is a distant horizon—and politics, a close one. Most major change initiatives here have had, at best, rather lukewarm returns. Governments and councils mostly only have time for *change* and *shift*, not transformation.

And anyway, transformation to what? Something incrementally better? Words like 'innovation', 'process improvements' and 'transition' might lead people to expect that the project for southern transformation helmed by the supercity would give rise to something altogether more promising. Officials are tempted to trumpet transformation as any old change, almost as if a chain of shifts can eventually get us to an indisputably different place. As evolutionary biologist Richard Dawkins describes it,[11] what inhabits the world today is due to persistent little accumulations of change, sometimes triggered by ruptures (geological or environmental or biological), but mostly because genetic material is endlessly recombined in 'inventive fertility'. Without taking the evolutionary metaphor too far, perhaps the social transformation that policymakers look for in South Auckland is embedded in what has gone on before.

But other theories about the process of change are possible. *Social reproduction theory* suggests parents and society pass on status and values to children, from one generation to the next. One sort of transmission is the everyday, taken-for-granted, this-is-how-we-do-things-around-here cultural kind. Another is essentially social engineering, transmitted through social institutions like schools, the media, churches, the state and the law, community and sports organisations, and so on. Social reproduction theory argues that the so-called institutions of change—schools and churches, for example—are inherently conservative. Schools don't create equal opportunity—instead, they perpetuate the status quo. Real change happens at the margins—or through revolution. Therefore, to transform you must disrupt.

But deliberate disruption, in schooling and social and economic lives, is politically dangerous and professionally scary. It tips over the known and invites in the unknown. Innovation doesn't always bring disruption (you can be incrementally innovative, a bit like the way traffic lights developed from fixed cycles to photosensitive cameras that triggered change, to central control of traffic flows via broadband signals—did you notice?). In scoping the future of secondary schooling in this country, New Zealand's Secondary Futures project (initiated in 2003) discovered that talking about the transformation of schools did not necessarily result in taking action about it. An evaluation of that project described the tension between the 'managerialist' set-up of our education system (a top-down approach, as in the charter to self-managing schools) and a more 'ecological' approach to change.[12] A less disruptive approach might be to look for bottom-up innovation, encouraged and dispersed through the networks of power. 'Visioning' a preferred future, as this project suggested, and then going for it is complex. Schools, especially secondary schools, are trains with carriages fixed by the system, and rearranging them on the academic track takes a lot of back-and-forth shuffling. There's little incentive to reshuffle for the benefit of passengers—the students; it's too disruptive. Metamorphosis is unimaginable shift, and visioning for change is valuable, but insufficient.

Another way of thinking about transformation is through the fashionable global discussion about *convergence*, which describes how governments, mission-led not-for-profits and market-led businesses are coming together to find a common language, a common purpose, and win–win solutions to some of the most intractable problems of education and the world. Harvard University professors and other authoritative eminences point out that governments can't afford to 'own' problems and their solutions any more; not-for-profits must demonstrate value, just like businesses. Businesses, in turn, must recognise shared value as the way to 'fix' the failures of capitalism.[13] Leaders of transformation in all fields must be adept at operating *across* disciplines, like triathletes. Operating from their helicopter vantage point, leaders ought to be able to figure out how all stakeholders can work together.

It's true: the most promising efforts to do something about what policymakers call the 'wicked' issues of learning in communities all seem to involve a multi-partner approach, which offers a rounder view of the shared problem, and catalytic leadership.[14] Convergence is the crucible for social entrepreneurship—

but it needs two things: a new kind of governance over learning, and a new kind of leadership in education. So how do governments and existing educational and community leaders respond to that need?

It seems that while all transformation is change, not all change is transformation.[15] 'Breakthrough innovation'—as the shift to self-managing schools might have been called—has not delivered equity for every student. And, as systems scientist Béla Bánáthy suggests, the history of 'improvement' in South Auckland education hasn't changed the caterpillar into a butterfly—although it may have made the caterpillar faster. Inequalities have widened, not narrowed. So what was the point?

Public policy tinkers at the edges of South Auckland communities. Governments and sector professionals play it safe. They like discrete and limited projects that don't rattle existing power-settings. Projects may add up to a worthy commitment, a gathering up of alliances, each delivering 'measurables'; the KPIs of action. But unfortunately flagship programmes for change, like the government's Investing in Educational Success initiative, become the tomato sauce sloshed on top of everything, improving the taste yet disguising the whiffy stuff beneath. What could governance over *learning* in South Auckland (as distinct from governance over institutions) look like? The central government's urgency for its targets and the Auckland Council's urgency for a southern transformation must surely involve some deeper, more painful and more politically dangerous shifts. Where is the catalytic leadership for this?

Community has a difficult meaning for educators: a community, for schools, is simply the parents or guardians. To principals and boards, community governance screams interference with all of their responsibilities. It suggests a war zone of competing interests. 'Community' feels complicated for education leaders and policymakers, because it takes them outside their silo.[16]

In the community development and economic development contexts, community is a network of geographic, ethnic or social group members. A community-led problem-solving approach requires an understanding of the role of intermediaries, why existing power-holders in the system should accept one, why central government and local government politicians and policymakers might work with one, and how they should do so. Educators need to be part of it. However, policymakers, politicians and institutional leaders like quick wins and visible outcomes. They also want to fund things that make a measurable and immediate difference, not woolly words like 'co-ordinating' or 'community leadership'. As for connecting learning to the big picture of health, jobs and poverty—well, in reality that seems too vague and too hard.

There is a legitimate public interest in how well our schools compare internationally, whether our education system is 'improving' (especially for the disadvantaged), and whether public services meet the needs of the economy. But there is a tension between public and private domains. We get drawn into debating matters of private interest: How is *my* child doing compared with other children at school? And compared with other children across the country? And compared globally? Is the neighbourhood public school a good option for *my* child? This clash between the public interest and the private interest gets in the way of community problem-solving.

The bigger, rounder picture of learning in South Auckland points to the need for a new kind of governance for education. The challenges of education in this country are challenges of *communities*. An adaptive response could be to reshape the relationship between schools and communities in the widest sense—and to rethink altogether the governance settings that shape decision-making across educational institutions. Local government might genuinely be part of the transformation journey.

In this book, the pillar for the theory of educational transformation in South Auckland is the sum of all of the above: the history, the present and the destiny; the pilots, projects and programmes; the structures and processes that create change or block it. To transform, a constellation of approaches will be needed. It seems to me that there is no one set of stars to follow, no one way. Efforts must involve institutions and organisations of all kinds, and different ways of working. Together, these networks and their actions constitute a form of *community governance* over the learning and skills goals for Auckland's south.

Community governance is not a structure in itself, nor is it even a single process. It is a form of collective problem-solving in empowered communities. It involves working and managing networks—the champions, influencers, road-blockers, providers of services and organised lobby groups—that make a place tick. It is also about understanding data and measuring outcomes, getting things done, delivering results that matter. It is the state working with, alongside and through other agencies—public, private, not-for-profit—to get 'desired outcomes'.[17] Desired outcomes are what the government wants (with the democratic mandate of the people), *and* what communities want. When I suggest community governance in this book, I'm really talking about getting to better educational outcomes via community collaboration and a different kind of education policy-making.

So what might be the message to the minister of education from the learning narrative of South Auckland?

Here it is. First, let's begin with the mothers of South Auckland. Intergenerational learning is a critically underdeveloped policy area, and without it South Auckland's potential will not be realised.

Second, learn from experience. The 'back story' of what happened in South Auckland as the early childhood education market failed has contributed to the talent shortfalls we currently face in the labour market. New kinds of learning services are needed, and at scale, to serve the uniquely urbanised social and cultural heritages within South Auckland's families and to grow the economic potential within them.

Third, the self-managing schools model, now a quarter century old, must become next-generation governance. The market's reach has tipped into dysfunctional societal relationships that undermine the public project for learning. Issues of power are central to any model's effectiveness. Too many school boards in South Auckland are unable to fulfill their complex statutory role. To re-empower and refocus them on the things that matter most, there needs to be a powerful intermediary that understands how community inquiry and collaboration works.

Fourth, delete policies with unintended consequences—like the school decile system—and redesign policies with poorly understood outcomes—like attendance services.

Fifth, define what education is for. Is it about jobs? Poverty reduction? Personal or cultural empowerment? Allow communities to own their schools as networks of services that are pitched to success, not failure. Factor in the socio-cultural context in which influence is exerted in South Auckland.

Finally, local governments have a critical role in shaping learning outcomes. Wellington and Auckland must come together to shape better community engagement with the economic and social mission of learning in places where inequalities are now endemic.

I'm mindful, however, of a core Tuesday message from the people I met in Ōtara: *Don't tell our stories for us. Tell your own.* So this is my version of what I've learnt about the potential for transformational shifts for learning in South Auckland.

There are, of course, always other versions.

2

Learning is intergenerational

Why the mothers of South Auckland matter

Hūtia te rito o te harakeke
Kei hea te kōmako e kō?
If you remove the heart of the flax bush
From where will the bellbird sing?

Bro'Town, Mo'Town

Make a difference to the mothers of South Auckland and the impacts can be felt in their families for generations to come.

Take *bro'Town*—the first mainstream, prime-time portrayal of Pacific people on television. It's the [mis]adventures of five Auckland-born fourteen-year-olds, their shared urban home, Morningside, and their daily interactions that make them bros, if not family. The creators of this animated comedy turned the bros into recognisable, archetypal urban Aucklanders that a certain audience could identify with. *Bro'Town*'s stereotype of urban masculinity features also at the movies—in the box-office success of *Sione's Wedding* and later spinoffs. *Bro'Town* is loud and obvious and visible. *Bro'Town* is outside—at school, playing sport, hanging out with mates, forever young and in trouble. Here, street families and blood families exist side by side.

New Zealand's first female Pacific Island judge, Ida Malosi, pithily recognises the influences on the young men who appear before her: 'On Saturday night he committed an egregious violent offence. On Sunday he dutifully did as his mother said, got up and got dressed in his Sunday best and went to Sunday school. On Monday he appeared in court.'[1] She is describing the real-life clout of *bro'Town*'s opposite: mo'Town. Mo'Town is about women and girls. Mo'Town is *inside*, about responsibility and children and making ends meet.

Malosi is part of the august company that calls for greater attention to the mothers of our boys. The late Celia Lashlie wrote powerfully of her belief that it is women who have the power to change the lives of at-risk families, especially children and boys.[2] *Bro'Town* is set in the fictional Morningside. Mo'Town is set in real life, southside. Lashlie recounts the dismal lives of real boys and real mothers. *Bro'Town* is a media hit. Mo'Town isn't. A mo'Town woman is undereducated, unemployable, and scrabbles to live, let alone get ahead. Her needs are largely ignored in our public policy settings. Over the next ten years, Auckland's Māori population is projected to increase by 43,000 people to a population of around 199,000. Pacific people will number 290,000. Most will live southside. The women of these ethnicities will have a bigger influence on Auckland's future than any other single demographic. What are we doing to support them in their motherhood?

The kick-start for transformation is an intense, burning fervour that triggers an overwhelming thirst for something different. Meleane Pau'uvale was once a high school teacher in Tonga. In 1995 she migrated with her teacher husband and children to New Zealand. Meleane found it difficult to get a job with her island qualifications, but she did observe how children in her adopted community of Ōtara missed out on preschool, even when both parents were working. So Meleane began to run an informal playgroup in the family garage. As these things do, the playgroup began to get a life of its own. Meleane's husband was the only one working in the family, and the playgroup was not a financial proposition, although sometimes donations from local families helped. Transcending the financial struggle, though, was a collective vision emerging amongst the women in her playgroup. Tied through family and church and culture, the women started to dream and pray for the opportunity to start their own early childhood education centre.

To get an early childhood education licence (the ticket for entry into the business), Meleane needed a proper qualification, recognised in New Zealand. She made a huge three-year commitment to go back to university and retrain. English is not Meleane's first language, she was a migrant in an alien culture, and her obligations to family and to leadership of the playgroup were considerable. Yet she stuck with the vision, she had support from the group, and her graduation became a milestone for everyone.

Akoteu Kato Kakala (basket of fragrant flowers) is today a Tongan bilingual early childhood education centre in a smart, converted house on Bairds Road, Ōtara. The group purchase of the house and the establishment of the centre was a 'project' of Kakala Malie, the incorporated society set up to realise this Tongan community's dream for their new life in Aotearoa. Meleane's legacy is ongoing; education has got into the family bloodstream. Sulieti, formerly the centre administrator, has a management degree. Her younger sisters, Lorraine and Jeanne, have graduated as educators.

This centre is not merely a service. It is a community collective. This is an important distinction. 'We don't own this centre; the community does. It's a very unselfish process. And it should be like that,' says Sulieti. 'In Tonga, land is very important. You're not somebody until you have a piece of land. To be given the opportunity to establish an early childhood centre represents so many things for all of the women involved here, not just for our families. It is not just a place for the learning of their children; the land on which it sits generates a sense of belonging, of being part of a community, of being valued and of being committed to being New Zealanders (but bilingually and biculturally Tongan ones).' Sulieti pauses. 'This project opens doors to further learning for the mothers—to see that anything is possible, that there is hope.'

That the focus of the Kakala Malie project has been on the mothers as much as the children or the business opportunity ought not to be a surprise. 'Building community is important to us, everything comes from that! What [lots of New Zealanders] see is our [Tongan] colourfulness, and our poverty. By working together, we have made something happen. But we are individuals too, with dreams and aspirations of our own!' Adds Sulieti: 'Lots of those mothers, cleaners, factory workers; they never think of being educated themselves. But now they can imagine themselves getting a qualification and working in the centre.'

These women are creators of wealth, in all senses of the word. They know, from experience, what it is to be an Aucklander, a New Zealander, and a citizen of a diverse community. They have learnt how to set up a collective business that grows their economic and social independence. The physical, social and economic transformations made by the project involved a communal sacrifice in which every member of the Kakala Malie contributed to the transformation of others. Their project illustrates how the DNA for transformation already exists in the mothers of South Auckland.

Thinking intergenerationally

There's a learning challenge in Auckland that can be described via statistics. Of the approximately 60,000 students in each year's national cohort, around 7000 will not achieve NCEA Level 2, and 87% of those students will have a primary caregiver with less than an NCEA Level 1 qualification.[3] In Auckland, 410,000 adults have low literacy.[4] There are over 10,000 families where parents do not have qualifications, a statistical substitute for low literacy. From the Growing Up in New Zealand study, we know that 16% of mothers and 38% of fathers seldom or never read to their children. New Zealand's rate of single parenthood is relatively high (compared to similar countries)—the OECD ranks us third (after the US and Ireland)[5]—nearly a quarter of parents must cope on their own. As child poverty advocates point out, around 175,000 New Zealand children, or 16% of the total, live in poverty.[6] Poverty and poor literacy (and learning achievement) are intergenerational matters.

Regular patterns, as in a fractal image, underlie the deficits. There's a now-famous American study which shows that at age three, children from wealthy homes have heard 30 million more words than children from less affluent homes.[7] Children living in poverty hear less than a third of the words heard by children from higher-income families. This gap arises from habits of interaction between parent and child, and the gap grows as the years go on. In the same vein, eminent Harvard University political scientist Robert Putnam (who famously wrote about the decline of social capital in America), showed that more affluent parents are investing much more heavily in their children's futures than less wealthy parents.[8] They invest more time (in reading to their children) and more money (in enrolling them in piano lessons, dance classes and sports clubs, for example). This enrichment of their children's growing-up years offers them advantages that pile up like an inheritance for later generations. The link between poverty and education can be demonstrated in New Zealand too, reflected in data from the 2009 international PISA study on New Zealand's educational system performance.[9] Poor kids don't do as well as rich ones. The 2011 Green Paper for Vulnerable Children from the Ministry of Social Development pointed out that although there are many 'risk factors' for children's vulnerability, and any one risk may only raise concern fractionally, stacked-up risks make it much more likely that children won't do so well. And according to Statistics New Zealand,[10] one in four children live in medium- to high-risk households, and those in the most high-risk category are beneficiaries of the state, mostly solo parents who had their children young.

All these facts shape a picture of complex cause and effect, boiling down to the health of the flax bush: the whānau. Childcare and preschool programmes don't outweigh parenting. Some researchers estimate that the contribution of parents to young children's development may be three or four times that of the 'professionals' in institutions for early learning—apparently a conservative reading of the evidence. Even high-quality childcare won't offset the negative effects of poor parenting.[11] The cycle of poorly educated adults begetting poorly educated children is not inevitable, but is certainly predictable.

Yet programmes for the learning of mothers are a forlorn wallflower of public policy.

*

I'm looking at photographs taken in 2003 on the first day of the Manukau Family Literacy Programme at Rowandale Primary. That day, the welcome protocols felt tentative and unpracticed, the waiata ragged, the smiles weak.

The rawness of the start created tension and excitement all at once. Here is Cook Islander Metua gazing shyly out from the group photo. She first came to live in New Zealand in 2000; she needed a kidney transplant. Metua was a reluctant rope-in to her grandson's school programme. Like all the parents here, Metua turned up because her grandson persuaded her to, because she really wants to help him learn; not out of any particular personal ambition of her own. And in this photo we see her four days a week with a dozen other mothers and a tutor in a refurnished classroom at her grandson's primary school. It is fairly basic, but was one of the few classrooms in any primary school, anywhere in the country, where adults have been invited to formally learn alongside their children.

Having adults doing a university programme in a school crosses an invisible line. Schools are for children, not adults. Universities have campuses, not classrooms in the community. But this programme locks together multiple schooling, early childhood, employment and social development goals: better childhood learning, better skills for better jobs and positive parenting. The glue is whānaungatanga, the deliberate nurturing of learning relationships in the family unit. So what was the motivation for Metua to come to school now?

Adult education policymakers call people like Metua one of the 'hardest to reach' groups in the community. Her child is the entry point to learning for herself. Says her adult tutor, Sharon Alderson: 'To start with, it wasn't about what we were doing, it was about the kids . . . Everyone wanted the same thing; every single parent in this programme wanted their child to succeed. But then, we put in place a whole pile of things because it wasn't just about the kids, it became about *us*.' Almost all of the 14 parents signed up on that first day, at stages in their lives of benefit dependency and low-income jobs, have gone on to become social and economic contributors in their community. Metua became a social worker. Helen is a primary school teacher. Tina became a team leader at New Zealand Post. Nagamma is an early childhood educator. Rachel became a teacher aide and an elected school trustee. The programme added measurable value to their lives. Over time, at programmes in other schools dotted around Manukau, husband-and-wife teams, sisters and brothers, grandmothers, daughters and granddaughters worked together. They learnt about childhood development, the philosophy of early childhood education programmes, and shared parenting practices. They learnt basic skills in mathematics, about family health and nutrition, computing and career planning. They regularly visited classrooms to observe and help their children learn. They were affirmed in their parenting roles. At the same time, they gained proper qualifications that entitled them to enrol in higher-level training programmes. To help them affordably sustain their dreams, they also held down jobs doing cleaning work and night shifts in factories.[12]

This gig started as an idea about the importance of families as the cradle of education. If parents lack skills in literacy, so will their children. If parents lack support for their own learning, how can we expect them to grow literacy and life skills into their parenting? According to advocate Dame Lesley Max, we should not be releasing parents of their responsibilities to parent just because they are beneficiaries or because by our lights they do it badly.[13] She argues that we should be making it as easy as possible for parents to make good decisions about learning for their children, and to affirm them in that role by good *adult* learning policy. As Celia Lashlie also argued, we have over-relied on Child Youth and Family (CYF) services and early childhood policy to compensate for poor parenting and dysfunctional home environments. A 2014 parliamentary select committee inquiry into engaging parents in the education of their children seemed to agree.[14] It recommended stronger efforts to engage parents and families throughout the education sector, and quoted initiatives where some success appeared evident. But its recommendations missed the point: intergenerational learning remains to this day merely a byproduct of other 'interventions'.

Yet intergenerational family learning programmes have good investment credentials. A 2006 PWC study of the return of investment for Metua's programme showed that families could improve their income by over $200 per week. For every dollar invested, the government could get a $9.31 return—a result of reduced benefit payments, increased tax take, more positive health outcomes associated with higher incomes, and reduced spending on other social services.[15] Even if the assumptions behind this rate of return were halved, this is still extraordinary value for money. In 2015, 175 families participated in Whānau Ara Mua, now funded by the Tertiary Education Commission as a Level 2 foundation education programme that uses the intergenerational learning model first developed in Manukau. Dame Lesley Max's Home Interaction Programme for Parents and Youngsters (HIPPY) also offers similar opportunities for adult personal development and growth alongside the needs of children. There are few other practical expressions of joined-up thinking that make the *mothers* of mo'Town central to the urge for change in education in South Auckland. At this rate of intervention, it would take 40 years plus, or two generations, to address the hopes for mothers here.

The continuum of collaboration

Intergenerational work can't be done without partners. But 'partnership' is often oversimplified. Metua's family learning programme taught me and my colleagues—almost by accident—about the continuum of collaboration[16] and how hard it is to work together.

Contact Networking Sharing Cooperation Collaborating Collective action

Figure 1: The continuum of collaboration

The continuum starts with the independent and free-wheeling institutions that operate in a market or in a place. *Contact* is nothing more than understanding that there are other players and that you have to know what they are doing in order to be competitive and stay competitive. We observed schools in 'contact' all the time. They share a twice-yearly morning tea with the early childhood centre at the other end of the school site, host the occasional visit from the police officer down the road, make phone calls to the truancy service, participate in the professional network of teachers—all are contacts.

When you deliberately set out to learn something from these morning-tea contacts, you are then purposefully *networking*. South Auckland operates in networks, both formal and informal, inside the education sector and across the community. These networks have names that reflect their project: the Ōtara Community Network; the Manurewa Principals' Association; the Māngere Schools Cluster; the Manukau Early Childhood Education Taskforce. 'I think I can see the point of being part of a network,' said one primary principal to me in a tone of doubt. His partnership with an early childhood service and a tertiary institution could never have happened without a matchmaker, because his networks matched his closed sphere of professional contacts and left out to the broader networks for learning in his community.

It's not too big a leap from being networked to *sharing*. Sharing is voluntary, like going to the library to borrow a book, sharing your photos on Facebook, writing a blog or hiring out your school hall. Sharing creates few demands. It may even have a patronising big brother–little sister quality about it. Sharing organisations appreciate they have a part to play—but always on their terms.

Participants in deliberate transformation efforts recognise that change doesn't happen just by what they do, but by what they do alongside others. *Co-operation* describes an escalating commitment to social change that goes beyond sharing. The education sector is full of 'co-operating' entities, clusters of learners, communities of practice. Co-operating is harder than sharing, because it involves changing your behaviour so that you are in sync with other people who are in turn harmonising with you. Co-operating is like a rolling mud-ball; it gathers up mass. Schools don't have to have a written agreement to be playing nicely side-by-side, and initially it doesn't require any greater sacrifice than being socially aware of those around you, or clustering to tap into a particular fund or resource. So a school principal who agrees to a family learning programme, for example, which shifts the vision for the school from being solely about the learning of children to being about the learning of families, is gifting his or her co-operation to the community. It is an entirely voluntary act.

Collaborating, however, is a much more formal commitment that requires a division of labour and teamwork. At some point, as principals and schools get more deeply involved in family learning programmes or other partnerships for learning, individual and group goals inevitably come into tension. Here's the test for a truly collaborative operation: can one single person or organisation take the credit (or blame) for the outcome? This is a really big political question. Careers are built or destroyed by success or failure in collaborative effort. Ownership is less clear when you collaborate, which is why the education sector has always found it so hard to move beyond co-operation. Collaborating involves a deeper commitment to professional success—for others, too.

Collective action, at the far end of the continuum, is hardest of all to achieve, because it means you have to commit to something that is binding on the whole—even when it goes against your shorter-term interests.

The real point of the continuum is that people will collaborate mostly when there is something in it for them. We could observe partners persisting in the family learning venture because it delivered satisfying and effective results, we could offer tools and external support to help overcome the difficulties that inevitably arise and arrange public visibility for the work. But it's a big ask for institutions to step outside their traditional mandates and autonomies. Understanding what collective action for intergenerational learning looks like in theory is not the same as making it work in practice. Bringing a successful intergenerational family learning pilot to scale became a hurdle too far.

However, a continuum is linear. It does not suggest the almost invisible unity of purpose, form and effort that impacts individuals and families and empowers communities to act for themselves. Strong communities network. More than a buzzword, a network is social mobilisation—powerful enough to shape thinking and action.

Schools such as Victory Primary School in Nelson and Manurewa Intermediate have tried to restructure themselves as community hubs, providing one-to-one health services for residents as well as many recreational and social programmes and community events. In this sense, these schools have attempted to de-privatise themselves; making their services open to all the people living in the community, not just those who have children enrolled at the school, and somewhat opening themselves to adult learning and the nurturing of 'family'. Their success is in their leadership for using networks to shape change. While there was initially only a gut feeling that teachers, principals, police, nurses, doctors and social workers all needed to work together around the needs of individuals and their families, the hunch at Victory School worked its way into evidence about what works and what doesn't. *People* make it work. And perhaps that's especially true because it is a community where you can (relatively easily) identify who the leaders, brokers and partners might be. This school has discovered, as others have, that far from being a distraction to 'core business', inclusion of the needs of mums comes with a bonus for the learning of children. It's like discovering an unopened present on Boxing Day. Parents as critical partners have always been there, but have somehow been overlooked.

We have separated out learning into buckets for babies, for children, for youth and for adults. Each bucket has its own 'practice', determined by sector rules, its own pedagogy and its own professional culture. These silos are reinforced by the focus on 'student achievement', because data on outcomes is almost single-mindedly fixed on what happens for the individual and not on the overall context in which they do their learning.

To take adult learning and children's learning out of their silos and put them together takes a fundamental change of policy mindset—and shifts in the practices of most education providers. Early childhood centres and schools are not generally designed for adult learners; and there are powerful myopias which require schools to focus only on what they can directly influence; and that makes a school only about the children. Adults learn in tertiary learning environments—wananga, universities and other institutions—and only rarely with reference to their children's learning. And what of the adults who do no formal learning at all?

The lives of mothers tell us a lot about the destinies of South Auckland's children.

As the Wriggle and Rhyme session at Te Matariki Clendon Library ends on a wet and cold Monday morning in June, Becky[17] comes in with Sandy, her carer, and her two-year-old son Hiran. She diffidently carries him into the circle just in time for the final song. Hiran comes up with a book—a 'touching' book—for me to read as I sit on the sofa nearby. We say some of the words, 'furry', 'soft', 'hard', and he is delighted to repeat them. Becky's disorganised entry is partly an escape from miserable weather outside, and partly due to Sandy's encouragement to get her out of the house. Twenty-four-year-old Becky has special needs and Sandy is helping her achieve some simple goals. Becky tells me that she lives with her mum, dad and sister. Now she triumphantly shares that she has a husband. She met him on Skype because he lives in India. She went to India with her mum, and has now married him. Woo hoo! It was his dream to come to New Zealand, and now she is going to help him, she tells me. My dad is Fijian Indian and my mum is Jewish, she tells me, apropos of no question at all. This theme of Indian–Jewishness is repeated in our conversation several times. It is clear that Becky is in a good space right now. Her dream— marriage and a driver's licence—is about to come true.

Sandy is paid ($14 an hour, 2014 rate) to work with Becky several times a week. Ideally she would like to be a nurse, but 'it's hard to drop a wage for three years while you study,' she says. She at least has credits at NCEA Level 2. Her son, now five, is at school. Working with Becky is an expression of her growing ambition to make something of her own life. 'On this job they gave me ten weeks of training and now I am helping to train others,' she says proudly. Her role includes teaching adults with special needs how to cook dinner, do housework or manage their budget. 'Yes,' confirms Becky with equal pride. 'I can cook curries now.' I ask Sandy about her ambitions. 'Before,' says Sandy, 'I wouldn't have bothered to learn science and all that. But now I would. I'm thinking about the Open Polytechnic or something like that,' she says. When Sandy's shift with Becky finishes at midday, Becky scoops up Hiran and puts his pink-and-grey woolly hat back on. He looks very warm, much warmer than his mum, who's in a sweatshirt and, incongruously, a pair of maroon satin pyjama shorts and jandals with daisies.

Pushing for productivity

Approximately 80% of the developed world's three- to six-year-olds are now in some form of early childhood education and care. About one quarter of OECD children under the age of three are in childcare.[18] The drive to encourage women like Sandy and Becky into jobs is politically bipartisan. Former prime minister Helen Clark and minister for state services Paula Bennett both received flak for suggesting that public policy should encourage women to return to work earlier after giving birth. There's a relationship between women in the workforce and national wealth. The economic rationale runs like this: when all else is supposedly equal, more women working leads to an increase in hours worked across the country, which in turn leads to an increase in GDP. So for New Zealand to get richer, we need our women back in the labour market, and therefore we need early childhood services that are flexible and responsive to working parents.

It seems that Kiwis are somewhat ambivalent about women going back to work when children are young. Our child-rearing pattern is changing, though; perhaps counterintuitively, if they have a partner, the more educated our young women are, the more likely it is that they will go back into the labour market when children are small.[19] Why? You could reasonably suppose that educated young women don't want to compromise careers or mortgage long-term. They are also more likely to return to an attractive wage. They are more likely to be able to afford elite childcare services. Parents like Becky, with a preschool child and no school qualification—and no partner, or an unreliable one—are *least* likely to be in the workforce and to return to it early. The best reason for this that the Treasury analysis could suggest was the 'relative generosity' of New Zealand's benefit system.[20] Restricted ongoing learning opportunities for mothers with low employability didn't rate a mention.

In the era of president Lyndon B. Johnson, the American War on Poverty came with a sense of moral obligation. Today, the social responsibility argument holds no water. Instead, reducing inequalities is about getting a better economic return on investment. President Barack Obama calls it this way: 'Every dollar that we spend on these [early childhood] programs saves as much as $10 in reduced health care costs, crime, and welfare later on.'[21] Cases for investment are built on productivity and value for money. Here, too, we're replacing moral imperatives with scientific ones. The New Zealand government's chief science advisor, Sir Peter Gluckman, argues that science applies to social policy.[22] Advances in the science of early brain development, for example,[23] now provide backup to the assertions of educators that early learning, especially oral language fluency, is crucial.

Economists help to build the case. Nobel laureate James Heckman points out that if advantage accumulates for children through early learning, so does disadvantage.[24] High-quality early childcare in the first years of life has beneficial effects that carry into adulthood. Services are a 'protective factor' for children at risk.[25] So it makes sense to match early learning services to the Ministry of Social Development agenda for 'vulnerable children'. In February 2012, the Welfare Working Group recommended that all recipients of welfare payments who are caring for young children be *required* to send their kids to preschool once their child reaches three years of age. And so it has come to pass. Since July 2013, beneficiaries must enrol their children in an early childhood education service for at least 15 hours per week from the age of three years. They have no choice. Beneficiary parents have social obligations—indeed, 'reciprocal obligations'—for their children, which none of the rest of us have.

Electorate finger-wagging about the shortcomings of parenting among beneficiaries often has a holier-than-thou tone. Unfortunately, we know that children in state care get a very raw deal,[26] and that being on a benefit is connected to a litany of social problems longer than a soap opera. After a trawl through the 'big data' of the Ministry of Social Development, the New Zealand Treasury found three danger flags: those children who by age five were known to CYF, had a parent or caregiver who had a corrections sentencing history, and had been supported by a benefit for most of their childhood were twice as likely not to get NCEA Level 2 by the age of 21, were five times more likely to have been on a benefit themselves for more than two years before age 21, and were an astonishing seven times more likely to have been in prison before age 21.[27]

The policy of compulsory early childhood education for the children of beneficiaries sits uncomfortably in the platform of a party that once had a phobia of the nanny state. Exacting a *quid pro quo* from the state's largesse could be labelled beneficiary-bashing or an abuse of some vague human right to rear children as we see fit. Perhaps its aim is to transfer some of the social capital of most middle-class parents to the (largely Māori and Pasifika) poor, rather like forcing you to take medicine that tastes awful but is good for you. Becky is left un-empowered in the learning project for her children.

Yet the ideological policy divide here is curiously difficult to define. Intergenerational services are a fundamental long-term intervention strategy. Early investment in family wellbeing and learning for Becky alongside her children will save taxpayer dollars in the long run. The investment case is made. The evidence is there. The resources needed to make it work are there. Unfortunately, Becky's own productivity as a mother remains unaddressed in the policy story.

Intergenerational learning should be the starting point, not the forgotten point, for social transformation.

Part 2:
From Markets to Networks

3

Early learning

What happened to the plan for early childhood education?

My colleague Robin, a long-time activist in early childhood education, clatters into my COMET office in Ōtara one morning and relays her astonishment at the closure of a nearby early childhood service. 'How can that be?' she asks crossly, plonking down her blue plastic basket of books. 'If there are more babies being born here than anywhere else in the country, why are services closing? That's the *third* service I've heard of that's closed in recent months,' she says. Something in her tone makes me listen up. '*Who* is keeping tally?' she wonders. '*Whatever* happened to the [government's strategic] plan here?'[1]

Good questions. Over cake and morning tea, the lubricants for all good thinking in our tiny office, we consider what these service closures mean. The government's plan had three goals: to increase participation, improve quality and promote collaborative relationships. On the surface, six years into the ten-year plan the government's goals for early childhood education are looking good. Government is driving up both quality and choice by setting up a market of professional services. More children are being enrolled than ever before, there are more services for parents to choose from, the system is becoming more responsive to the needs of working mothers, and quality is rising.

Or is it? In our Manukau neighbourhood, something seems not quite right. Cake and tea aside, we decide that a discovery process is in order. What exactly is the problem? What could the community do to support early learning? Einstein said the formulation of the problem is often more important than the solution. Would this be true for us?

Defining the problem

Parents and children are the primary consumers of early learning. Costs are subsidised by the government to the tune of over a billion dollars (so perhaps the 'consumer' is actually taxpayers).[2] The 'providers' in this market are the kindergartens, kōhanga reo and kindercare owners. Providers of services must meet the purchasing requirements of government and the expectations of parents. No one is forcing parents to participate in this market. Nevertheless, growing participation in early childhood education is *public* policy.

We've attended a fair few public openings of new preschool services. But when a service closes, we hear only a discreet and gentle sigh. Failure must mean that the market is working! After all, the market is an arc of efficiency and accountability matched to consumer demand. So why does it seem that the supply of early childhood services is not keeping up with demand? At first, the answer looks relatively straightforward to us. Nearby Middlemore Hospital is New Zealand's baby factory. Blame population growth. While fertility rates in New Zealand have been reducing, in Counties Manukau the curve goes the opposite way. Every week, more than 162 babies are being born at Middlemore or its satellite units in Pukekohe, Papakura and Botany. This amounts to about 8500 babies every year.[3] It doesn't match Jakarta, but it's New Zealand's version of urban explosion.

In 2004 there were 252 early childhood learning centres in Manukau, with 11,276 enrolments. We discover that, a whole three years later, despite the push from the Ministry of Education for increasing participation and a baby boom in the area, there is a net gain of only two more centres and 174 more enrolments.[4] A Ministry of Education official comments, somewhat helplessly, that actually there was a history of underused services in Manukau—what would be the economic point in building more services? It seems that, paradoxically, supply *was* keeping up with demand.

That Māori and Pasifika children are less likely to participate than other children is a general statement of fact. But in our office we want to know what the data looks like at the *community* level. The ministry's data for 'Auckland' is not local information. With the generous help of ministry officials, we laboriously split the data out between the suburban areas of Manukau City. Startling differences in participation rates start to emerge. In 'catchment areas' like Howick, the participation rate is 99%; in Māngere, samples show an overall participation rate of 79%.

Is this believable? We get anecdotal feedback from teachers and school principals in high-poverty communities. Their new entrant surveys indicate even lower participation rates. This is what they tell us:

> Attendance depends on movement in the community. At the moment [winter] it is very, very low . . . getting people to come is a challenge. They come irregularly, then they are removed from the roll, then suddenly they reappear. Sometimes there are family issues, but other times because it [ECE] is not compulsory they can't be bothered. The weather can be a big indicator. Sometimes we have only 10 attending, when the roll is actually 30.

> Of the new entrants to our school last year, 50% had been to an early childhood centre. But we are aware that deeper analysis will probably show that they haven't in fact attended very much at all . . .

> Only one in three among those arriving in our new entrant class has been properly enrolled in an early childhood centre . . . we know there is a problem, but we don't have the data to back it up.[5]

It is beginning to seem as if the ministry's 'participation' data doesn't really tell the full story. If a child enrolled, but didn't turn up very often, that child is still counted as having participated in early learning. Some children can be counted twice, for example, if they enrolled in two services (say, a morning session at kindy on Tuesdays and Thursdays, but full days somewhere else on Mondays). The participation evidence can't be validated. Did you attend a service?—Yes. This question to new entrant parents can hardly count as serious science.

The Education Review Office points out that there are quality issues in Pasifika services.[6] Many are struggling to cope with the licensing paperwork. The ministry puts in place financial and advisory supports so centres can move from being an unlicensed 'language nest' to a formally licensed service. This process, however, offers no information about the quality of teaching and learning going on in each centre in our patch.

As for establishing new services: well, it seems just an add-on to the ministry's role. The market is supposed to be self-regulating. The Ministry of Education does have a 'discretionary' funding pool which it uses to support community-led groups to build new services, with underserved communities a priority. But the fund is modest and oversubscribed too, so there is a set of ranked priority criteria for meeting 'need'. Manukau has 41 priority catchment areas for new ECE services, with seven of them given the highest priority ranking. Only one or two applications are successful each funding round. At that rate, Manukau wouldn't catch up for generations.

The market isn't designed to meet the needs of the least advantaged babies in our communities. Even in the flash new subdivisions of South Auckland, there isn't any service planning. In Flat Bush, where a town the size of Nelson is under construction, over 1300 preschool children are expected to arrive in the next six years. There are nine licensed services, with just 350 places. New schools can be built faster than early childhood education services, even when land on school sites is set aside for them.

The story of early childhood education in Manukau was revealing uncomfortable evidence of market failure. But nobody was calling it 'failure'.

Anecdotal gems arrived in our office between 2004 and 2005. Despite the rising birth-rate, the Manukau Central Kindergarten was unable to fill rolls. Making 'donations' compulsory helped the service's viability, because then parents could access WINZ subsidies. By changing 'session' operations so that there was more flexibility for parents, the roll increased further. Eighteen months later, the number of children had increased to 44. This seemed promising but underwhelming progress.[7]

And then, from a bit of bagginess between supply and demand, available child places in Manukau suddenly began to shrink like clingwrap under heat. The net effect of the new 20 Hours ECE policy, strangely enough, encouraged parents who already sent their children to a service to *increase* their hours, thereby leaving *fewer* places for those who weren't already enrolled. The actual rolls had dropped but children were attending more regularly, the number of families accessing WINZ subsidies had dropped—and the waiting list had climbed.

Other providers told us of their problems recruiting teachers. Despite an increase in the number of Māori and Pacific educator trainees, community-based centres were finding it hardest to attract staff. They simply couldn't match the premium rates of pay of corporate providers. There were more Māori and Pacific trained educators in *mainstream* services than there were in kōhanga reo and Pasifika services.

It seemed that the government's ten-year plan was going nowhere in South Auckland. Instead, we could write a set of nine problem statements about the market:

- *The baby factory*: Children were being born faster in South Auckland than investors could build services.
- *Supply and demand*: There were empty places in existing services, suggesting low demand; or parents didn't want to send their kids to the services that were already there.
- *Inadequate data*: Local pockets of low participation were hidden inside the regional data. Apparent enrolment did not mean kids were regularly attending a service.
- *Uneven quality*: Quality services for Pasifika children were the exception rather than the norm.
- *Slow investment*: Private providers were unwilling to invest in poor areas.

- *No sector planning*: There was no way of matching growth predictions to service development.
- *Adaptation gap:* Traditional services like kindergartens needed to adapt their services to meet a changed funding environment and changing demand.
- *Policy shift*: The flagship policy of 20 hours' free ECE increased demand, but shrank places.
- *Teacher shortage*: Who would teach Māori and Pasifika children? Who wanted to?

I was outraged that the power over early childhood learning seemed to lie outside the community's control. Haphazard social infrastructure was everywhere in Manukau—no one led it; faceless officials in Wellington owned it. Where was the thundering community debate about the problem of participation in early learning? How could one even discuss the problem without good data? Where was the forum in which to craft solutions? What were the mechanisms for working together to implement change?

I realised that if the early childhood story in Manukau was only known to policymakers, nothing much would change. I could not think of any forum where the Ministry of Education could have or would have shared data with the community for joint problem-solving. In fact, the local circumstances in South Auckland were actually invisible in their data. It struck me, then, that the community's sense of helplessness was perhaps part of the ministry's universe too. I guessed that those Auckland officials could not publicly tell a bad news story that could embarrass their minister. They were working extremely hard on the problem; their data-sets were complex and difficult to reconcile with the reality on the ground. As well intentioned as they were, local officials could not lead a problem-*sharing* approach; nor could they publicly 'advocate' for stuff that wasn't policy. I added problem number ten to my set of bullet points:

- *Policy constipation:* Government policymakers had no mandate to address market failure. They could not even admit that there was failure in South Auckland.

Four more bullet points would soon emerge for my problem statement list. Among them:

- *Social class* and early childhood services;
- *Lack of co-ordinating structures* for working together;
- *Collaborative dysfunction*: the inability of government agencies to work together and with community long enough to achieve efficiency and effectiveness; and
- *Council processes* and early learning priorities.

Social class and early childhood services

The big ideas of community development and economic development, and the work on intergenerational learning, highlighted for me the challenge of a market of services focused on early learning alone. It's not immediately obvious how these ideas are connected. To round out the picture, I take time in this chapter to explore some of the complexities facing policymakers when 'services' are singularly focused on the learning of very young children.

Somehow, when the rest of us weren't looking, 'education services' and 'care services' became one. Childcare is not simply a babysitting service. Preschool centres and home-based services must get a licence to plan for and deliver learning for children, even the babies. The benefits of joined-up policy-making come backed by evidence, quoted by Treasury no less, that early childhood services make a difference, 'especially for children from low-income families and children whose parents have low levels of education'.[8]

So, what Jesuits instinctively understood ('give me the child until he is seven and I will give you the man'),[9] we now put into effect through public policy. We have a proper learning framework (New Zealand's early childhood curriculum, Te Whāriki); people working in centres are (mostly) trained and qualified; we have a centre licensing system which guarantees minimum quality; and we have a monitoring system in the Education Review Office (ERO).

We have indeed raised participation through establishing a market. Early childhood services are charter schools for babies. All services, whether centre-based, home-based, kōhanga reo or hospital-based, for-profit or not-for-profit, are businesses in a contract with the state. To be successful in running your enterprise, business models need apply. The government purchases (through subsidy for services) over $1.3 billion of services from this market each year.[10] This has more than trebled since the beginning of the millennium.

If you run a business, you will readily recognise how this market works. You will compete on brand, like Lollipops Educare, PORSE and Au Pair Link, owned by Evolve Education Group, a listed company on the stock exchange; or the BestStart education and care centres. You will offer your services where there is demand and where there is profit. You will see yourself as being in competition with community-owned services run by charitable groups or incorporated societies like the New Zealand Playcentre Federation and the kindergarten associations. They too have to operate on a business footing or face loss of 'market share'. Even language nests must operate as competing businesses in the early childhood market. The effect of having a single early childhood market, with government as purchaser, has been to force all 'providers' to meet a curriculum, a set of philosophies and a set of standards. And on the surface that looks like a success story.

However, the market is more complex than a Wasgij puzzle; the picture on the box is *not* what you get. The picture suggests an economic model where, all things being equal, everyone could choose an early childhood service that meets their needs. 'All things being equal' means: all services are of equivalent quality and value to parents. So in Devonport and Howick, the data shows almost 100% of children attend an early childhood service before they go to school. Here, there are strong social norms encouraging enrolment. Advertising in contemporary literature and magazines and other digital media reinforces the message. In this sense, the government policy drive towards mass participation in early learning has been largely pulled off in middle-class areas. But not in South Auckland.

Markets are about choice. So how and what do people choose? I run an anecdotal survey. My hairdresser Breanna from Māngere Bridge wants to enrol her child at the nearby kindergarten, where her husband went as a child, but there is a waiting list. A home-care service works out especially well for her, because the home-care provider can work around Breanna's work hours and could also be available for other babysitting services. Single mum Kirstin's choices narrow down to affordability and a vacant place in a kindergarten with a good reputation. Rachael from Panmure looks for all-day convenience and a quality reputation. Mother-of-four Elise supports the local playcentre, rapidly running out of families with time and energy to support it, and a local kindergarten on off-days. I extend my unscientific enquiries further afield. As a resident of Remuera and a fulltime professional worker, Anne-Marie enrols her children in a private, fulltime service, with meals included and close to work; there is a three-month waiting list so she plans early. Hurana, a Samoan primary school teacher in Māngere, has responsibility for the care of her daughter and granddaughter. Because her daughter works, the baby goes to the Pasifika daycare centre next door to Hurana's school. She shrugs at my question about language learning. She doesn't think her granddaughter's fluency in English or Samoan is an issue—she sends her granddaughter there not because the service is Pasifika, but because it is conveniently next door. In Ōtara, Samoan woman Maire tells me that she was put off by a local service because it was too, well, Samoan. 'At lunch they serve only Samoan food!' she tells me flatly. Maybe palagi food represents a better class of care. Maire was the only person in my informal sample who admitted that the backgrounds of other children mattered to her.

For professional leaders and researchers, quality is behind the policy of choice in early childhood services. What is quality, exactly? Researchers doubt whether parents can readily identify indicators of quality.[11] I have a summary of the research; it is as user-friendly to parents as Arabic instructions.[12] Quality is a judgement most parents expect 'the experts' and ERO reviewers to make.[13] Parents assume quality. I don't mean to suggest here that parents don't care about quality. Of course they do. This is why early childhood corporates emphasise quality in their marketing materials, and why kindergartens (with teachers 'fully trained and qualified') have such a long and illustrious history of committed parent involvement and support. Ministry of Education research in 2006 confirmed quality is a core preference of parents.[14] That same study also mentioned practical considerations: opening hours, location and cost. But we shouldn't be surprised that choosing an early childhood service is a remarkably pragmatic decision for many parents. If providers focused *only* on quality, they would be at risk of missing the market.

That is because quality is a disputed term. The 'Q word' is prescribed by government based on *the science* about what constitutes quality. There's a checklist, as in some quality control lab. But, like the white-coated professional who only looks for red markers without recognising the significance of the blue ones, quality inspectors don't always recognise the bias of the checklist.

For example, the Te Kōhanga Reo National Trust Board does not see itself as being in the early childhood market, but in the business of language and cultural maintenance through whānau. According to the trust, which uses its own quality criteria, ERO reviews miss the point. In its own words,

> when the Kōhanga movement was established in 1982, it was established as a whānau development initiative, operating under the former Department of Māori Affairs, not an ECE service. In 1990, without consultation, all Kōhanga Reo were brought within the ECE framework under the Ministry of Education, despite the fact that the nature and purpose of Kōhanga Reo and their kaupapa are inconsistent with that framework.[15]

In other words, when parents choose kōhanga reo, they are not choosing an early childhood service, but making a commitment to culture.

The same talking-past-each-other issue can be found in Pasifika centres. Modern early childhood practice focuses on child-centred learning. Teachers are encouraged to follow the interests of the child—indeed, it's part of their formal training. Mat time is supposed to be short and sweet; a story-time perhaps, or a song to mark the beginning or end of the session. In Tongan culture, mat time relates to being together 'as a family', and is often more extended than at other services. Children share in Bible verses, prayers, hymns and songs. If you have ever been part of Pasifika churches or formal functions, then you get a sense of the timeframes involved. A teacher confided her dismay to me about the way ERO reviewers dismiss mat time as 'a Tongan way of thinking' rather than a sign of valued cultural practice reinforcing home expectations. Similarly, the official disapproval of shared sleeping places for babies and their siblings bewilders some Tongan parents and dismays some Tongan educators.[16] It is common practice for parents to allow preschool siblings to sleep together; so why is this not permitted at a centre?

This is not a scientific paper about quality in early learning. We all know that coffee groups, workplaces, social media and the internet are excellent sources of community information. A parenting conversation on one of the many websites I peruse recently suggested that a service offering soup and sandwiches at lunchtime would add convenience but also dollars to your bill, and 'may' be a sign of service quality. Such an opinion carries weight. Conversations, even electronic ones, are personal and meaningful peer influence. The conclusion anyone might draw is: parents choose mostly through that most scientific of educational reviews—word of mouth.

Veblen's theory of the 'leisure class' doesn't get explored in the Ministry of Education's research about parent choices.[17] Thorstein Veblen, a Chicago economist, suggested over a century ago that consumption of some services—like schooling—is about class as much as it is about value. Veblen's work has been the starting point for many socio-economic studies ever since. There are differences in consumption patterns between those of different ethnicities and between the haves and the have-nots. A good that gets *more* desirable the more expensive it gets, like a Louis Vuitton handbag or a Mercedes car, is called a 'Veblen good'. Veblen argued that attention-seeking is characteristic of upwardly mobile purchasing behaviour. People spend lavishly on things that other people will notice in order to prove that they are prosperous. Explains one expert: 'You have to be able to demonstrate your wealth; otherwise it's no fun being rich'.[18] This counterintuitive element in the economic law of demand—that you will choose to pay more for something, even if you can get a cheaper version of it somewhere else—drives 'conspicuous consumption' (a term that Veblen invented). People like to outdo those with whom they would like to class themselves.

In the case of early childhood services, do we really want to know what it is that makes parents choose some services over others, or no services at all? The fact that the ministry's research ignores selection of an early childhood service on the basis of class or ethnicity seems somewhat surprising. Unfortunately the ministry did not commission its research in order to find out the deeper *class* motivations that accompany choices for children, perhaps because of the underlying assumption that class and quality is the same thing.

So Veblen's theory leads to another definition of quality in early childhood services, which sits alongside the educational one. It is market competition at work to get your child into the 'best' early childhood service and thereafter to the 'best' school. What is 'best'? To choose well reflects well on you; hence what Veblen terms 'vicarious consumption', as distinct from 'conspicuous consumption'. On this basis, if there's a long waiting list for an early childhood service, it's a good sign. Your peers want their children to go there too. It becomes a mark of exclusivity if you get in. I met this phenomenon among new migrant parents in East Auckland. Like a version of the 'tiger mom' Amy Chua, who wrote frankly about the extraordinary lengths she took to advance the prospects of her children,[19] one well spoken Indian migrant phoned me at my office one afternoon to enquire if I had a grading system for early childhood services in the area. When I said that I did not, she asked me to express an expert opinion about where the 'best' service was. I referred her to the ERO reports and she became very agitated. These did not tell her where the 'best families' sent their children.

We Pākehā New Zealanders are uncomfortable talking about elites. The very word 'elite' implies that access is the preserve of the well-to-do and talented, structured to be only available for some. It offends our sense of fair play and perhaps even undermines our vision of ourselves as a classless society. All the same, even a policy for free and universal early childhood education does not reduce the market for elite services, distinguishable by steep fees and long waiting lists. Fees allow some services to capture rationed resources, such as fully qualified teachers when there's a labour market shortage, and to add 'extras' like sophisticated digital technologies, cooked meals, smart equipment and furnishings. Fees keep out the riff-raff. Statistics confirm the interweaving of peer pressure, class and culture. Participation rates are highest in richer communities, lowest in poorer neighbourhoods.

Is quality a purchase of government or parents? Politicians and policymakers agree—why would you spend $1.3 billion of taxpayer dollars on poor quality services that don't add value to children's futures? Government buys quality through its system of licensing and review. In this sense, government is the one making a trade-off between the quality and costs of services, and quality and parent choice.

Co-ordinating structures for a collective approach

Agenda-setting theory describes how certain topics get public currency. The more often the topic is discussed and the bigger the headline, the more likely it is that the audience will believe the issue is important. To make participation in early learning a public topic,[20] in 2007 our trust somewhat unimaginatively issued a 'report'. Nowadays one might use a blog, a web platform, an infographic or Tweets to tell the story. Believing this had to be a community conversation, not just one for the policy people in education, we naively waved our story in front of various audiences, including councillors and council officials.

It was fortuitous timing. Manukau City Council was about to move into a new phase of its strategic plan. With stewardship from then chief executive Leigh Auton, early childhood education could become a council-sponsored project. In 2008 an ad hoc organising group funded by the council hosted a well-attended one-day community summit in the heart of Manukau—a community-led forum for on-the-ground 'experts', not a conference for the delivery of academic papers to a polite audience of researchers and policymakers. Despite the Ministry of Education's distinct nervousness that this could become a complaints fest, the community-focused event had startling results.

Firstly, the summit encouraged community *leadership*. If powerful community leaders don't understand the real issues, how can we expect them to act in support of them? Mayor Len Brown was relatively new to his Manukau mayoralty when we invited him to be part of the summit opening ceremony. His opening address included a call to 'lift the game' for the youngest children of his city. We did not expect he would stay to listen; after all, a mayor has lots of calls on his time. But he proved sincere. For the next hour he listened intently and asked questions as the story of poor participation was laid out. His later willingness to lend his weight to the issues facing this sector now only underlines for me how important it is that not just sector professionals but community leaders, too, know about them and are regularly updated.

Secondly, distinctive and powerful messages came from *community voices*. It is important to record them here, because they represent the community's expertise on the problem. The Kōhanga Reo Tāmaki Makaurau demonstrated what a whānau-led approach looked like and meant, with tamariki and whānau reminding us that kōhanga reo is more than an early childhood 'service'. Thelma Chapman, an Ōtara identity, focused on bicultural approaches in her centre's vision for learning. A Manukau-based case study of the impact of the 20 Hours ECE policy on kindergarten enrolments, delivered by Franklin Kindergarten Association chief executive Karen Shields, told a powerful story of successful service improvement at the cost of child places. A panel of Pasifika voices shared perspectives on governance, service choices and self-empowerment. A teacher from Clendon Park School talked about her school's view of the effects of poor participation on later schooling achievement and a collaborative Manurewa schools' effort to understand new entrants' early childhood experiences. All of these contributions painted a rounder picture of the complexity of community aspiration for early childhood learning in Manukau.

Thirdly, the summit was *a catalyst for change*. Michelle Pratt, a director for a privately owned provider company and a trustee of the Living and Learning Foundation, detailed in a punchy address her grievances about the petty obstructions in the council's district plan. Council had to take some ownership for its part in the problem of poor participation in communities, she said—and her call triggered Manukau City Council action.

Finally, the summit was *a community call to Wellington* to take notice. It did. A flurry of secret policy work soon resulted in a commitment to build nine new centres.

Community governance requires structures to make things happen. Two new structures hatched out of the summit: a task force providing an advisory and 'champion' role, linking practitioners and providers to each other and to local and central government; and a Ministry of Education 'project implementation group' to build the nine new centres. By working in tandem, the two groups created some entrepreneurial responses to the participation question.

Driving up demand for early childhood services can be both a government goal and a community development action. However, the structures for community-owned action and government-owned action are very different. The difference between governing over communities and governance from within communities emerges from these two ways of working.

The Promoting Participation Project was originally designed as an 'information and brokerage' intervention by the Ministry of Education. In its policy design it adopted a tell-'em-and-hook-'em-up approach to non-participating families. Community providers ('local solutions to local reasons') were contracted as 'placement services' to reel families in. Parental disinterest remained discouragingly high. After a controversial beginning to the project and an even more controversial elimination of its focus on ethnicity, the findings of an evaluation were, at best, lukewarm.[21] Yes, children were being recruited, although sometimes at a younger age than originally envisaged; and yes, more children participated. But not enough places in centres in the largest targeted communities stifled the programme. The evaluation neatly sidestepped bigger issues for 'non-participation', such as parents not liking the quality or cultural context of available services,[22] or having philosophical or cultural objections to sending their 'babies' to services outside the home. Without community development in mind, the project sat outside any other actions.

Playgroups are part of community-building. Coffee groups, the Plunket Society and other local networks sustain good parenting and trigger early learning. Community development workers know how important these local organisations are for social wellbeing. They connect mothers and young families to others in their community. A colleague, Allen, came into my office one September afternoon, having partnered with Ministry of Education officials all morning on a pilot exercise involving 'reaching out' to families. What did 'reaching out' look like? On this occasion, it involved setting up a sample playgroup in the middle of Southmall Manurewa, with pamphlets and display boards about playgroup options—a relatively simple exercise. Over twenty young mothers, most still teenagers, none of whom had their children enrolled in any early childhood services, sauntered by on this particular Thursday. Several dropped their children off at the playgroup as though it were a convenient babysitting service, and promptly disappeared around the back of the mall to smoke. Allen grinned, generous in his interpretation. Children are everywhere in malls. They are with their parents in league clubs, in churches, in the Manukau District Court, in parks and homes too. How simple might it be to raise awareness of the importance of early learning by running playgroups for children *where the parents are*?

A mobile playgroup seemed the obvious answer. Manukau's 'project implementation' team set to work to champion a play-truck. The efforts to co-ordinate funding and opportunity resulted in the Counties Manukau Kindergarten Association purchasing a secondhand delivery vehicle and fitting it out as a warm and inviting play space. Running on a carefully pre-arranged timetable, the truck began visiting various unserved corners of South Auckland. The project was deemed an early success. Except one day, a second truck was cheekily parked immediately behind the play-truck: this one, a mobile shopping truck. Clearly, temptations to get into debt follow poor parents everywhere.

Playgroups are also economic development springboards. As the story of the Akoteu Kato Kakala in chapter two illustrates, many Pasifika groups over the years have stretched their horizons and gained licences to become formal services. The Tongan mothers are now business owners, with skills and contributions that far exceed their own expectations.

For a while, schools sponsored their own projects to drive up demand. They did it, of course, to help their new entrants get off to a good start. The Parent Mentoring Project in Manukau involved about a dozen schools in Māngere and Ōtara, all of whom had received Ministry of Education funding for a community liaison worker or playgroup leader to run an on-site playgroup. This anecdotally helped parents to grow their awareness of what they could do to support their child's learning before primary school. The schools had a gut feeling that this effort was valuable and important. But 'projects' have a finite life. Schools did not feel that they could sustainably invest more of their own money into preschool learning,[23] and they certainly had no money to carefully gather evidence to justify their continuing investment in the effort. The Ministry of Education found, when it evaluated the effects of playgroups, that over time they did indeed make a difference.[24] But did schools have to run them?

A focus only on the schools' efforts to improve preschool learning fails to appreciate the importance of local community knowledge. The SPACE programme run by Playcentre[25] and other parenting initiatives like these comfortably straddle the fence between 'community development' and 'education service provision'. Playgroups are a parent's first experience of organised early learning. Parents form friendships, their children grow older, and the families move on to the next stage. Communities operate in a natural life cycle; thriving networks build on existing resources, mature, regenerate and rework over time. Like a Venn diagram, playgroups and playcentres and kindergartens intersect with sports clubs and churches. Many of these organisations have well-developed 'training' systems, organisational patterns and discipline processes which shape the lives of those involved. They *are* community; and they are influential. There's no surprise in finding that significant organisations like Auckland Rugby League express in their mission statements passion and dedication to providing their people with opportunities and skills to help them achieve success in sport—and life.[26] Playgroup project possibilities have indeed been explored with local sports organisations. However, cross-community structures to facilitate working together are weaker than the barriers. Although playgroups help to drive up demand, in the end they are only small-scale solutions to the goal of full participation in early learning.[27]

Community development needs policy-making to nurture it. Instead, there is an enduring tendency of bureaucracies to want to replace community-led efforts with structures that are predetermined and centrally controlled. With the arrival of the supercity, the Manukau City-led initiative to increase participation evolved with the same uncertainty as stepchildren at a remarriage. Bigger initiatives squashed existing working relationships, and a shared problem-solving approach, relevant to place and local networks, disappeared into the bowels of the new Auckland Council bureaucracy.

Local government and early learning

It is surprising to consider the extent to which a council's core business intersects with early learning services.

Imagine, if you will, a large oak tree on a piece of development land. Long ago a Flat Bush settler planted it, and in its modern environment it provides shade and splendour in the middle of Goodwood Heights, a new subdivision which looks down on the south Ōtara flats. A church group applies for resource consent to build a new early childhood service on this land. A neighbour objects, citing the importance of the tree. The church group, after amending plans to preserve the oak, waits. The Manukau City Council calls in an arborist. The oak tree has a deck around it, on which children could sit and play. Is this safe? 'What will you do with the acorns when they fall?' asks the arborist, bemusing the applicant. The centre manager consults with the Ministry of Education about whether their suggestion is okay: they would sweep up the acorns and dispose of them safely so no harm could come to the children. The ministry agrees that this is an appropriate response. The answer is relayed back to the arborist, who then officially asks, on behalf of the objector: 'Ah! And what will you do with the aphid droppings?' Could the arborist be serious? This promises further delay in a process that has already taken months. Without resource consent the community group's eligibility for its funding from the Ministry of Education is at risk. Delay could collapse the project—the community group would have to reapply, again in a competitive process, for funding from the ministry the following year.

There's a desperate shortage of early childhood services in South Auckland. How do you efficiently lift the paperwork barriers? On 14 November 2008 a high-level meeting chaired by the mayor, with providers, the Ministry of Education and senior Manukau City Council officials present, establishes a 'technical working group' so that a three-way process solution can be negotiated, streamlining consents and prioritising support for all early childhood applications.[28] A ministry official, in an aside, tells me that they have been trying to 'sort this out' for years.

Where should early childhood centres be located? An elderly couple in Saint Heliers is horrified that a preschool is to be established next to their home. There is to be a high fence—for acoustic reasons, it's a requirement for resource consent. They are faced with Hobson's choice: visual fence monstrosity or noise nuisance. This catch-22 apparently lowers their home's amenity value.[29] The Saint Heliers couple has a first-world problem: the luxuries of retirement in that lovely suburb must sit alongside the modern urban community need for services for young children. Should the good folk of Saint Heliers have random commercial establishments in the middle of their residential zones? Clearly not. But here's a challenging public policy question: is learning for children, for profit or not, an activity that should be *excluded* from residential areas?

If it's not okay in Saint Heliers to have a licensed early childhood education centre in a residential area, is it also not okay in Clendon or Ranui? The legacy district plans of all the former councils of Auckland took a variety of positions on the location of early childhood education services. In parts of the city, children were deemed a potential nuisance; the decibels of children playing the equivalent of industrial activity. In other parts of the city, expensive resource consent processes, subject to grumpy neighbours' objections and lengthy delays, relegated new early childhood education services to commercially zoned areas. This is not where the children are.

How safe is safe? In March 2007, prime minister Helen Clark opens a new early childhood education centre, Jump and Jive, in South Auckland. Splendid, you might think, when you are trying to encourage the market to deliver more places for underserved communities. Getting a licence is a rigorous process—and rightly so: the safety of our children is paramount. Still, it seems almost as difficult as building a power station. At the final hurdle, Jump and Jive has to get a sign-off from the Auckland Regional Public Health Service. (They are the people who protect you in the event of a flu epidemic or a cholera outbreak.) It turns out that traffic is a health hazard, and this particular centre, near a busy intersection and a petrol station, suffers a bit of a problem—from air pollution.

At a Manukau City Council forum, a public health official explains their position statement on this matter.[30] Apparently you shouldn't locate early childhood services near railways, arterial routes or petrol stations, or in heavy industrial areas. This news is received in astonished silence. You, too, would mentally click through the implications. How many preschool services do you know of on main roads? I live in a cul-de-sac. I guess there are some particulates in the air there. But not as many as in the houses that face major routes all across the city. Perhaps this is why you should not buy a house next to a busy road, or send your children to a school next to a motorway—like Auckland Grammar, for example. Sure, particulates from vehicle emissions have a health impact. In Auckland, infectious and respiratory diseases among children are among the more frequent causes of acute hospital admissions.[31] It is a serious issue. Even so, the Auckland Regional Public Health Service's position makes little practical sense. At what point do we concentrate our attention not on the victims, who may have very little choice in where they live, work and play, to the perpetrators of the pollution?

Count the officials: the Ministry of Education (1) demands that every application for a licence be accompanied by a report from the director-general of health (2) to make sure health and safety standards are likely to be complied with and that the premises are suitable for their intended use. But they don't monitor air quality—the Ministry for the Environment (3) does. And if you have a complaint, like a bad smell wafting across your centre, then you must go to the Auckland Council (4).

Jump and Jive waits months for permission to open. According to the jungle rumble of the day, the centre's private owner is forking out thousands of dollars in rent—an unsustainable line item for a business not yet open. Questions in the House of Representatives are embarrassing.[32] The centre owner tries to cut through the red tape by taking her own measurements of the particulates in the air.[33] Pollution levels are shown to not be significantly alarming, but no one takes her word for it.

Who gets learning priority? Point Chevalier is an inner-city suburb, once working class but now enjoying a real-estate renaissance. Household income is relatively high and next-generation growth means that many young families moving into the area are looking for education services. Four decision-makers are involved in this story.

Decision-maker 1: The Auckland Kindergarten Association. Point Chevalier has had kindy services since the 1930s, and since 1984 the kindergarten has been located in the grounds of Point Chevalier School, under a property occupancy document (POD) negotiated through the Ministry of Education. In

2011 the kindergarten has a roll of 90 and a waiting list of 160.

Decision-maker 2: The Point Chevalier Primary School Board of Trustees must address the growing pressure on its burgeoning roll. It has a 'zone', but to shrink that is unpalatable to parents. The board applies for funding from the Ministry of Education for more classrooms to accommodate growth.

Decision-maker 3: The Ministry of Education agrees that expansion at the school is warranted and allocates funding for capital works.

Decision-maker 4: The Auckland Council's district plan says that to get a resource consent to build, you need to make sure there is enough car parking space on-site.

The power balance among these four decision-makers is very uneven. The schools division and the early childhood division of the Ministry of Education don't work together. The school board of trustees and the kindergarten committee don't work together. The Ministry of Education advises the kindergarten in August 2011 that it is to be evicted by the end of 2012. The school needs the land for a car park.

This is bizarre. In a press release, the general manager of the Auckland Kindergarten Association asks pertinent questions about civic values. Why do the ministry and the school think a car park is more important than an early childhood service? Why do the ministry and the school think the school swimming pool is more important to the community than early childhood education for thousands of children, she asks?[34]

Land in Point Chevalier is demonstrably expensive and scarce. Moving the kindergarten is an option, but who will fund the space or the place in order to preserve the service? Other voices join in. The chair of the Albert–Eden Local Board, Peter Haynes, and the local MP, David Shearer, attend public meetings. Someone calls on the mayor to do something—he responds that he will intervene if he can 'add value'. All decision-makers, the kindergarten, the school, the Ministry of Education, and the council, had neither mechanism nor incentive to jointly solve the common problem in a timely way. But this is a community with the capacity to look after its interests. It forces a solution: the kindy's relocation to a new 'education hub' on expensive, recently purchased land nearby.[35]

These stories illustrate the point that early learning services are not islands of operation. There are good reasons why the Auckland Council needs mature and considered policy that specifically supports its engagement in the sector, including for its community development and economic development interests, as the last chapter explains.

Why vulnerable children (still) miss out on early learning opportunities

Assembling the evidence for market failure led us to understand that solutions would be as complex as the problem itself. By one informal estimate, at the time of writing, over 2000 South Auckland preschoolers still miss out on early childhood services. Some of those children are the most vulnerable in our communities. A confusion of policy innovations, political ideologies and social cultures colours their story. As already described, the push for productivity, the movement for children's rights and the protection of vulnerable children imply changes for the early childhood education sector. So too do changes to the benefit system, the clash of parental values and service philosophies, and the failure of local government and central government to work together.

Home-based services and the entrepreneurial spirit

Neuroscientists emphasise that the first five years 'last a lifetime'.[36] The research is compelling: nurturing relationships; consistently warm, loving behaviour; and attachment to adults and carers matter to brain development. In-home services seem ideal to parents. They provide attachment-based relationships in small settings. The carer can be related to one or more of your children—a parent or grandparent, for example. And when your child is over three, you can access government subsidies. For middle-class mums with suitable homes, a subsidised live-in *au pair* is perfect. Such a service is essentially a privatised and personal service from the public purse—but what the heck, it appeals to middle-class voters. From a public policy point of view, these services need less capital and are more adaptable to changing population demands. Skilled women return earlier to the workforce. So, over the last 15 years the number of home-based services in the Auckland region has trebled.[37]

But as a solution for disadvantage, the market fails here too. The government's participation target groups may be Māori and Pasifika children, but they have not been part of the growth in home-based services. In 2012, 17% of the children enrolled in home-based services were Māori and only 3% were Pasifika. In 2011, of more than 18,000 children, just over 3000 were Māori and only 510 Pasifika.[38] Few of the major providers, mostly privately owned companies or franchises, target the vulnerable and the poor. Yet these home-care businesses swallow up $107 million of government funding every year.

I hear two streams of anecdotal stories about in-home care. From an exclusive enclave on the North Shore, parents are converting their private *au pair* arrangements into government-funded subsidies. In South Auckland, parents are dubious about the quality of what they are being offered through private in-home care. Anecdotes are poor substitutes for evidence, but I haven't been the only one smelling something fishy. In 2012 the Ministry of Education advised the minister that it was concerned about quality and 'irregular practices' in home-based care—for example, *au pairs* who do cleaning, cooking and other housework, but are being paid as educators; and providers recruiting the aunties who care for kids anyway, turning them overnight into paid educators. Sector leaders, too, wrote to the minister to express their dismay at the directions home-based services were taking. Should *au pair* services be defined as ECE services? What are appropriate qualifications for home-based educators? What supervision do they have? Are there any guarantees for parents? Who is monitoring them?

So the minister agreed to take a closer look. Unfortunately, a review of home-based early childhood education services struck early problems.[39] Its timeframe seemed tight. 'Consultation' with the sector coincided with Christmas 2012–New Year 2013. Private providers got jumpy—could this be about cutting funding? Millions of dollars were at stake, so they hauled in lobbyists and lawyers. The Ministry of Social Development also asked questions about what this review was all about. Were vulnerable children participating in home-based services? If so, were poor-quality home-based services adding to their vulnerability? If not, how could home-based services add value to the rising agenda for vulnerable children?

It's moments like these you need Minties. The Better Public Services target for increased participation had been set. If you reviewed funding for home-based services, the target might look sick. In July 2013 the review was canned. The Ministry of Education defended its about-turn: home-based services had 'an important role to play' in achieving the Better Public Services target of 98% prior participation in ECE in 2016, it said. A new data-gathering system was due to come live in 2015,[40] and other 'transformative' sector funding reviews were underway. Home-based services 'contributed' to government priorities. They were apparently helping beneficiary parents fulfil the proposed social obligation to take reasonable steps to enrol their three- and four-year-old children in ECE; and it could contribute to the range of support available to vulnerable children as set out in the White Paper.[41] It was rather too politically convenient to leave $107 million in public funding unchallenged and unscrutinised over the election season. Vulnerable children weren't being well served through home-based services—and even today there are still no guarantees that they are safe there.

Better public services

How will we know that the government's public service target[42] for early childhood education has been reached? Until the ministry's new electronic data-gathering system became fully operational, only estimates were possible. Participation in 2013 was around 95%, so the target didn't seem a great stretch then. However, nationally around 3500 children hadn't accessed ECE at all, and if you counted those who only occasionally accessed it, you would get to about 12,000 children missing out. Of those, about 6000 are in southern and western Auckland. That's a lot of early childhood places to find in a short space of time! In the hottest spots of Auckland, where participation is lowest, services appeared full.

On the Weymouth peninsula there are 924 children between zero and four years old.[43] Solo mum Darlene joins many other beneficiary parents there looking for a place. In mid-2013 there was one privately owned service and two community-owned services in the area, with places for about 90 children. Darlene is faced with a catch-22: she must find a service in which to enrol her child, which may or may not be high-quality, or fit her cultural aspirations. Darlene says that her preferred service was too expensive for her and too far away. She did not care for the services closest to her. She tells me that she felt lucky to get her daughter Roxanne enrolled in an out-of-area kindergarten on Wednesdays, Thursdays and Fridays.

Darlene cares about which service Roxanne attends, but she can only choose what service providers offer and what she can afford. Poor-quality services are bad news for small kids. It is in everyone's interest that the services in places like Weymouth are the best they can be. However, the ministry won't refuse to purchase crappy services when its much-vaunted target will only be met if all child places, and more, stay in the market. Services are demonstrably capable of becoming 'better' public services. But there's an assumption here that they are culturally appropriate and that they can meet the aspirations of communities. Are these services merely the fall-back position for those who have no choice?

Parental values and early learning

Different worldviews govern child-rearing practices in Western and Pacific cultures. Increasing opportunities for early childhood *learning* and increasing participation in early childhood *education* are two different things. 'Education' implies a system of service provision mandated by the state—with its own cultural norms. 'Learning' allows for a broad definition of how babies grow and thrive. Learning is embedded in nurture and care and is deeply influenced by whakapapa, intergenerational practice, changing patterns of ethnicity and identity, and philosophies of learning.

The ethnicity dimension in parenting practice is more complex in South Auckland than policy positions currently suggest. Social and cultural evolution is at work. Half of all the children born in Middlemore Hospital have more than one ethnicity. The dance group on the Niuean stage at the ASB Polyfest could have as many students of other ethnicities as it has people from the Rock. I recognise Pacific moves on the Māori stage. Bollywood and Cook

Island drumbeats mingle in a single sound-bowl. These are only outward expressions of a cultural shift in which identities become intermingled with urban allegiances—distinct from village or whānau or iwi belongingness. Being Māori or being Pasifika comes with connections to place—that is, place with a contemporary urban meaning. It's tangible everywhere. In the usual round of introductions at a community meeting in Ōtara, a group of young people finish their mihi with a phrase that sets a modern stamp on the 'who am I' set-piece. They say 'Two-seven-four rocks.'* They mean 'Ōtara is my place.' Former MP and media identity John Tamihere, chief executive for Te Whānau o Waipareira Trust, drily says that the 'Māoriness' of many whānau in his Westie patch comes from their urban memberships of rugby league, netball and touch clubs, not their connection to iwi. 'Whatever works' is his mantra for service design.[44] Others echo those pragmatic views. A Christchurch study of Pasifika parents and early childhood services found that choices available to parents are not simple.[45] Just because a parent is Pasifika or Māori does not mean she would choose a service where traditional practices of childrearing are followed. Mixed heritage and co-habitation adds more than flavour to cultural life. A new urban identity is emerging in South Auckland.

There are some contradictory messages here for policymakers. Should early childhood services reflect cultural essences? Māori and Pasifika parents, in whatever forums you might find them, express educational aspirations that are often no different to those of parents everywhere. Mostly they want their children to do well, finish school, go on to tertiary education and get a good job. On the other hand, many Māori and Pasifika leaders express an ultimate preference for competence and confidence working in *two* worlds. Even when they choose services for their children that are not expressly bilingual or bicultural, both parents and leaders want social and economic futures that include strong connections back to identity, ethnicity and class. Yet the debate about what kinds of services are suitable for Māori or Pasifika children seems to be much more in the academic domain than in the popular one or the commercial one.[46]

It seems that officialdom is looking for 'transformation' through participation to deliver future learning success. Commercial interests see the public agenda as a business opportunity. For Māori and Pasifika leaders, increasing participation must be about meeting aspirations for bilingual and bicultural futures first.[47] Only then can academic and social success follow.

In other words, the desired transformations are not the same for parents, officials, business owners and ethnic leaders. There is no shared statement of outcome.

* The digits 274 mark Ōtara telephone numbers.

Supply-side tensions

New start-up services cost a lot of money. Remember, government doesn't want to own these services. An $11 million public investment in 2011 ended up being dished out to both private and community groups in 'targeted' communities.[48] Others got money to create less formal playgroups and parent-directed services. Even more funding ($23.6 million) was invested the following year, most (but not all) of it in Auckland.[49] After ten years that investment is deemed to have delivered its return—more child places. Private proprietors ended up with an asset. Contracts through this fund (called the Targeted Assistance for Participation Fund) seemed to be, in effect, a form of public–private partnership, but with more limited time horizons. These new places could demonstrably show 'increased participation'. But would they meet the bigger need?

There's a supply-side irony. In well-to-do suburbs, competition among services has become fierce, especially as the birth-rate drops. Enrolments are becoming so tightly contested that the business case for smaller services is collapsing. Since there is no limit to the number of licences that can be issued in an area, the market opportunities for significant profits are closing up.[50] This is, of course, classic market operation. Is this 'market failure'? Transparently not. Big business, having squeezed out the smaller community operations, wants shareholder returns. One corporate buying up early childhood services is forecasting a profit of $16.6 million and dividend yields of 4.7%. At least some in the sector are not comfortable that the money is being diverted from families and services, its original place,[51] into private pockets. Nor does this privatising process solve the general supply problem in low socio-economic communities.

One political approach to supply problems is to enrol children in schools earlier—say, at four years old. This is common in other OECD countries. In the Netherlands, children from age four can attend (for free) any of a number of different *basisscholen*, or primary schools, although it is not compulsory until age five. In France, compulsory schooling begins at age six, but almost all children attend an *école maternelle* from three years old. It's free. In Auckland, one political advocate for the early enrolment solution[52] has some endorsement from Manurewa school principals. Other stakeholders suggest that schools have a lot to learn about the ECE curriculum, Te Whāriki, a document internationally praised but not what school teachers are trained to teach. Specific curriculum management skills, and philosophies underpinning the early childhood curriculum, are not generally applied in school settings. If early school enrolment reduces costs for early childhood services, there are clearly advantages for government. However, welcoming children in South Auckland schools from the age of four would require schools to more actively address aspirations for bilingual and bicultural futures for the children of the south, and would require new policies related to licensing, teacher training and qualifications. That could be rewarding, but would certainly have to edge out current priorities. At the very least, this suggested solution would require more than a superficial debate conducted via media or consideration by principals without reference to community aspirations. Badly implemented, this idea could become simply a perpetuation of failed social policy in South Auckland.

Juggling priorities: prisons or early childhood services?

The Wiri area is New Zealand's largest prison precinct. There are three prisons: a women's prison, a men's prison and a youth prison; with 1600 prisoners in total. Within a 5 km radius of these three South Auckland corrections facilities there are more than 40,000 people, a population larger than the populations of Taupō or Queenstown. Wiri is the polar opposite of those other two places, disregarding the absence of snow. This block includes the suburbs of Clendon, Burbank, Rowandale, Homai, Manurewa Central, Hillpark, Wiri, plus the Manukau city centre area. The minister of corrections set up a fast-track board of inquiry to deal with objections to the latest build.[53] The board of inquiry's breathless reflection on the social problems of the area makes depressing reading:

> characteristics of these communities include lower levels of formal qualifications, lower numbers of professionals and higher numbers in service industries, lower levels of volunteers, lower participation in early childhood education, poor access to health services, higher rates of teenage pregnancy, higher numbers of single parent families and absent fathers, higher levels of mental illness, drug and alcohol addiction, more social issues concerning crime, gangs, policing, prostitution, visual untidiness of neighbourhoods, high numbers of liquor stores and numerous youth issues, fewer opportunities for training and education, higher numbers of low decile schools, lower levels of self-esteem and civic responsibility among Māori and Pacific Island youth, higher rates of stand-downs, exclusions and expulsions from schools for Māori and Pacific Island youth, and higher absence and truancy rates.[54]

A litany of disadvantage that focuses on problems, like the concept of the prison itself, casts promise or potential aside. The cradle-to-prison pipeline is not inevitable, but a growing number of children will live and learn right here. Statistics New Zealand forecasts that by 2031 this community could grow by another 23,750 people, a growth rate of nearly 60%, compared to only 40% for the rest of Auckland. In the Manurewa–Papakura ward, which includes the 'immediately impacted area' of the prison, there were 486 Pasifika four-year-olds enrolled in services (2011 figures),[55] but there were only two Pasifika-led services in the area. By June 2015, 89.3% of Pasifika children arrived at school with at least some early childhood education, but this is still the lowest rate in the country (and it is perhaps a generous interpretation of the data). Prison facilities represent expenditure on social failure. How much expenditure? In March 2012 the government estimated the maximum potential cost of the men's prison alone at $900 million over 25 years.[56]

And the return on investment? You could build a lot of early childhood services for that money. As former local board member Colleen Brown rails: 'When you build early childhood centres you are expressing hope and belief in the potential of the community. Building a prison sends the opposite message.'

Even so, building more new services, not prisons, might not be the whole answer to the issue of low participation.

Change and scale

The early childhood participation story is changing. Birth-rates over the last couple of years have dropped all over the country, including in South Auckland. The babies of the mini-boom are turning five. Services are getting larger—up to 150 children in a centre—because it is more economic for providers that way. The corporatisation of the sector is gaining pace, with overseas investors buying up services to roll them into new companies that will become listed on the stock exchange.[57] Housing intensification in parts of Auckland is likely to result in demand for more childcare places, but only commercial services will be able to afford to build. Some new centres are catering to identity, language and culture, and addressing the needs of struggling families—but not nearly enough. The interconnection between health and learning is being drawn more tightly—we now know that poor attendance at early learning services is not just a question of 'bad parenting'. Highly infectious skin diseases and respiratory illnesses associated with poor housing conditions impact on participation rates. The ministry is encouraging groups of services to collaborate as a network, using 'improvement methodology' to raise attendance rates and the quality of services.[58] New stories of disadvantage and inequality emerge from all of these developments. Participation rates are successfully up in parts of the country—but in South Auckland those rates are still not equal to levels of other groups in other parts of the city

I like the utopian idea that we could just step out of the market model picture and walk into a new scene; one which is more marked by collaboration and accommodation of the needs of the most disadvantaged. But, as Albert Einstein reminds us, we can't solve our problems with the same thinking we used when we created them, nor can we simply return to 'as you were'. Unlike moving from one slide to another on Microsoft PowerPoint, dissolving the market approach will take more effort. Wresting the model away from its failures will be no easy task. It is not possible to start with a blank sheet of paper. What is feasible? Three interrelated policy directions spring to mind.

The first is to think of early learning services in South Auckland as more than an educational opportunity for children. The sector also holds economic potential specific to people and place. Consider the population weight of South Auckland as a viable laboratory for a significant economic development initiative *through* early learning services. The majority of urban Māori and Pasifika children and their families use services owned by corporates and non-Māori organisations. These others own service design—and retain profits. The big idea of economic development within the Crown–Māori Economic Growth Partnership, He Kai Kei Aku Ringa,[59] suggests why and how Māori might take the front foot in developing entrepreneurial, managerial and governance capabilities. Service redesign doesn't take defeat of the market as its goal. Nor does it require *more* investment—just a different kind of investment. As He Kai Kei Aku Ringa literally suggests—to provide the food you need with your own hands—ownership and responsibility are important to economic wellbeing.

So we already know that high-quality early learning is a proven investment with an excellent rate of return.[60] The whole industry of early childhood services adds significantly to country GDP. In fact, *not* investing in early learning robs taxpayers of the opportunity to invest wisely, a bit like getting a piddly interest return from the bank when you could be a getting a higher return elsewhere. Governments all over the world recognise this. Although the business case is muscular, the current capacity for Māori or Pasifika-owned business interests to step into service delivery in the early childhood sector as it is currently structured is relatively weak. An excellent prospect, you might think, for a public–private partnership (PPP).

Developed by governments of all hues to share risk and reward, PPPs also empower. The World Bank defines them as 'long-term contract[s] between a private party and a government entity, for providing a public asset or service'. In New Zealand, PPPs are currently being tested in the construction of prisons and schools; both physical infrastructures. The private party bears significant risk and management responsibility, but under a well-structured contract would be empowered to shape service delivery as long as it could show performance outcomes. There is certainly interest in development of the Māori economy, with long-term horizons for returns to Māori interests. Bilingual competency, early literacy and growing family incomes through professional capability and business skills—iwi investors aspire to this. Māori interests meet market opportunities right here. It is easy to imagine Tainui or other tribal entities being shareholders in significant proportions of the early learning services in South Auckland and using them as springboards for whānau independence, as the Kakala Malie did for its community.

Of course, a PPP is not the only way to do this. The social investment bond,[61] currently under trial in the health sector, could just as neatly raise the funds needed. The bond shifts the focus from service delivery to outcomes; to holistic, multi-goal approaches that go beyond the early childhood silo. A back-of-the-envelope calculation of an investment in the order of $25 million is not unreasonable in the context of clearly defined deliverables that meet government aspirations (in social development and education terms), match local and Māori economic development strategies and support community empowerment approaches. Cross-sector, multi-layered outcomes nested within a single project are challenging. With intermediary support, South Auckland would be an ideal crucible for innovation of this kind. It is certainly a policy avenue worth exploring.

The second policy approach takes local and central government collaboration as its departure point. People who made submissions to the Auckland Plan gave surprisingly strong endorsements for weaving early childhood provision into the city's vision. The priorities explicitly mention the council's interest in ensuring 'strong family attachment and early intervention for children before school'. What does that imply? An Auckland Council policy on early learning that straddles the strategic, social development and planning portfolios within council ought to be a priority. The council needs to fill that policy gap. This doesn't imply that ratepayers should directly fund services. However, local government can, and should, play an important facilitative role in shaping communities that 'work' for learning. At the very least, a community governance framework for early learning (as expressed in policies for the plan's implementation) should be explicit about the mayor's role and the role of officials, council organisations and networks in early learning (see the final chapter).

Policymakers need a mandate for Wellington to talk to Auckland about early learning. This is yet to be crafted. An agreement between the mayor of Auckland and the minister of education about collaborative approaches to achieving the Better Public Services target for early learning ought to be transformative. But it needs a mechanism for bringing both interests together—that is, a special-purpose incubator for innovative use of financing tools, delivery models and community inclusion in policy redevelopment. This is intermediary work, a consistently missing ingredient in the South Auckland recipe. A mutually mandated go-between ought at least to be able to draw all of the above approaches together.

4

Broken partnerships

How South Auckland's schools almost fell over

Human history becomes more and more a race between education and catastrophe.
— H. G. Wells, *The Outline of History*[1]

First efforts at partnership

On the bright spring morning of 1 October 1989, the principal of the intermediate bounded cheerfully into his school. Today he was self-managing. He was running a Tomorrow's School. How different would it be? He was waiting for the usual regional board of education letter to appoint two staff members for next year. 'I'm so looking forward to getting new first-years from the training college,' he'd told his fresh board of trustees. Perhaps a phone call would arrive today. But there were more immediate issues that morning: a student had a problem that needed to be referred to a social worker; and there was a problem on the far field—he would have to walk over there to sort it out. He paused in the sunshine. New setting, new technology. Wouldn't it be great to have one of those new mobile phones? Yesterday, he would have simply signed this off from the hidden bank account, a PTA-owned pot of local fundraising money that the Board of Education didn't know about. But not now. Here was an instruction from the minister that specified that if there were any secret stashes of gold (heaven forbid!) they were to be declared—to the new board. Now the convenience of a mobile phone had to be put up as a business case to people he'd never before had to be accountable to.

I was on his board. The request arrived on a busy Monday afternoon as a note to the agenda. We dutifully sat down to discuss priorities, just as the trustee recruitment advertisement glamorously suggested. We didn't even have a budget yet. We looked at each other. Didn't boards have a duty to manage a budget? Without a budget, how could we approve the purchase of a mobile phone? It felt mean to say no. We were at a system transformation point. Could we parents really make a difference to our children's schooling? Would buying that mobile brick for the principal improve the learning outcomes for my son? Self-managing power had sounded so appealing! Would it really work out? I could see the disappointment, even bewilderment, in the principal's face. I had similar feelings myself.

Schools once nested in a stable and insulated world. New Zealanders believed we were an egalitarian society, socially cohesive and prosperous. As the post-war baby boomers arrived, towns and cities expanded. New schools sprang up in icons of Kiwi suburbia like Pakuranga, Papatoetoe, Te Atatu and Manurewa. In this world, transformation was less important than modernity. By the 1970s 'community engagement' was as hip an educational theme as bell-bottoms. High schools enrolled adults alongside the regular students. Other modern secondary schools started up crèches for children of staff and pupils. Still others experimented with school marae or wharenui. Some even ran community newspapers. Community secondary schools were 'in'. The Department of Education's resident expert in the continuing education unit,[2] Charlie Herbert, sent regular letters to the fraternity. 'A school is much more effective if it establishes partnerships or networks with parents, with community groups, with other learning agencies rather than trying to operate like an "island apart",' he advised.

Charlie Herbert knew South Auckland. He'd been foundation principal at Aorere College in 1964, pioneering the concept of secondary schools having community education programmes stitched together by a co-ordinator. The co-ordinator 'had a leadership role' in encouraging learning in the community. (Even local government caught on to this idea. Many community houses began as community learning spaces sponsored by local high schools.) Charlie Herbert also understood, perhaps better than most, about the new kinds of communities arising in Auckland. The city's faces were changing. An educational makeover was definitely on the way. Tangaroa College and Ngā Tapuwae College were established in 1976; then in 1978 came Macleans College, its buildings the ultimate expression of the whānau philosophy.[3] (Although these schools had much in common when they first started, everyone in Auckland knows how different they've turned out to be.)

Secondary principals used to report to boards of governors, but those boards did not shoulder the levels of responsibility and oversight that boards of trustees have today. No one expected much 'community' consultation when a new school was to be built. The Department of Education needed its cohort of principals to be able to translate its philosophy of community engagement into practice—but not all of them could, or did. Having been selected by the wise bureaucrats in the Department of Education to lead its new secondary schools, foundation principals had authority to lead. Anecdotes abound of the actions of powerful foundation principals and their relationships with community. Some saw parent–teacher associations as an impediment to decision-making or a pointless waste of time. In keeping with the practice of the time, few of these Auckland principals consulted Māori on the names of their schools, a matter of some cultural importance. Mostly, despite the *theory* of community engagement, the community was invisible and disempowered.

At Ngā Tapuwae College, partnership—as educators then understood it—was incorporated into the construction programme. The school was to have a swimming pool, a library and a community centre paid for by the Manukau City Council. It was to be open 24/7 to its community. The school was cutting-edge in other ways. The Department of Education appointed Ann Gluckman to become the first ever female principal of an Auckland co-educational school, a move greeted with some excitement among the profession. Gluckman and her husband, a distinguished physician and psychiatrist, were well known in Auckland circles and were part of the Jewish community. By New Zealand standards, Ann Gluckman was a woman with an exceptional career path and an unconventional history. But her networks had little in common with Māngere, the community in which she found herself. The school was supposed to be a model for the 'new society'; more connected, more inclusive. But exactly *how* does a school interface with its community?

No one anticipated the challenges this school would face, nor understood how to address them. Middle-class values and aspirations drove the development of the school. Like a badly woven mat, partnership began to unravel. The management of a community library inside the school became technically impossible. Eventually, the Manukau City Council gave its ownership share of the Hugh Lambie (Ngā Tupuwae College) Library away, opting instead to offer public services at a shopping centre nearby. The second casualty, the swimming pool, was trickier for the school board to shrug off. The council and the school struggled to agree on terms of joint operation. The council had paid for the facility; the school did not have the operational funding to maintain it. This expensive fixture inside the grounds was in danger of becoming a white elephant. The third tension was over the community centre. According to one view, the community education co-ordinator was presiding over a cheap social venue and glorified bingo hall. The school seemingly had no control over its community outreach. And finally, the school's Māori bilingual unit, with powerfully articulate leadership, demanded increasing autonomy over the curriculum for Māori students.

At Ngā Tapuwae, power and control became pivotal issues. Struggles of various kinds raged over the artwork, relationships with Māori and Pasifika communities, the facilities and the curriculum itself. All this raruraru (dispute) undermined the school's capacity to deliver anything, shaking community confidence in the school. While she was up for the leadership challenge, Ann Gluckman's operational managers struggled to make the educational reality on the ground match her vision. Through sheer force of personality, Ann Gluckman kept the school together. As it failed to meet expectations, the Department of Education became increasingly concerned about the school's direction.

I'm underplaying the issues here, because the long story of Ngā Tapuwae College—its icons and personalities, the cultural offences given and taken over the course of its history—deserves its own scribe and place. According to many who were closely connected to education in South Auckland at that time, the idea of a community school was right and the timing was right. But could the people involved negotiate the major potholes in their road?

Partnership with community requires more than the idea of working together. The former Manukau City Council, the former Department of Education and schools had never before had to accommodate each other's perspectives on what made a 'community school'. The processes of local government clashed with the diktats of education. The culture of teachers and their professional leaders did not facilitate community integration one jot. To the community, the school's efforts at consultation lacked conviction. What 'partnership' actually meant was never agreed upon. Whatever it was, it could not be rescued from the growing shambles.

Naturally, the arguments and infighting at Ngā Tapuwae College spilled over into the electorate office of the local MP, David Lange. Over the years the department had weakly wrung its hands about the college's tribulations; its solutions involved pouring in 'discretionary staffing' and special compensatory deals. Enter the curriculum review. The old Department of Education was noted for its careful, long-winded processes. The curriculum review was an interminable exercise resulting in a long, long sweep of recommendations reflecting liberal high-mindedness. Words like 'community' and 'empowerment' were scattered throughout. The proposed reforms were supposed to be 'transformative', but apparently not a single one was costed. The 1984–87 term of the fourth Labour government was nearing its toxic end. Minister of education Russell Marshall wanted to start implementing the reforms. Minister of finance Roger Douglas was obstinate; apparently education's direction could cost more than the country's GDP. Prime minister David Lange threw up his hands—perhaps he could see that you can't just keep throwing money at problems, hoping they will go away. The too-powerful Department of Education had few friends among the public, or even inside schools. Everything else was being rejigged into a market; education must have its turn too.

Confided an Auckland official:

> We [officers of the Department of Education] knew something was up. We thought that the promised reforms were likely to give more autonomy

> to the Auckland region, a bit like the District Health Boards. But no. Everything was set to be atomised and there arrived a sense of absurd urgency and crisis. All the discretionary funding for South Auckland [which had been carefully accrued by making special cases for assistance] was hastily bundled up and redistributed across the system, one size fits all. And then parents were told—it's all over to you.

Given autonomy, power, and trustee meeting fees, wouldn't you fall for it too? It was pure Orwell. The reforms had public appeal, accompanied as they were by a television campaign that showed parents making decisions about real spending and school priorities. It seemed like participatory democracy at its best when the first round of trustee elections was declared a resounding success.

Luddites may still believe that the education reforms of 1989 should never have happened. Don't underestimate Ngā Tapuwae College's role in triggering them. I recall attending speeches where David Lange expressed his great frustration at the intractable problems at that college. The old Department of Education seemed incapable of resolving them. Having appointed himself as minister of education, he believed he was dealing with the festering sores at the school by accepting the recommendations of the Picot Report, the blueprint for the reform. The influential voices in support of the curriculum review and its myriad recommendations were all for shift. It is a matter of historical record that, in cabinet, Russell Marshall lost and Roger Douglas won. The prime minister gave Marshall the foreign affairs portfolio, and made himself minister of education. Not since Peter Fraser had a prime minister taken education into his charge. It was a move at least partly explained by Lange's conviction that the challenges in his own electorate would never be solved by the systems in place at the time.

However it was initially envisaged, the new model for education soon departed radically from the previous mission for social equity and shared citizenship.

The market tragedy unfolds

As John Hattie reminded us, Tomorrow's Schools is yesterday's news.[4] The backstory behind the failure of reform to advance learning in pockets of social and economic deprivation across New Zealand sheds light on the circumstances of today's schools. The logic of self-management is simple enough: we live in a diverse world, and those who work at the school level are best placed to decide how to match the resources at hand to the learning needs of students.[5] Unfortunately, for a long time it was hard to tell whether the logic was playing out, because there were few measures to tell whether learning had actually improved. (And as it turns out, according to international tests, Kiwi students perform apparently no better or worse than before the reforms.)[6] When New Zealand's education bureaucracy splintered into a network of hundreds of school 'providers' of education services, few could foresee the tragedy for South Auckland. Peter Ramsay, a member of the task force that drew up the reforms, described the two rival political agendas in play at that time.[7] The first agenda, favoured by educators, was for a partnership with parents and the community and the fostering of equity ('parents as partners'); the other agenda, favoured by the Treasury and business, was for competition and choice ('parents as customers'). These agendas tussled for dominance.

You know how the story ends. The reforms redefined the relationship between schools, the government and the community so that schools became chartered agents in a contract with the state. Yes, they are actually chartered. Technically, all schools in New Zealand are charter schools. Government still holds the power—except now it is further removed from the action. When schools make up their own minds about what the state wants them to do, they miss the point of the system. To deliver on its charter, a school is supposed to meet a set of key public service 'purchasing' criteria, known as guidelines. They are also supposed to follow the national curriculum. They are nudged into line by threat of a negative education review. While parents may consider themselves partners with government in a shared education project, and ministry officials suggest they are forging partnerships to improve schools, in reality parents in the governance role are merely acting as contracted agents of the state. All other parents simply become 'consumers' of state-provided services.

Today, different strands of politics and ideology influence educational policy direction:[8]

- The 'we're-all-in-it-together' conviction (*the social democratic perspective*) aspires to equal opportunity, inclusion and parity of outcomes. Government has a duty to alleviate social injustice, to protect liberty and prevent harm. Clarence Beeby's famous mission statement for Peter Fraser expresses it best:[9]

  > The government's objective, broadly expressed, is that every person, whatever his level of academic ability, whether he be rich or poor, whether he live in town or country, has a right, as a citizen, to a free education of the kind for which he is best fitted, and to the fullest extent of his powers.

- The *capitalist perspective* supports a free market of education options, which will result in everyone getting what they want (the choice argument); or it offers an egalitarian approach to social disadvantage, expressed as: 'everyone ought to have an equal chance to become better off than everyone else.'

- The *conservative* or *libertarian* argument seeks to prevent the Big Brother state imposing [other people's] educational agendas on you. The role of government should be minimal. People should be free to pursue their own goals as individuals.
- The final creed is the agenda for *Māori cultural renaissance*, expressed as a grievance that mainstream schools don't respond well enough to Māori learning needs,[10] or as a movement of self-determinism; and more recently through co-option of the libertarian or capitalist arguments, applied to collective iwi or hapu ends.

Underpinning each of these perspectives are very different visions of what our schools should be like and what their outcomes should be. No wonder ministers of education get a hard time. Kiwi schools are in ideological and cultural ferment.

The whole point of reform was to improve learning, no? The reforms in South Auckland were transformational in one key respect—quality schooling was no longer viewed as a public given, but parents' responsibility. Between 1989 and 1995, the government's policy was not to interfere in school governance,[11] presumably to let the market develop and settle. Schools in South Auckland who asked for help were, in effect, refused it. Schools were supposed to either confront the reality of markets: self-manage or die.

So, ironically, the reforms compounded the issues facing Ngā Tapuwae College in Māngere. The school received two bad ERO reports in a row. The first one, in 1992, was invisible in much the same way as the old inspectorate had kept in-house its uncomfortable truths about schools. The school roll was dropping at an alarming rate. By November 1994 the college had halved to a roll of 542, now almost exclusively Māori and Pasifika children. But by publicly releasing its second report, ERO was signalling its intention for transparency and purposeful analysis of a *public* school that was supposed to be using *public* money for the benefit of local children. The report summary included this: 'Successive administrations of the school have failed to address effectively serious and persistent reservations as to the competence of its governing authorities and managers.'[12]

No individual school had ever before had such public damnation. The power plays at the school came at the expense of children's learning. In a war over control, children were, in effect, collateral damage. David Lange's reforms appeared to be an ambulance too late. Pessimistically, the ERO report claimed that there were no incentives 'to ensure that the College becomes a useful, productive, and sound provider of education in the foreseeable future.' In other words, in the opinion of ERO, the school was a write-off. The report recommended that, except for the development of a separate facility for Māori bilingual education, it be closed; and until that point arrived the ministry should sack the board and appoint a commissioner.

Famously, the former principal of Auckland Grammar, John Graham, took on the commissioner role.[13] Graham's appointment was controversial; his role there took him out of his Auckland Grammar cultural milieu. It became, literally, an extraordinary experience. His biographer writes:

> His thinking on many aspects of New Zealand's social structure was changed forever as he absorbed first-hand knowledge of the impact poverty and unemployment were having on the lives of many. 'I was not aware of the extent of deprivation at lower-decile schools. It was a huge learning experience and what was needed was the zeal of a missionary to help the disadvantaged.'[14]

From the very first day there was a face-off over Māori educational empowerment. The kura unit, led by Te Kepa Stirling, was supposed to be one of the most effective in the country. Yet here it was on the brink of closure, paralysing Māori ambition. Although John Graham's appointment ensured that administrative improvements were evident and the school remained open, subsequent ERO reports trace roll decline to 405 in 1995, sliding further to 381 in June 1996. An Auckland Grammar in Māngere it could never have been.

In the vicinity, Southern Cross Primary School was also a cot case. Two commissioners had made limited progress. A couple of neighbouring intermediate schools had falling rolls and ambitions to become middle schools. The minister considered closure for them too. Fifteen hundred students teetered at the edge of an educational desert. Where else could they enrol? Would they bother? The Ministry of Education was in a bind. It would be a travesty for the ministry to shut down a well-performing Māori bilingual unit. Here was a classic case of adaptive challenge[15]—there had to be a solution, but it would test legal boundaries, be risky and perhaps open up new problems.

The decision of the minister to combine three schools and the unit into one single complex area school was disappointing for Māori. To be named Southern Cross, the reorganised school would be overwhelmingly Pasifika. Still, it was better than complete closure. Yet how do you create one cohesive board from four previously dysfunctional and non-collaborative bodies? There was a one-off deal: the ministry would fund a change manager for a two-year term. As for the new board, few Pasifika families had governance ambitions. In contrast, the minority of Māori families at the school were well-organised and politically savvy. Māori trustees came to dominate the board. It was no surprise, then, that board decisions about resources were driven by the aspirations of Māori leaders. The Māori bilingual unit's position within the whole became powerfully unassailable because its academic results remained relatively sound. Māori students travelled from all over the city to access education there; their families were educated and competent advocates for the needs of the unit, their social capital significantly greater than among the Pasifika families in the mainstream part of the school.

But applying a rural governance model to an urban setting was like stretching a too-small jersey out of shape. Layers of patches covered the bad fit. A school is only funded for one principal, but this school needed strong curriculum leadership across all age groups. Stability and succession issues tested the board. Distortions in the school's funding and staffing entitlements led to money woes. Because media interest doesn't normally differentiate outcomes according to ethnicity, the success of Māori students became an *insider* story. In the end, the limitations in the governance model got to the Southern Cross board. It decided in 2010 that the interests of Māori students would be best served if Te Kura Māori o Ngā Tapuwae became its own separate school. This long-awaited moemoeā (dream) finally became official in February 2011.

At the same time, school traumas in Ōtara were taking their toll. Tangaroa College's principal had been sacked in 1994 after being found guilty of defrauding the college[16]—and as he had also been a Manukau City councillor and deputy mayor, and a role model for Māori, Kuku Wawatai's sudden fall from grace brought shame to his family and community. Tangaroa College's roll had dramatically plummeted to close to 400 students, and accompanying that roll drop was loss of funding for investment in building upgrades and new resources. At what point would alarm bells sound in the ministry? The appointment of the new principal, Jim Peters, was contentious—a palagi principal in a largely Pasifika community did not go down well, especially as the deputy principal, herself Pasifika and highly respected, had been passed over by the board.[17] When Peters arrived, the school was at its nadir. Requests to the Ministry of Education for help fell on deaf ears. The ministry would only look at helping the school to work within the funding available,[18] as though the child had misspent her pocket money.

When schools enter a spiral of decay, it's very hard to reverse.[19] Ōtara's other secondary school, Hillary College, was effectively a 'dead school'.[20] Once, it had been the poster school for modern schooling in a multi-racial urban environment. Ministers brought international visitors there to illustrate the strengths of education in New Zealand. But by the end of 1996 the school's woes were legion. There were bad ERO reviews, a ministry 'intervention team' had come in to assist the board, the principal had left, one hundred students had left en masse in protest over his untoward departure, the board had failed to attract sufficient quality leadership to be able to appoint a new principal, and the Treasury was pushing the minister of education to complete a business case for closure.

As these two schools atrophied, the costs of closure mounted. Anyone with a nose to the political wind knew there would be significant community opposition to secondary school closures.[21] It was unacceptable that a whole suburb the size of New Plymouth or Napier could be stripped of all its secondary schooling options. Besides, what would neighbouring communities make of an influx of the suburb's brown kids into their schools?

Among the most senior and well-respected principals of Auckland, the recently retired Charmaine Pountney agreed at short notice to run a rescue mission for Hillary College. Her three-term experience left her seething with anger. Her story of the school's pullback from disaster is recorded in her book, *Learning Our Living*.[22] A 'business plan' drawn up by an accountant was stuck in interminable bureaucracy in Wellington, and only media interest in Pountney's appointment could trigger a tiny dollop of interim rescue money. The 'diabolical process' of school rescue was accompanied by demands by the ministry and the Treasury for seemingly pointless input and output statements which were meant to show that if you spent money here, the result would be so many students (define the number) with higher qualifications, or a better relationship with your school community (define the relationship). Almost-dead schools involve a lot of work. Getting rid of useless teachers and employing new ones, getting the school accredited to provide qualifications, dealing to complex student needs—these were exhausting enough, without absurd bureaucratic justifications to get the support so clearly needed. Charmaine Pountney's experience was searing. 'Schools take a long time to die, and a lot of children suffer along the way,' she sadly relates.

Hers is just one account of what happened to Ngā Tapuwae College, Hillary College, Tangaroa College and their feeder primary and intermediate schools in the Ōtara and Māngere areas during the 1990s. In a *Metro* magazine article in 1994, Jim Peters, principal at Tangaroa College, summed up the feelings of the beleaguered leadership in schools in Māngere and Ōtara at that time: abandoned by the state, deserted by their communities and exhausted by the efforts they had to make to serve the children enrolled with them.[23]

The sweep of educational reform served the middle class just fine. What is not to like about self-managing schools? In the forefront of boards' and principals' minds in the more affluent suburbs was making the roll grow so you did not look like a failing school. Confidence is everything. Schools with rising rolls were busy building fancy fronts and expanding office space.[24] Tidy, attractive schools grew enrolments. It was a virtuous cycle of increasing advantage. Schools with falling rolls had no money for building improvements and often looked shabby, a sign they were in a vicious counter-cycle of diminishing investment. In 1992, when zoning was abolished, schools in the poorest communities in the city and with the highest proportions of Māori and Pasifika students in the country battled for survival. Aspirational families with the motivation and the money chose to enrol their children in more affluent neighbouring areas. Thousands of students began travelling out of the poorer suburbs of Auckland every day, noticeably adding to traffic congestion (today, more than half of Auckland's 260,000 schoolchildren make the school run by car). They leave behind those young people most at risk, the children who are the statistics of poverty and disadvantage.

This downward spiral is the stuff of education legend, explained by the now-famous 'cautionary tale' of Americans Ted Fiske and Helen Ladd. The Fulbright grantees came to New Zealand to check out our educational experiment:

> Changes in enrollment patterns show that parents appear to be trying to move their children up the decile ranking of schools; further, it is quite rational for them to do so. Although some minority and low-income families clearly benefit from having choice, nonetheless parental choice increases the concentration of minority and disadvantaged students by more than can be explained by changes in residential patterns alone. In addition, disadvantaged students are significantly over-represented in the schools that are least able to compete for students and hence, by the market definition of success, are failing schools. Because the playing field is not level, competition is not healthy, and it leads to a situation in which the benefits to the schools serving advantaged students are intensified and the problems of the schools serving disadvantaged students are exacerbated.[25]

Forgive me if this recent history seems obscure to the present task. To make transformation meaningful, there has to be deep change, so deep that it constitutes a complete break from the past. Paradoxically, the past often explains the present. Transformations are built on the attitudinal shifts that people make, the relationships organisations have with each other and the experiences that colour those relationships as change happens. The experience of the 1989 reforms on schooling in South Auckland was indeed transformational—although not in the way policymakers envisaged.

A community education forum, in which matters of school reorganisation were theoretically decided by the community, was written into the school reforms of 1989. The problem with asking a community what it wants is that you then have to listen to what it tells you. The first forum, in Christchurch, related to the many empty spaces in schools across that city and the required earthquake strengthening of Hagley High School. The cheapest idea was to close Hagley and redistribute its pupils among the remaining secondary schools. The 'consultation' did not go the Ministry of Education's way, however. Astute political lobbying kept Hagley open, and the experience cost the ministry many millions it had not envisaged spending. Ouch. How could the Ministry of Education rein in its capital spending if it had no control over network reorganisation? Community forums were deleted from the legislation, and the ministry designed new policy for reorganising schooling.

All across the country school principals, excited by competition and self-management, now turned their attention to restructuring themselves. Markets offered new possibilities. Primary schools could pitch to keep their Year 7 and 8 students, intermediate schools could apply to become middle schools, and secondary schools could restructure if they dared. The market theory is that communities reshape schooling networks so that they are more effective and responsive to customer demand. In reality, principals take the lead for largely self-interested reasons. From the kick-off, policies for 'change of class' gouged enrolments in neighbourhood schools and ruined collegial relationships. In the suburbs of Ōtara and Māngere, Bairds Intermediate School and Fergusson Intermediate were trying to become middle schools, as Clover Park Intermediate had. At recruitment time, contributing primary schools refused certain intermediates access to their students—a clear sign of network breakdown. Change efforts appeared to be driven by roll protection and principal self-interest. The signals to all school leaders were plain—the system encourages you to go hard out for enrolments, but watch your back.

Gutted school rolls and poorly maintained buildings are a sure sign of system inefficiency. In Ōtara, the change-of-class application from two intermediate schools provided the Ministry of Education with the perfect excuse to suggest an Ōtara plan. Under legal obligation for the minister to 'consult', the ministry appointed two facilitators. Their job was to feed to the minister the community's views on how best to deliver education in the area.[26] Community has no general meaning in education legislation. Teachers and principals in the applicant schools asked why they could not use the permissions in the legislation to self-manage—after all, they were being 'responsive' to their school community. What business was it of Wellington bureaucrats to come in and tell them how to organise themselves?

But what I really want may not be what others really want. And just as the schools in post-earthquake Christchurch have since appreciated, the law sets out how consultation must happen. The Ministry of Education's consultants are paid to listen to what people say. As a consultant you write it down, you keep your mouth shut, you summarise everyone's arguments. You certainly don't challenge the squabbling players as you interview them one by one and then go away and write a report with recommendations. Imposed solutions, even compromises, didn't please the Balkans, and nor did they here. There's nothing about this process that invites people inside schools to take leadership or responsibility for the big picture. When the minister proposed a decision, everyone in Ōtara universally rejected it, but for a fistful of different reasons.

David Lange, now from his vantage point on the opposition backbenches, had his own analysis of what was going wrong in his backyard. The Ministry of Education had withdrawn from sector leadership and the government's ideology was making them withdraw even more. In Lange's view, the ministry had lost its spine. It ought to be 'an ongoing partner in the contract. That's who the charter is signed with—and they have withdrawn. I envisaged them there in the front row and far from staying there, they became the referee, then the linesmen,' he quipped, 'and now they're watching the whole thing on satellite TV.'[27]

In the wake of the consultants' recommendations, trustees of South Auckland schools paddled furiously to prevent their collective waka from sinking. The elected chairs of all 17 Ōtara schools agreed that it was *their* community problem, *their* prerogative to exercise leadership and *they* wanted to do something about it. They proposed to jointly recommend to the minister what they wanted for Ōtara. The minister agreed that they could do this—provided they took 'quality' into account.

Excuse me? Since when was *quality* a consideration in school reorganisation?

Over the next ten months the ministry facilitated a commission-style process in Ōtara, whereby expert evidence and the views of a range of school stakeholders were put together and analysed by a forum of board chairs. By hearing each other's voices, forum members began to see that 'a community of interest' could exist outside of their own individual school concerns.[28] The forum overwhelmingly rejected the applications of the two intermediate schools to become middle schools, and recommended that the minister do the same. The minister agreed to decline the applications; transparency in the process enabled people to see why.

(It is possible to argue that the reorganisation of Christchurch schools might have followed a very different path in 2012 if the lessons learnt from Ōtara had been injected back into the system. However, it seems our system is unable to learn from its mistakes.)

The forum in Ōtara encountered a depressing statistic: not a single student from any of the Ōtara secondary schools had got University Entrance or Bursary over the previous three years. *All* schools had contributed to this educational disaster. All that rucking and mauling for a nil score! The assumption underneath the reforms, that you can separate the administration of schools from what a school is for—the teaching of children—was patently wrong.

Local trustees called for an ongoing forum for debate about schools in their area. The Ōtara Boards Forum banner proclaimed its three founding purposes: 'Increasing Student Achievement; Supporting School Boards of Trustees; Area-wide Co-operation in Education'. And then across the bottom, the strap line: 'Building Education in Ōtara'. While it initially received encouragement and support from the Ministry of Education, the forum's continuing existence would depend on voluntary commitment of trustees and principals to work together. The motivation for change was certainly there. But as we shall later see, when the forum lost its connection to the policy decision-makers in the Ministry of Education, it lost its transformative power. The forum could reproduce its learning, but it could not advance it. Today it has shrivelled to archival interest only.

Outcomes for students were not just an issue in South Auckland. In early April 1993, deputy principal Susan Cave at Porirua College in Wellington hosted a well-attended national forum about 'at risk' secondary students: the educationally underperforming, the socially maladjusted, the economically deprived. There was a data vacuum. Without statistics, the case for political attention was difficult to make. Actually, who was 'at risk' and how many? School leaders were wary of the ministry's attitude to research—it had already withheld the results of a study called the Smithfield Project,[29] and concluded that marketisation did not sit comfortably alongside the government's policy goals. A school-led and independently analysed survey of the extent of at-risk young people in secondary schools identified that 20% of students were leaving schools without formal qualifications and were without systemic support.[30] That they would be permanently economically disadvantaged was self-evident. That this represented some 50,000 young people every year across the country seemed outrageous.

Policy-making is often pushed along by public outcry. Public release of the schools' evidence dismayed the Ministry of Education,[31] and finally persuaded the government to adopt a mitigation strategy. Decile funding, in more or less the form in which it exists today, arrived in schools in 1995.

The term 'at risk' was coloured by the intensifying debates around school qualifications. A group of influential and wealthy schools led by Auckland Grammar actively resisted the introduction of NCEA and defended the status quo exams. The annual School Certificate, University Entrance and Bursary round-ups included drafting gates that allowed middle-class kids through, but put South Auckland kids off school altogether. As the knowledge wave kicked in, there were good economic as well as social reasons for keeping kids in learning for longer. The qualifications system clearly needed reworking. At the same time, educational leadership for social justice needed particular effort in Auckland. For principals to speak out about the professional issues confronting leaders and teachers in the lowest-decile schools (and respond to the escalating ethical abuses of colleagues regarding questions of zoning or school reorganisation) carried career complications. The Auckland Secondary Principals' Association became a difficult meeting ground as various personalities clashed over the ethical and social issues facing the profession. The divide between high-decile and low-decile school leadership was increasingly obvious. Many committed professionals came to believe they were taking on a career risk in accepting principalship in a low-decile school.

Hence arose the Auckland At-Risk Committee. It concentrated its efforts on support networks for leaders of secondary schools who worked in the most challenging communities and on the effects of education's increasingly public battles with the government. The committee attempted to rework the collectivist ethos of the profession and to address social distress among young people.[32] During its short but focused life, the Auckland At-Risk Committee marked the beginning of co-ordinated health and social services in schools, a more collaborative approach to the youth mentoring movement in New Zealand (as further described in chapter six), and the establishment of alternative education units for the most at-risk students.

The turning point

Schools are incredibly sensitive to discussions about failure, and research being conducted in schools in South Auckland often includes conditions of anonymity. The traumas of the three secondary schools of Ōtara and Māngere are already in the public domain. The woes of primary and intermediate schools are less well known. Kay Hawk, in her doctoral study on the downward slide some schools experience, found that each failing school's situation was in some way unique, and that factors leading up to their decline and fall are devilishly complex.[33] The challenges of Hillary, Tangaroa and Ngā Tapuwae were each different (and remain so), but had social and economic poverty in their communities in common. Less visibly, a number of primary and intermediate schools across both suburbs had equally awful ERO reports and internal struggles or external issues to address. The point of this chapter is not to pull scabs off old wounds, but to insist that while individual schools may have failed, the whole network of social, economic and cultural supports for schooling in South Auckland had disintegrated. We now know, to the cost of the potential of young people in those areas, what *didn't* raise educational achievement in South Auckland. Paternalistic ideals of community schools ('partnership' schools), as Ngā Tapuwae College illustrated, were not the answer. Leaving struggling schools to cope alone in a rapacious market was not the answer either.

Out of the fire of the governance changes in South Auckland popped the hot coal of accountability. The ERO report *Schooling in Māngere and Ōtara* called it what it was: seriously deficient education across the network.[34] The ERO chief executive, Judith Aitken, ripped open the veils of in-house consternation about schooling in South Auckland and deliberately turned school performance into a public conversation. Schools had poor trusteeship, lousy principals and 'weak or failed' teaching. Her office found that boards didn't know how to effectively manage the performance of their principals and that principals' management of the performance of teachers was abysmal. Social support networks were disconnected and ineffective. Her policy shift on the audience for her reports saw her being named as a whistleblower of national significance.[35]

Her report was a watershed in many ways. Firstly, ERO had never expressed concerns about a whole network of schools before. Secondly, the report scarcely named a single school, yet seemed to run right over the top of the ministry's efforts with the most egregiously failing schools. Surely the ministry had to accept some culpability for failure. Thirdly, ERO widened its lens just ever so slightly to consider social circumstances as a contributing factor in school performance:

> It is acknowledged that all 45 schools are located in disadvantaged socio-economic settings; thirty-seven are classified as having the highest level of socio-economic disadvantage nationally. Accordingly these schools operate in the social context of low incomes, high rates of unemployment, crowded housing and poor child health.

But there was to be no excuse:

> It is commonly asserted that there is a strong link between school failure and the degree of disadvantage in a socio-economic setting. There are, however, some 20 per cent of the schools in these two districts that provide an effective education for their students. Their boards, principals and teachers have, with various degrees of success, met the challenges of their students' backgrounds and concentrated on teaching and learning to the benefit of their students.[36]

In other words, if some schools can do it, why can't everyone else?

The recommendations ERO offered were more top-down, market-based solutions: tightening helplines through 'supply agreements', appointing ministerial monitors and commissioners to boards and paying them properly, setting up an area-wide services agency that would broker quality educational services and which schools could purchase; restructuring schools, firing teachers and paying to attract quality staff; and so on.[37] The report barely alluded to the bitter fights between the schools for students. The report did not explore *why* some schools could be successful and other schools not. It merely pointed a generic finger at governance and management failures as though these could be addressed by simply emulating the successful 20%. How schools could learn *from each other* was not addressed in the recommendations. Poverty and the marketisation of schools were effectively dismissed as irrelevant.

School trustees had 'no idea' how to respond.[38] While the report put a spotlight on extensive failures of governance, recommended solutions were nested in a managerial philosophy totally alien to the social norms of South Auckland. How could a board act as the employer and appraiser of a principal in a cultural environment where principals have mana and status? Trustees had no idea what was going on in terms of staff performance. Why would they? This was surely the principal's area of expertise. Trustees claimed that the report generated hundreds of hours of unpaid volunteer time—and that actually they were working in a fog of incomprehensible or unrealistic expectations. Yes, there were certainly issues for many of the 17,000 children attending schools in the area. Yes, some principals and teachers ought to lose their jobs (and did). Yes, some boards did get the boot. And yes, the ministry's hand was forced. Like a gunshot in the playground, the report jolted everyone into action. Judith Aitken's outspoken backing of the report triggered the most concentrated and sustained investments in schooling improvement this country had seen.

So what does a non-interventionist government do if it wants to shift failing schools?

The change trajectory

The Ministry of Education needed a new theory to improve schools that matched the self-managing schools model. The theory needed to be a set of chained-together ideas to explain what should happen next. In summary, the ministry's theory posited that there can be only two reasons for poor achievement—it was either the home or the school's teaching and learning practices. Evidence could point either way. Decile funding is supposed to address the disadvantages of home, the government's first intervention point. That leaves the school's teaching and learning practices as the government's second intervention point.

So who is the expert on supporting teaching and learning in New Zealand schools? The universities and private professional development experts were (and still are) contracted providers, themselves competing in a market. They could provide advice to individual schools, but they could not steer improvement across the whole system. Schools could not speak for the system and address its overall quality; they could only speak for themselves. The running of the hounds requires the alpha-dog to take charge. But the ministry would not intervene. What, interfere in the market? No, no! But by 1994, 'in response to a Government request',[39] the ministry's dilemma became a dipping of toes into new water: a School Support division inside the Ministry of Education. The theory of school improvement advanced a step further: if possible failure in schools could be identified earlier, then white knights could come riding in to help them develop 'self-management capability' (a safety-net strategy); or the ministry could put in place a 'preventative strategy' (known around the house as schooling improvement).

Safety-net strategies and schooling improvement work crescendo-ed until by 2004 over 300 schools had become a part of 16 schooling improvement initiatives.[40] The theory got more legs: getting quality teaching and learning into schools ought to be a fixable and therefore short-term problem. Schooling improvement work, therefore, was 'project-based'; not a long-term solution.

To kick off its school support work, Ministry of Education officials invited the lowest-decile secondary schools in the country to co-operate in a new initiative called Achievement in Multicultural High Schools (AIMHI).[41] The schools were initially suspicious. Lumping all the lowest-decile secondary schools in the country together might give the public the impression that they were all failing, and at least two of the original eight schools felt emphatically that they were *not* failing in the contemporary definition of the term—in fact their rolls were stable or growing. Three of the schools were indeed in serious trouble. Three were fragile, their reputations fading and rolls falling away. It was an artificial grouping. It was not about 'community', because the invited schools were not all geographically together. Porirua College in Wellington was included; Aorere College in Auckland was excluded. Insofar as competing low-decile secondary schools could of themselves be considered a community, this was a new way of thinking.

Some principals were blunt. If this was meant to be just another self-help or self-improvement project, why bother? To other schools, absolutely strapped for support and cash, the ministry's proposition was attractive. After internal debate, the principals collectively agreed that the ministry's invitation ought not to be ignored, but that a strong, *co-ordinated* schools-led approach would be needed. Power relations gave the project a rocky start however. Project governance evolved as the ministry and the schools learnt how to work together;[42] a steering group later became the AIMHI Forum. The word 'partnership' was bandied about, but few project participants truly believed in it.

The ministry contracted researchers Kay Hawk and Jan Hill to provide feedback about what was and wasn't working in the AIMHI project. Three research reports laid out the issues confronting students and their teachers. As in-school processes were examined and adjusted, the wider social challenges facing these schools also came under scrutiny. Health emerged as a major issue. An astonishing 50% of students in these schools needed primary healthcare.[43] Penrose High School and Tāmaki College had already piloted a model of full service delivery that located health, social and education services together; but it still took some years for the penny to drop in policy circles that *youth health and education outcomes were connected*.

What was the fate of the Hawk and Hill feedback reports? Only following a change of government (the new minister of education, Trevor Mallard, announced in 2001 a Full Service Schools initiative) would there be an attempt to take a more consistently holistic approach to the needs of students in these secondary schools. Youth workers and school nurses were appointed to serve in each of them, and every Year 9 student received a full health assessment. The positive effect of this on student learning could be counted—school NCEA results were slowly shifting upwards,[44] although it would be difficult to attribute the rising results to health interventions alone. But here's the rub: the Ministry of Education resented having to find money for health outcomes from Vote: Education. Only after several years of testy negotiation did the Ministry of Health and local health boards pick up resposibility for these services.

According to Bill Gavin, the former principal of Ōtāhuhu College, the ministry appeared to take fright from the conclusions of the AIMHI researchers—including that 'the difficulties (for student achievement) are complex and many of them are external to the school's control'. The ministry sent the researchers' final report out for peer review (perhaps the researchers had been captured by the schools and could no longer see dispassionately what had changed, or what ought to change).

The spat over the research report highlighted the clash of theories governing the relationship between the ministry and the schools. For the ministry, non-intervention was emphatically the default setting for the relationship. Decile funding had been intended to address the issues of community disadvantage; schools ought to be able to get stability at least, and thereafter sustainability in achievement, from within their budgets. For the schools, wise and effective use of project funding had enabled them to make measurable improvements. So why would the ministry withdraw from a collaborative project that was making a difference? The ministry's theory prevailed. After nearly ten years it decided that the AIMHI 'project' needed to end. The schools were collectively no longer exhibiting symptoms of imminent collapse, and achievement and other data were trending upwards. The schools were to cease asking for money each year; they had to stand alone. If the AIMHI collective wanted to continue to work together, it was up to them.

The Strengthening Education in Māngere and Ōtara (SEMO) project, unlike the AIMHI initiative, was directly triggered by the ERO report and largely focused on what was happening in the primary and intermediate schools. It had an inauspicious beginning, embedded as it was in enrolment rivalries, lack of trust and the ground zero of Judith Aitken's report. Where to begin? Kids here were behind before they even started school, and they remained behind. Was 'being behind' as a new entrant a permanent handicap? Could schools make a difference? If new entrant teachers got targeted professional development and support, could more children reach expected levels for their age at school entry and at six years old?

To tease out a practical response to those questions, the University of

Auckland's Woolf Fisher Research Centre and the Ministry of Education worked with schools and early childhood services to pilot an 'intervention'. Some years later, *Picking up the Pace* pithily reported the results.[45] No, it didn't have to be like this. Yes, teachers and schools could make a measurable difference. Low rates of progress in literacy were neither inevitable nor unchangeable in low-decile schools. Educators could bring children up to scratch. How? Well, the educators needed a specific set of skills and special coaching and support from professional leaders. They were working with children who needed 'a special kind of speeding-up in order to "pick up" the expected rate of progress in their literacy achievement' as soon as possible after entry to school, thereby guaranteeing development in literacy over the rest of their school careers. What's more, to make changes in their practice, teachers needed to be part of a 'community of learning'.

This research was not without its critics. First of all, there was only partial reference to *why* children were already behind when they arrived at school, although there was tacit admission that early childhood education policy had failed these children before they even got to school. Secondly, another group of academics did not agree that this research was sufficiently rigorous to provide 'evidence' that shift is possible or sustainable.[46] Nor did they agree with the sweeping assumptions of the researchers that changing teachers' expectations might have had something to do with success. Despite improvements, they argued, those kids were still in the tail end of achievement.

So whose fault is poor school performance? *Picking up the Pace* highlighted a two-camp debate: those who blame poor performance on principals and teachers, and those who blame it on the social and economic conditions in which schools operate. The answers the Woolf Fisher Research Centre researchers came up with were certainly convenient for a schooling improvement agenda increasingly focused on the technical skills of teachers in the classroom.

It is indisputable: teachers and schools make a difference,[47] as do families and communities with social capital. Rather than weighing up whether one thing is more important than another and building policy that falls to one side of this blame game, there had to be some other 'story' by which South Auckland's particular educational challenges could be explained.

A confusing array of other schooling improvement research projects in South Auckland with complicated histories reported similar results. We want these kids to *read* well, right? In Māngere,[48] a project to improve reading comprehension across a group of seven decile 1 primary schools showed that by building a teacher's and school's capacities to understand the evidence about student learning,[49] you could make gains in student achievement over and above the gains you might normally get. How? You needed good leadership in schools; strong collaborations among teachers; lots of professional input to give teachers quality feedback about what they were doing right; high quality, shared student assessment data; and the involvement of parents. This is a more complex solution than focusing on a single teacher's performance.

We want these kids to *write* well, right? Under the auspices of the Ōtara Boards Forum and a project called Ōtara: The Learning Community (OTLC), a collaboration of six Ōtara schools and 29 teachers worked with professional development facilitators and researchers to see if they could raise the writing skills of children in their schools.[50] Again, the research showed good results. You could improve kids' writing scores through intensive on-the-ground professional support of the teachers; the creation of a 'professional learning community'; and committed school leadership. Again, the research reinforced the emerging story about how nested the student gains were in the 'community' of professional networks around the teachers and how closely they worked together.

To cut a long story short, the suite of research commissioned by the Ministry of Education, potted across 'clusters' of schools right across South Auckland as well as national clusters (in projects for raising literacy and numeracy), proved that teachers could teach kids better—*given a particular set of supportive professional circumstances.*

Evidence is important to policymakers. What evidence did this or that intervention show of improved student learning? Were teachers learning too? Here is the news: for the 35,000 children in these two suburbs, the evidence of these research studies is that effective schooling improvement rests on something bigger than what is going on inside individual classrooms and in stand-alone schools. South Auckland's problems lie not simply in poor teaching, poor principalship, poor governance or poor people. Firing teachers and principals and closing down failing schools was not then, and is not now, an effective or practical solution. At its heart, classrooms are parts of schools, and schools are elements in a system whole, and how the parts work together and learn together is almost more important than how bits of the system work as stand-alone units.

As this work marched forwards, the notions of 'partnership in transformation' and 'communities of learning' began to emerge. The irony of these phrases will not be lost on many of the readers of this book.

Partnership schools and communities of learners

Strengthening Education in Māngere and Ōtara was a *project.* SEMO project official Brian Annan wrote that the ministry's ambition was to 'craft a partnership' that would develop comprehensive solutions.[51] Projects by definition have a beginning, a middle and an end. According to the ministry's schooling improvement theory, its intervention was to create a set of circumstances that would have long-lasting ownership and impacts across all of the schools in Māngere and Ōtara. The Ministry of Education's involvement was explicitly finite. It wanted 'partnership' but not 'dependence'; partnership to the extent that the Ministry of Education's primary responsibility is *not* to students or schools or communities, but to the minister—a point made clear at the time by the secretary for education.

So what did the SEMO local-level partnership look like in practice? Everyone was nervous about stepping onto the partnership escalator. Although they asked for help, the principals wanted to remain self-managing and didn't want to be told what to do. For this reason, schools themselves initially designed in-house projects to build the participation of parents in their schools and build community confidence in them. There was a pot of money to support this work, over and above school entitlement, but it had to be defined in a contract. It seemed simple at first: all schools were to fill out a submission for a 'funding provision agreement'. But to principals it felt like a top-down exercise of managerial power. Some principals suspected from the outset that once the contract finished and the money disappeared, the initiatives could fall apart (most later did). If this was 'partnership', then was giving out extra money but not telling the schools what to do satisfactory? Although schools borrowed ideas from each other about what they could do, they apparently didn't base their project idea on any evidence about its effectiveness.[52] Nor was 'collaboration' a part of their thinking.

A year later, the ministry team took a more hands-on approach to disbursing the money. So then, could you call it 'partnership' when the ministry challenged schools about their educational practice?

This was a delicate dance. After a year, schools apparently felt a hands-on ministry was preferable to hands-off,[53] because now the ministry was sharing its knowledge rather than sitting back and waiting for the schools to come up with solutions. At what point would the schools 'own' their own practice and become accountable for it? For how long would the Ministry of Education stay on the playing field?

Terry Bates, formerly a project manager for the ministry, describes his career in education as being deeply involved with the 'policy crucible of schooling improvement initiatives'. The high-minded principles on which the ministry based its schooling improvement work included 'purposeful intervention, evidence-based work programmes, measurable outcomes, reciprocal benefits, fiscal transparency, and lifting teacher skill and competence'. All very well, according to Bates, except that he ran into constant blockages put up by school principals. They were almost uniformly distrustful of the ministry's motives, resented being 'coerced' into participation and disagreed with each other about what the real issues were. They were incredibly fearful of public scrutiny; some were actively and openly resistant to intervention, some demonstrated 'cavalier' attitudes to contractual obligations, and principals backed each other in a spirit of professional collegiality but refused to be professionally accountable. In other words, it was a leadership mess. He writes:

> If the point of schooling improvement . . . is to make a greater difference . . . in every classroom in every school, the response seems to be 'only to the extent that individual principals are prepared to allow.[54]

'Partnership', then, could not be a word you could use for the relationship between the ministry and its schools.

Manurewa is a southern suburb of 80,000 people and growing, bigger than the city of Palmerston North. Thirty-two schools educate over 16,000 children in mostly either decile 2 or 3 schools, with a couple of high-decile schools (the sharp divide is typical of Auckland). In September 2002, the minister launched with fanfare a schooling improvement initiative there. Unlike the Māngere and Ōtara experience, this project was not born out of crisis. The sensitivities about this among school principals were clear from the start. They did not want their schools to be tarred with the brush of schooling *improvement,* implying dissatisfaction about the educational offerings in the suburb. No, this was schooling *enhancement,* with funding injected to help schools work together and offer them professional support.

Whatever the name, the ministry's theory of schooling improvement would apply to the Manurewa Enhancement Initiative (MEI)—and it, too, would be a finite project. All schools signed a formal memorandum of understanding identifying the goal (raising student achievement, especially for Māori and Pasifika students). The scoping phase set up five 'working parties'. Workshops and meetings across the suburb's schools decided what the projects should be. A 'steering committee' agreed on guiding principles and by 2004 the project strands got under way, among them improving school attendance, literacy and numeracy outcomes. There was much goodwill. Researchers were appointed to track progress and outcomes.

The issue of data management quickly became a key frustration. It's important to this story to recognise that in 2004 many of these schools were only at the beginning stages of using electronic data-gathering systems. Gathering data about attendance relied on someone accurately completing the school roll each day. Secondly, analysing school rolls without computer support was a lengthy and expensive process—therefore not top of anybody's to-do list. Thirdly, measuring learning was a sensitive question. 'How well is our school doing in relation to yours?' was not a question competing schools could directly ask each other. Schools monitored students' literacy and numeracy progress with a variety of assessment tools; so you couldn't compare apples with apples.

Schools were all over the place in their data-gathering and recording practices. This doesn't mean that the teaching was bad (or good), or that the students were making good (or poor) progress. It was just that it was difficult to tell. Schools were very guarded about who had access to their data and why. 'It's like herding cats,' confided one researcher at a report meeting I attended. Even an agreed list of tools did not allow researchers to confidently assess the progress of the project in improving literacy or numeracy outcomes Manurewa-wide.

Project governance got complicated too. The ministry was co-ordinating the project, creating a connecting infrastructure that had been only lightly sketched in Ōtara and Māngere and in the AIMHI project. But principals were suspicious of the ministry's intentions, and their commitment to a collaborative vision remained limited to the 'extra resources' that the MEI offered. Inevitably, professional tensions impacted on the willingness of school leaders and trustees to see beyond their own schools. As one Manurewa principal tells me, 'I learnt a lot from working with the researchers and other principals, and the professional development my staff got was focused and high quality, but the governance side of [the project] was diabolically difficult.' Principals felt involved in endless meetings, and the topics were not always relevant to the immediate needs of their school. On the continuum of collaboration, would the MEI go any further than surface co-operation?

Experimental design in the sciences involves control groups and study groups, start points and end points, consistency and a thousand other requirements. When clusters of schools work together to design better learning, the researchers and experts supporting them must travel and co-ordinate timetables and agree upon purposes and goals. Schools are very busy work sites, dynamic institutions with personality. Teachers come and go. Students come and go. Even principals move on. Rigorous academic practice and the needs of researchers get in the way of the day-to-day responsibilities of a school. Sometimes it all seems too hard. But here is the irony: despite the difficulties, researchers across all of the projects identified partnership as a *strength* in getting improved results—that is, partnership as defined by the working relationship between the researchers, the Ministry of Education and the schools around the shared goal of kids learning better. The reports pointed to the pick-me-ups and increasingly effective teaching practices in schools in South Auckland.[55]

But the rush of expensive research projects, university contracts and mahi together was not sustainable over time. Since the system's default settings had a longer life than the research projects themselves, the risk was that without the presence of a co-ordinator with clout (the Ministry of Education) and the luxury of researchers funded to operate closely alongside schools, the schools would fail to develop among themselves the will to continue to work together or to maintain the gains that they had made in student achievement. Without the financial carrot (or coercion) that a schooling improvement initiative offers, few schools were able to define, develop and fund a learning agenda that helps them and colleagues in other schools to achieve better results. Unless you get a really bad ERO report, why bother?

Six years later, the MEI had done its dash. A consistent cross-school approach to truancy and absenteeism had triggered improvement in attendance statistics (although evidence for that being sustained across the suburb remains almost impossible to pin down even today). All through the life of the MEI, some schools weren't ready to be truly collaborative. The consensus around working together was fragile enough to allow some schools to walk away from the project. It was never really clear how much 'improvement' was made to learning outcomes across the whole suburb, although individual schools could point to significant shifts.

The lesson from the MEI is that under the devolved schools structure, collaboration is hard to sustain because the glue that keeps people working together and the system incentives for joined-up effort are missing. Gary Hawke, formerly the head of the School of Government at Victoria University of Wellington, would argue that the original intent of the devolution of administration to schools was always for schools to be seen as part of a whole. Core elements of public service operation were either completely ignored or never understood by those charged with making the reforms work.[56] The management culture inside education has never learnt how to collaborate around government goals, says Hawke; indeed, it too often refuses to acknowledge that the *quid pro quo* of being self-managing is to be 'accountable' for achieving system objectives (as set by the politics of the day). The quality of teaching and learning in South Auckland schools has had its greatest advance through the research and efforts of 'action learning' leaders working collaboratively—and perhaps more often in South Auckland schools than in their equivalents in many of the more comfortable suburbs—but scarcely with the *government*'s goals in mind.

The idea of a 'partnership' approach to schooling—and schooling improvement in particular—is confusing. Who is supposed to be partnering with whom? In the schooling improvement work, much earnest discussion focused on the relationship between researchers, the principal, the teachers and the ministry. But partnership *with parents* was the founding rationale for the 1989 reform. No one told schools what the information to parents or communities should look like.

There's a piece of paper in the partnership with parents called the school report. Three evaluation studies from the University of Auckland included the reporting practices of primary schools in Māngere and Ōtara.[57] The first evaluation report showed parents and teachers talking past each other. A school could say to parents that their child Semisi was doing very well, but compared with what? Was he was doing well in relation to other students in the class, the school or the country? As Semisi's parents, you could send him to secondary school believing he was doing very well, and then be shocked to discover from his first high school report how far behind he really is. A 'standard' in one school could have very different meaning in another. By the time a child reaches secondary school, catch-up help might be too little or too late.

Realising that schools should report to parents against some sort of benchmark or standard is one thing; turning the school report into a crucial element in the parent–child–school partnership is quite another. Would legal coercion be a tool to make partnership with parents work? Yet another evaluation study two years later showed that primary schools were being driven to change their reporting practices, but it wasn't because they wanted to improve their partnership with parents.[58] Rather, the government had strengthened legal requirements around school reports.

The third study was focused on two schools that believed parents had a right to know how their children were really doing. Their willingness to share information with parents did not, however, make the task any easier. The principal and teachers confronted an ethical dilemma: how to report low achievement honestly but safely and constructively. There weren't any tools to help the teachers to reference their results against the broad national curriculum levels. They wanted to approach their task professionally, but would parents understand them?

The technical dilemmas in these schools had wider meaning. The drive for national standards is a global one, but in New Zealand it coincided with our own realisation from this kind of research that we didn't have good student achievement data to understand our own school reforms. We could test student learning, but our diagnosis was flawed. We couldn't benchmark learning against normal progress, nor could we identify what learning should happen next. We'd devolved decision-making down to schools, but schools were unable to tell parents, community, or government how students were really doing. Schools could maintain that most of their students are working 'at the standard' for their age, without moderation of their judgements or critique of their statistics. What could blow the whistle?

Change versus transformation

Did 20 years of extra energy and investment in the schools of South Auckland make a difference? It's hard to tell. What we do know is that not even among the most outstanding examples of classroom practice can you find the magical transformation that *sustainably* removes the effects of economic poverty, social dislocation and a disconnected system.

We've also learnt that partnership or collaboration depends on good information-sharing and evidence—at the school level *and* the community level. Knowing that South Auckland's schools can improve through creating clusters of professional practice is not the same as showing that South Auckland schools have improved, even on a school-by-school basis, and certainly not as a network of schools on a suburb-by-suburb basis.

The major insight from the South Auckland research isn't the predictable solution to fire the teachers who are no good and get in new ones (as though enough good teachers come pouring out of the universities ready to teach Māori and Pasifika students in our most disadvantaged communities anyway); or to put school boards in the naughty corner while a commissioner sorts out the school; or to shame principals whose schools are at the bottom of the league table; or to teach schools about how to use data properly; or to import change-principals. In zooming in on the learning process in the classroom, researchers were able to show how important it was across the profession to have *real* conversations about learning, how teachers could grow their expertise as a consequence and modernise their teaching practices in response to changing government and societal expectations. People learn. Schools learn. Yet the conditions for ongoing system improvement are opaque.

All that extra investment in education in South Auckland might have made a difference, but on the surface, everything looks as it was—or worse. Many people still don't want to send their kids to schools in South Auckland, and the improving NCEA results still show Māori and Pasifika kids are not achieving at the same levels as their Asian and Pākehā peers. Inequality persists. What other evidence do we need to show that the yawning gaps between those who have educational capital and those who don't are not being filled?

International system thinkers like Andy Hargreaves and Michael Fullan discuss how the 'professional capital' available to a community, as well as the skills and knowledge of individual teachers, are both important to the transformational task.[59] Others cite social capital and even 'spiritual capital' as germane to the task.[60] All this capital must be shared before it can become transformative, they tell us.

Sharing professional capital is, of course, the point to the latest ministerial push to invest additional resources into educational achievement. The point in describing some of this arcane educational research in South Auckland is that there are no quick fixes to be found. The 2014 policy shift to 'making best practice universal practice' (Investing in Educational Success, IES) is yet to prove the answer. The policy attempts to establish collaborative cross-school 'Communities of Learning'—but without fundamentally changing the patterns of cop-out that already exist, or the underlying market drivers towards competition and silos of practice. Calling them Communities of Learning has a research-backed, collaborative ring. But co-operation across schools is still a voluntary gift from the principal and the board. Interest from South Auckland schools in establishing and participating in the minister's Communities of Learning is currently low. I can see why. At a primary school in Papakura I observed a board struggling to come to terms with teacher quality and resources for a new entrant intake in which 100% of students arrive at the school 'below the standard' and 280 of the 350 students in the school have special needs or are at high risk of a low-achievement outcome. Not every school needs additional staffing and support in the way that this school does. For schools in the most distressed communities, however, already facing competitive pressures from their neighbours for staffing and relentless pressure to deliver outcomes that are unrealistic in the face of community disinterest and professional exhaustion, the roundabout, jump-the-hoops way of getting the resources that the IES policy promises just adds complications. Time to collaborate? Yeah, right.

The rush of 'solutionitis' in the IES policy reflects a partial understanding of the problem and an incomplete assessment of the alternatives.[61] South Auckland schools are indeed interested in better outcomes for their students. Although the policy has apparently been informed by their own participation in high-quality research, schools in South Auckland are wary to share, afraid to again expose their learning challenges for fear of even more rejection from their communities.

A three-year political term is not long enough to turn discovery into policy. No political party has put on their policy agenda a fundamental change to the way schools are run. Politicians only campaign on one or two headline issues, and these become the policy directions for their term of office. When a political leader makes a public promise, it is very difficult for her to later listen to actual research, perhaps because changing tack is so hard on votes; because good research sometimes takes too long to come to a conclusion; because the research does not fit the prevailing philosophy for schools; or because research doesn't carry the emotional appeal that is the essence of public balloting. How to get students up to standard remains a press-button political issue, but it seems that the answers are less electorally appealing than the question. You can't mobilise knowledge gained without mobilising the electorate; just as a car that needs petrol needs a service station too. Having poorly understood evidence about the shifts that have taken place across schools in South Auckland creates a climate ripe for 'political' solutions rather than ones that actually work. Transformation involves not just knowing what we have to do to fix things, but turning that into publicly agreed-upon understandings and politically winnable solutions.

Principals in South Auckland, teacher unions, researchers and ministry officials buried the outcomes of the South Auckland research (perhaps it was too academic, too complex, too equivocal and too embarrassing) so that it became impossible to create a climate of new policy expectation in line with the findings. The lack of a public narrative about the learning going on in South Auckland schools became a perfect medium in which to grow alternative political agendas. It was as though appalling schools and terrible teachers were still so rife in the public mind that we needed to start from scratch.

Like chess aficionados, policy buffs admire smart moves. When the window of policy opportunity opened, there was a ready solution to the problem of failure in South Auckland:[62] the charter school.

5
Governance and power

How the self-governing schools model works in communities in South Auckland

Nā tō rourou, nā taku rourou
ka ora ai te iwi
—With your food basket and my food basket
the people will thrive.

Governance design is the way we set the rules for how the system operates, and how people exercise power. Governance by the market is supposed to empower consumers and sideline the state. But as we have seen already, markets have limits. Charter schools are about creating an education market. To understand the failure of the market and charter schools in South Auckland, we need to pay more attention to how various stakeholders exercise power in the governance of schools. This chapter is about how the system works and the role of system leaders in shaping good governance. Is this governance we have the most effective we can find? What alternatives are there?

Private versus public

Governance is at the core of the debate about public education systems and their purpose. I am in Washington, DC, visiting the Public Education Network (PEN), which was then the peak body for organisations across America called Local Education Funds (LEFs).[1] Ginger groups with fundraising clout, LEFs were operating in school districts to advance the quality of public schools. The president of PEN, Wendy Puriefoy, invites me to explain how education works in New Zealand. My story is that most children attend self-managing public schools, each with a board of trustees that employs the principal and has responsibility for delivering the curriculum. We chat about the role of parents, the principal, the Ministry of Education and the public accountability requirements of boards. At the end of our discussion she says to me in her Southern accent, 'Why, honey, I do believe you've got a privatised education system. This is exactly what we are not about!'

A privatised education system? I was startled. Didn't we have an overarching, connected network of schools owned by the state? Were schools not accountable to the Ministry of Education and its minister? Didn't we pay taxes to get good quality education services for our children?

Wait a minute: *all* of the 2500 state schools in New Zealand are charter schools. All have a board of trustees mostly made up of parents (around 14,500 elected trustees across the country), all have a contract with the state (yes, called a charter)[2] and all are required to report as public entities back to the minister. A charter is really a performance contract that must meet the National Administration Guidelines. I realise now that the debate about charter schools in this country has become lost in the confusion about what 'privatisation' of schooling actually involves. It is a governance question and highly politicised, too. During this conversation, Wendy Puriefoy commented that our education system being in the control of parents (in theory, at least) seemed rudderless and selfish. In her view, a *public* education system should benefit all children, not become part of parental game-playing in a search for *private* family advantage.

Why does the distinction between public and private matter? Don't we just need to 'fix' the poorly performing schools so that every child gets a good deal? Exactly what is the policy problem here?

Board power

In the last chapter, we saw how school reforms were seductively sold as 'partnerships'. Ten years after the reforms, a former president of the New Zealand School Trustees Association (NZSTA), Janet Kelly, would note that, in reality, trustees were being driven by 'accountability requirements'—and it felt like being ordered about.[3] Partnership depends on shared purpose, shared control and balanced powers. Schools and communities took some time to accommodate to the law that made parents the employers of the principal and teachers, owners of the curriculum but responsible to the minister for identifying and addressing barriers to student achievement. This is charter operation at work.

As it turns out, most boards do passably well with this responsibility, some even superbly. By 2007 the New Zealand Council for Educational Research[4] could report that, although lots of boards had significant issues, the system wasn't about to fall over. Follow-up stocktakes from the NZSTA (governance 'isn't rocket science')[5] and ERO were equally upbeat. As the foundations of school governance practice in this country were being laid, people tripped over the loose bricks—the nature of relationships between professionals and parents, and attitudes about competence, skills and control.

Schools feature regularly in community conversations. As I roam across the networks of South Auckland, the tales I hear of school governance are hairy and personal. At one school, the principal refuses to let the board see any student achievement data 'because they wouldn't understand it—they can't even read!' At another, a Samoan community identity controls board meetings by switching to business in the Samoan language, ostensibly to keep information about Samoan children and their families confidential—'he shuts out the principal and me,' whispers my Tongan confidant. At yet another school, the board members barely speak during the meeting and certainly would not ask questions of their principal—it would be culturally impertinent for them to do so. At another, the frequency of board meetings has gotten silly—the meeting fee is not large but constitutes a welcome contribution in a family with little other income. At yet another, the principal bullies the board into funding her annual overseas trip under the guise of her 'professional development'. At another, two board chairs have quit in quick succession because of the stress of the role, and the third is struggling to understand what to do. Board chairs may be absentee leaders or wield powers based on their mana, regardless of their competence. Extended families take over some boards and become active gatekeepers to prevent parent involvement in the school. In the 2016 school trustee elections, in many of these schools more than 90% of parents failed to return a valid voting paper.

The promise of self-management in education was to give even the poorest communities power in the democratic mainstream. School boards would help to grow governance skills within the community. Why did it work out that way in some communities, but not others?

Trusteeship is a skill set that can be learnt. Yet a 2002 study of a cluster of school board chairpersons in South Auckland reported a disturbing fact: only two of 16 chairpersons could accurately interpret their school's student achievement reports.[6] The matters facing boards are complex. Trustee training materials take no account of the low literacy and numeracy skills among the adult population in South Auckland;[7] of cultural patterns for decision-making; or of the sheer workloads facing trustees with limited time and social capital.

School governance within a charter offers trustees prestige and local-level power. When things go wrong, the Ministry of Education invokes the law to install a commissioner or apply statutory management. It is more than a removal of self-managing power—replacement of the board becomes, in effect, an insult to the mana of people and community. When they fall over, boards are dealt with as naughty children: they get a bad report, get supervision and lose the privilege of control. At any given time, the ERO judges around 16% of schools (nationally) as 'cause for concern'[8]—many of them are in high-poverty communities. While schools of any decile experience problems, the schools that struggle most with governance serve the very students that school reforms were most supposed to help. Trusteeship turns these parents into failures too.

The Ōtara Boards Forum (OBF) was an experiment that was, for a time, the showcase for collaborative systemic problem-solving. The previous chapter describes the lightbulb moment when the board chairs of 17 Ōtara schools agreed that they would work together to solve a problem. The OBF became its own official entity, registered as a not-for-profit trust. Forum leaders were invited to talk about their joint work to officials and international visitors at conferences. Articles appeared in newspapers and magazines about the area's combined efforts to improve learning. The minister of education, the mayor and local identities turned up to well-attended, collaboratively organised 'literacy days', where schools could jointly and powerfully send out community messages about the importance of learning. The OBF, it seemed, was a roaring success.

The common interest among these school boards held for some years, most especially while it was being actively nurtured and supported by the Ministry of Education. As crisis fades, the humdrum takes over. The ministry left the OBF to self-manage. It sweetened the withdrawal by awarding the OBF a local truancy contract. But a contract has a finite term. Without it, the constituent school 'owners' of the OBF can no longer see a reason to work together—the joint task has become too vague and too large and the requirement for them to commit resources too hard. All of the major schooling improvement initiatives in South Auckland demonstrated that collaboration via clusters of schools and teachers had benefits for student learning. On their own, boards, principals and teachers would have struggled to make any progress.[9] As a sort-of-voluntary community of practice, the Ōtara schools could box together and make enough improvements to keep ERO at bay. But eventually, without crisis or a clear purpose for working together, and without the co-ordinating glue, commitment to the community-of-practice idea went lukewarm.

In a sense, the OBF began as community governance 'lite', like Coca-Cola that isn't. The boards developed their own collective view about a preferred future for Ōtara. They had three levers: their mandate as elected representatives of parents in their schools, their joint commitment to the plan for schooling in Ōtara and to the forum itself, and the projects they worked on together. It was 'lite' because the process was closed to external input and scrutiny. These were public entities, chartered to deliver to the state. But who knew what was going on? Poor governance was not eliminated by the collective. At the time, I wondered aloud to a government official about this. 'The boards own this, and the community can butt out,' he told me firmly. Even as they fought to collaborate—I use the verb deliberately—these schools were acting as private enterprises.

The theory of social reproduction describes the ways in which the powerful and the privileged maintain their advantages over generations through control of systems and institutions.[10] In Ōtara I could observe that—no matter the rhetoric—power and control of schools rested not on parents but on the principals and the Ministry of Education. While parent trustees are nominally in charge, they don't all participate in 'board training' (an entirely voluntary activity), and the advice they receive about employment and curriculum matters is too often from the professionals who work for them and who have their own interests to protect.

Where is the real power to strengthen governance over schools and for learning? A community is more than parents. It includes local government officials and elected representatives, iwi and Māori urban authorities, leaders of community trusts, the CEOs of community agencies, business or workplace leaders who worry about the shape of the local economy and the skills needed for development, government agency leaders and community identities such as church pastors, kaumatua and the like. But these leaders are not often co-opted to school governance.

In enclaves of advantage in Auckland, trustees provide wonderful support to principals and teachers. These trustees attract competent educators and choose experienced principals as school leaders. They add the expertise of accountants, administrators and business managers to their board. But in other neighbourhoods underperforming principals are unchallenged, financial mismanagement is left unnoticed and what counts as professional competence and administrative process bewilders the uninitiated. Communities have no power to insist that governance quality is supported by system settings (as we expect for principal quality and teacher quality). The professional tasks of trusteeship, such as appraising the performance of a principal or ensuring that curriculum is delivered effectively, are only lightly sketched for board members.

To fix a general lack of governance capacity in places like South Auckland, it may be tempting to import a cadre of fully trained professional board advisors and trustees with the power to oversee the complex roles of employers and principals. Accredited professional governance support (yes, paid) could be a mandatory underpinning for all boards—a preventive medicine to the legal remedies normally applied when boards get into trouble. This is an approach adopted in the UK in the academy-as-a-market approach. Its vaunted purpose—professionalising trusteeship so that 'fully skills-based governance will become the norm'—looks attractive. But under this approach disempowered communities lose even the local-level powers they had. South Auckland's school governance challenges won't go away with this solution; disengagement simply transfers into a new setting.

So, just meddling in a school's autonomy is no answer to systemic dysfunction. The call here is for next-generation governance that includes a community empowerment approach at its most sophisticated and most inclusive, one that takes student achievement, professional quality and good governance as measurable system outcomes. This will test education policymakers for two reasons. A legislative shift in governance powers—especially for oversight of professional leadership—will certainly rattle existing power blocs. And secondly, education policymakers are not familiar with community empowerment principles and ways of working.

The powerlessness of community is further illustrated by the system's chronic inability to raise important educational conversations. The governance model encourages us to focus on the detail of individual schools at the expense of the bigger picture. Two Auckland illustrations make this point: the cases of Selwyn College and the Clover Park campus.

Selwyn College, in the heart of the desirable eastern suburbs, serves Ōrākei, Mission Bay, Kohimarama and Meadowbank. At the time of the 1989 reforms, over 80% of the school roll were Pākehā students; ten years later, this proportion had halved.[11] This could be attributed partly to aggressive enrolment strategies from neighbouring schools during the 1990s; partly to the liberal philosophy of the non-uniformed school; partly to a diversifying population; and partly to white flight. The school was Auckland's go-to school for refugees. It was famous, too, for its terrific performing arts programme. But, as Professor John Hattie remarked in one of the many media analyses of the school, it was most famous for 'clinging to a style and philosophy that the community no longer wanted.'[12]

Community views about how the school ought to be run seeped into the local MP's electorate office. Alan Peachey had himself been a secondary school principal, and his public statements were intended to apply pressure to the leadership of the school. Selwyn College worked exactly as the system intended it to work. But its mistake was to believe that the community would leave it to follow its own way. Essentially, community voices are irrelevant to the self-managing schools model; only *parents* (of children actually enrolled) can vote school boards in. In this sense, schools are almost private entities. Walk away, you lose your say. But actually, this community had plenty to say. Selwyn College became a battleground—attempts to capture the board and to redirect the school ripped the board apart. Eventually, after futile governance support and advice, the minister sacked the board and appointed a commissioner. Today, the community can breathe a sigh of relief. A new principal has turned around perceptions, spruced up buildings, smartened the uniform, posted better results, delivered better PR and improved community relations. Local real estate values climbed steeply. But the important conversation about how schools ought to respond to diversity and difference barely reached dinner tables. As noted historian James Belich wrote in *Metro* magazine in 2006:

> A lot of people are still in denial about the fact that Auckland has become a multi-ethnic place over the past 20 or 30 years. The proportion of other groups is now huge, and I think some Pākehā find that threatening. But the fact is, it's a reality and we've got to cope with it. If multi-ethnic schools like Selwyn don't work then Auckland is not going to work.[13]

That was ten years ago. No one took responsibility for steering that conversation to important and timely conclusions. A decade later, ethnic superdiversity is again a topic for city conversation[14]—but we are reluctant to connect it to educational choices.

A Samoan leader came into my office one morning. She wanted her local Ōtara primary school to adopt a bilingual philosophy. She understood how success for her children and grandchildren would hinge on their ability to operate equally competently in two worlds. 'I have no idea how to go about it,' she told me, 'but I can't get my local school principal to be interested in supporting the children's language.' She felt inadequate raising a topic that the principal would not understand and which the board felt powerless to do anything about.

Despite the 160 languages spoken in Tāmaki Makaurau/Auckland, English is almost universally the medium of instruction in schools. The merits of bilingual teaching and learning have not been central to the discussion about student achievement. Becoming educated in *two* languages is not a globally exceptional ideal—in fact, across the world education systems cope with multilingualism all the time. In a part of Auckland where more than a third of people are already bilingual,[15] fluency in two languages helps you to live in the English-speaking mainstream and to participate fully in the social, economic and cultural life of your ethnic community. But since in New Zealand the professional growth path that principals take to become leaders assumes monolingualism, few understand the differences between immersion schooling and bilingual schooling,[16] the pedagogies behind them or even why they are important.[17] So it is hard for principals to lead a community-wide debate about the place of language in learning. Individual schools and principals can develop a philosophy around bilingualism, but they only have a mandate to raise discussion within the confines of their own school community. It becomes almost a private debate.

The evolution of Kia Aroha College illustrates how important community conversations like this get lost inside the self-managing schools model. The Clover Park campus in Ōtara serves one of the poorest communities in Auckland. Like a shapeshifter hologram, over 20 or so years this school has morphed from an intermediate school to a school with an attached secondary unit, to a middle school, to a restricted composite school, to two schools, then to a secondary school campus. Its distinctive philosophy for bilingual learning drove these shifts.

Now, it is fair to say that the relationship between professional leaders in Ōtara has historically been one of distrust and poor communication. The Kia Aroha school principal and her board have long been isolated within the network in Ōtara. Their dream was to make this school a beacon for bilingual schooling in the area. At each of this school's transition stages, the minister had to consult 'the community'. But consultation is legally and narrowly defined, and deeply flawed. The wider community conversation, discussion and debate about 'being bilingual' and how to nurture that across the whole network of schools in Ōtara did not happen because other school leaders did not want it to, and because no community champions had the authority, or funding, to lead the task. There is nothing to support this school board's communications with its neighbouring schools, or for the schools in the network to consider the philosophical and educational integrity of the school's position on bilingual schooling. Each school is a separate body. So the Clover Park campus has had to develop its own spine.

If you are of the view that a lost language is no big deal, then the lack of community debate about bilingual learning opportunities across the network of schools won't matter to you either. However, loss of language and cultural identity is manifestly linked to poor social and economic outcomes. The irony is that student achievement, the thing that the minister expects most from schools, is so strongly linked to language development that leaving bilingual learning out of the policy mix looks almost deliberate.

But the affront is hidden. Student achievement data doesn't record language loss. The number of Māori who use te reo in Tāmaki Makaurau is shrinking, despite the rise in student numbers. The anodyne Pasifika Education Plan barely makes reference to bilingual learning. There is no community empowerment here. Boards, except in the most isolated of circumstances, are powerless to lead shift.

The power of data

Much of what we know about how to improve schools and learning is quite technical. The outcomes from schooling improvement work are like goldfish under a lilypad. The cognoscenti inside schools and the research departments of universities know about it. Few others do. 'Well, it's often complicated data,' excuses one principal. Yet in the 'Age of Big Data'[18] there must be some way to make all of this information publicly understandable. It's a public question for a public education system: Is the public investment in schooling delivering the outcomes we want?

The policy for National Standards represents the universal anxiety about how well schools are performing—at least, how well *my* child and *my* child's school is performing. The policy was built on the evidence that good teaching and learning depends on diagnostic tools that allow teachers to define what students know and what they should know next. Unfortunately, the public conversation on National Standards veered toward the more politically appealing view that parents have a 'right' to know how well their child is doing. Crucially, that is a private matter. We ought to distinguish between the private responsibility of schools to benchmark how well children are doing against National Standards and to design learning to help them meet the standards, and the public obligation of the state system to show that all children are achieving. While it might be possible to use the same data for both purposes, the anxiety of school principals and their professional associations is that publicising National Standards data will result in blunt and unfair league tables. Unfortunately, you can't have a useful public conversation about schools without facts. As education minister Hekia Parata insisted: 'I'm not publishing a league table; I'm publishing public achievement information.'[19] To be convinced that student achievement has improved, the public needs some critical evidence—more than the summative data of NCEA results at the end of more than ten years of educational input.

I came across a wonderful newsletter from a South Auckland primary school that reported how Māori children in the school were doing against National Standards. It was presented via a large graph with clear statements underneath. It was an effective piece of communication to parents. It was simple. It did not go into ifs, buts, maybes and technical mumbo-jumbo. I could not critique its accuracy, but I could see it would be a great starting point for a conversation with whānau about how their children were doing. This school has become particularly savvy about the use of data—as many involved in schooling improvement projects learnt to be. I pondered on how such a splendid graph could be incredibly useful in a more public conversation about how schools, collectively, in this neighbourhood were doing; especially if reported against the National Standards. But with poor, incomplete or overly complex information, it is no wonder the public concludes that schools are failing or that the government is failing to manage the schooling system properly. Who would *you* believe? The education sector professionals who say that New Zealand schools do really well in international comparisons? Or game-players pointing to appalling results in maths and science in South Auckland primary schools?

The fourth estate's powerful role in a democracy is to guard the public interest and act as a watchdog on the workings of democratic institutions. The public interest and the private aspirations of individual parents may be one and the same thing—but not always. League tables reinforce the private obsession with picking 'the best' schools (and, of course, they sell newspapers). That league tables are part of the system of checks and balances in a democratic society is a self-serving argument. All the same, we do need to have a public conversation on what National Standards reveal about the quality of the state's schools, suburb by suburb.

In fact, the developments in big data software have already triggered websites that begin to demonstrate the potential of educational data in the public domain. The *stuff.co.nz* website 'School Report' illustrates the possibilities.[20] On this website is more information about named primary schools than has ever before been publicly available in one place, although the fact that it exists in this form at all is due to remarkable persistence. In a climate of obstruction, the chief ombudsman eventually prised open the cache of data held by the Ministry of Education, pointing out that anybody asking for official information from a school board is making a legitimate request under the Official Information Act. It is no surprise that the school system leaves the impression it is made up of private institutions. However, public achievement information is more than the data for individual schools.

Data needs interpretation. The 'School Report' website is unable (yet) to tell you about the aggregate achievement in maths of all students in, say, Manurewa. Now, it is widely acknowledged that the National Standards data is flawed: it is not moderated (so that overall teacher judgements about what counts as achieved' in one school is the same as in another), and it is not based on a 'test', as in other countries. But growing transparency has sharp relevance, like the tang in a lemon tart. The conversation about how schools do, in general and in particular, is fundamental to community development. It can't be private information.

But just knowing about something doesn't necessarily translate into action. And as community development activists will tell you, public achievement information is not yet available in a form that is genuinely useful for collaborative action. Besides, the narrative of numbers is only the first step in longer conversations that flesh out the actual reality of student learning.

Partnership power

The 'partnership school'—kura hourua—is the latest version of governance by charter. Having sold the public on the idea that parent power could make a difference, in 2014 politicians told us that poor kids get a sad deal from the parent takeover of public schools. The answer, apparently, is that governance should now include 'sponsors'; that is, organisations other than parents as governors of a school.

These 'partnership schools' arrive in a community, somewhat ironically, without the consultation otherwise required for setting up new schools. Community ownership of schooling is thereby neatly sidelined. (The definition of consultation in education legislation has been found flawed in so many instances that, really, we ought to call it off altogether. How sadly naive, then, the expectations from professional leaders: 'We had no idea that there was a plan to license a new [partnership] school in our neighbourhood,' complained the Māngere Principals' Association just before Christmas 2013. 'There are 23 schools in our Māngere cluster and the professionals who work in them know, more than anyone, the educational needs of our community. Yet we were not consulted.')[21]

Could these new charter schools—excuse me, 'partnership schools'—be the answer to poor student achievement? Do 'partnership schools' open up our system, as some claim, to corporate takeovers of community democracy? Let's look at the five pilots in the first iteration of 'partnership schools'. The Vanguard Military School, zoneless in Auckland, is operated by a small private training business; it pinches the idea of the service-academy-within-the-school (already a successful initiative in over a dozen mainstream secondary schools) and spins it as its own idea. South Auckland Middle School is an expansion of the Villa Education Trust's private school in Remuera, and translates the idea of the sports academy to a target group of budding South Auckland sports stars. The Kura Hourua o Whangarei Terenga Paraoa, sponsored by the community-based He Puna Marama Charitable Trust, offers a programme for Years 7–13 with a focus on leadership and pride for Māori students and is run in partnership with a local secondary school. The Rise UP Academy, from the Rise UP Trust in Māngere, is a Pasifika community collaboration, formerly a community trust working alongside schools and now a competitor to them. Te Kura Hourua ki Whangaruru, sponsored by the Ngā Parirau Mātauranga Charitable Trust, owned and run by local whānau, was intended as a bilingual school and cannibalised the roll of the already small nearby state school.

None of these sponsors could be called big business. Rather, they represent community social entrepreneurship in action. That is, they are small enterprises with a faith-based or ethnic connection to target students and their families. These new schools will operate in a niche setting, will have a set of core values that are understood in their communities and will be conviction driven. Who is partnering with whom in this model?

The Rise UP Trust illustrates such tensions. The trust began in a garage in 2006, as Auntie Sita's Home School, running after-school programmes. It evolved as an outreach group that helped parents to support their children's learning ('We reap what we sow'—Galatians 6:7). It evolved into a formal entity that deliberately set out to build Christian community and intergenerational engagement in education (a Building Learning Communities programme). In 2009 this emergent collective received funding from the ASB Community Trust (now Foundation North) to advance their work with whānau. Activities included snappily named six- or seven-week evening and after school programmes. By November 2010 they offered these at two schools and two churches in Māngere and Manurewa, working with over 60 families. The ASB Community

Trust offered extra support to build good governance practices and sound management. But then, from being a community organisation that supported learning in local schools, the Rise UP Trust became a competitor in the South Auckland schooling market and was praised as social entrepreneurship in action. Although at time of writing, the Rise UP Academy schools a maximum of 40 students, apparently successfully, those students carry with them the whānau support and community connections once offered to the state schools nearby. While the trust has exciting community potential, the competitive model has destroyed bonds with other schools; replicating on a new level the education system's inability to cross-pollinate good practice, sustain collaboration and meaningfully reach out into communities.

The attractiveness of these new charter schools raises questions about power within communities. Why did Northland iwi Ngātiwai walk away from the local school already serving their children? For the controversial Whangaruru whānau, the rationale for change was certainly student achievement:

> Every (terrible) statistic represents a person—our sons, our daughters, our nieces, our nephews and our unborn descendants yet to come. These children make up our priority group and we are willing to work with you and others to provide an education that fits them.'[22]

The whānau's willingness to work 'with you and others' (that is, the Ministry of Education) sidelined the local public school. Is it because, despite the rhetoric of Tomorrow's Schools, the curriculum and its delivery at the local school have never truly been in the hands of parents or iwi? The whānau wanted to take back control because, says the group, 'We want to be part of the solution, we want to enable *our community* [emphasis added] to be a part of the solution. We want to be able to capitalise on the rich cultural history that must be utilised as part of the rongoā to the current situation.' Are mainstream schools, designed to be of the community, missing a trick here? Governance is about who owns and controls the curriculum and its outcomes. The difference between 'mainstream' charter schools and 'partnership' charter schools is only a minor shift of governance. The points at issue seem to be cultural responsiveness and pedagogy that engages and empowers. Ngātiwai seized the state's broken-down definitions of 'partnership' and 'community' and reinterpreted them for themselves. Their reasoning was obvious: since they could not exercise control over learning in the state's charter, perhaps their own private one would deliver better. We now know otherwise. In the end, alternative governance barely delivered for these Whangaruru children. Along the way, the whānau showed up the local school board as a self-governing sham unable to make a difference to the raruraru (problems) inside that community. The unspoken conclusion is that parent power *increases* social inequalities, because some parents are better at governing their schools and advocating for them and their children than others.

Still, the law of unintended consequences can deliver awesome benefits as well as awful detriments. These new charter schools may deliver in much the same way as the former Māori boarding schools once delivered Māori leadership and as prestigious schools in the Pacific deliver leadership—which is to say, imperfectly, but at least with a strong sense of identity and ownership. These schools create community and become integral to it. At the same time, they also privatise community so that the focus of the community organisation is . . . itself. Unfortunately, in a world where collaboration is not only highly desirable but necessary, splitting communities into self-focused competing entities is no answer to the need for a public education system with a fundamental purpose to build social cohesion and inclusion. Our public policy for governance of schools has patently failed in that purpose.

The market created problems in South Auckland and in other poor communities in Northland and the East Coast—and new versions of markets won't fix them. No matter how well these partnership schools meet individual community aspirations, they cannot solve the deep-rooted issues of unfair access to education. They won't provide the connective tissue needed for system transformation so that every child benefits from public education. They simply perpetuate—and exacerbate— the failures of the existing charter model.

State power and devolved responsibility

There's a bipolar tension in the market model between state control and school agency. The property portfolio illustrates this. Schools are the government's second largest property asset (after housing). The book value ($10.7 billion) alone doesn't represent fully the extent of public ownership in the property portfolio of the Ministry of Education. There are over 8000 hectares of land; 24,000 school buildings with 35,000 classrooms; not to mention the 1400 swimming pools and 900 schoolhouses. More than $500 million annually is spent on existing schools, and more millions are set aside for new schools.[23] If leaky schools didn't give the Treasury a fright, the Christchurch earthquakes sure did. The headaches afterwards included how to keep the whole education system internationally competitive in state-of-the-art buildings suited to new technologies (60% of schools are over 50 years old) while scrabbling around in an empty cashbox. They might well have asked: did the current asset management system offer value for money?

School boards manage this estate. Aside from the observation that, individually, schools with antiquated buildings seem reasonably maintained, the investment/divestment decisions about school property are peculiarly inward-looking. Is this efficient? Is governance of property absolutely necessary to the self-managing model?

As well as being a significant distraction from the priority for teaching and learning, there is no 'assurance' that boards manage property well. Nor do they have an overview of the bigger picture. Auckland is short of many thousands of student places in the most popular schools and has 32,000 surplus student places in the least popular ones. Parental perceptions and the policy of school choice certainly have something to do with it. Some schools want status and some build an empire. Few are content to be small, with an emphasis on quality. Shifting populations and social circumstances often mean that the classrooms the city needs are not in the places parents want. In sum, Auckland's schools are economically inefficient. To have large numbers of students bussing from the west and south of Auckland to central and eastern schools, and having some schools empty and others full to bursting, is wasted money and time.

Policymakers get this. The public doesn't always see it. With a billion dollars to spend on renewing 'infrastructure', system performance has to offer measurable value. The ministry intends for an attitudinal shift to change focus from it being a property funder to it being a 'high-performing asset manager'.[24] Can this state activism be as transformational as the new policy intends? Asset management involves disposing of assets as well as building new ones, shrinking zones as housing intensifies in inner suburbs, and reorienting boards to the creation of efficiencies in their suburb. Will schools and their communities allow the state to close uneconomic schools as parents bus students elsewhere, or will they re-bundle property assets as the long-term replacement of aging physical assets takes place? History shows that this is unlikely.

Infrastructure isn't the only issue. The 'shock drop' in the 2009 PISA results[25] added to the prevailing sense of a ministry in management crisis. Although the evidence for this fall apparently pointed to student performance in the lowest-decile communities, system performance is the sum total of performance of all individual schools. So what must our school system, sliding down against international benchmarks, do to become great? McKinsey and Company, a private global corporate services firm, asked precisely that question of school systems globally.[26] Analysts examined 20 systems from around the world at differing levels of performance to understand how each had achieved significant, sustained and widespread gains in student outcomes as measured by national and international assessments. (Because New Zealand can't show 'significant gains'—despite reform—we were not included as a case study.) That the world's most improved school systems keep getting better and better, the report said, comes down to three things: the way people in schools and across schools work together; the 'mediating layer' between the system leadership and the school; and the way the system grows its leaders. Let's analyse this a little more.

System improvement is something that happens at the front line of schools, they said. Improvement is not sprinkled about from a pepper pot; improvement involves professional movement and commitment across the whole system, like a popularity wave. It's useful to have decisions about what happens in classrooms being made at the school level,[27] they stated. That's a tick in the box for New Zealand—in Aotearoa our principals are as close to the classroom door as in any system in the world. But according to the McKinsey research, it is systemic collaboration that makes learning consistently and sustainably improve. That's not a check. Cathy Wylie of the New Zealand Council for Educational Research, whose work *Vital Connections* is the textbook on problems of self-managing schools, says that our schooling system collaborates only in pockets.[28] Our schools are competitive, disconnected and privatised to individual parent communities. Cross-fertilisation between schools has ended up 'too uneven in reach and quality'. Funding [for improvement efforts] is short-term, cluster operation always voluntary, and the commitment of 'self-managing schools' too variable to allow for hard-out transformational effort across the whole system, says Wylie.[29] Nevertheless, as research in South Auckland proved, when we create 'communities of teacher practice', we can make a measurable difference.

The second key characteristic of improving systems, said McKinsey, is how well the system leaders perform. The bridge on the ship ought to be for the best and brightest and wisest. By 'system leadership' McKinsey analysts didn't mean just the principals. Someone must steer policy, call the engine room for funding, amass evidence from the dials of system performance, and shape the environment in which principals, teachers and learners battle ignorance. The McKinsey report holds Singapore up as a top-performing system. There, the career path for system leaders goes from classroom to principalship, to principal supervisor, to system leadership, a career path demonstrably absent in this country. Singapore is a highly ordered society, lauded for its economic success and multi-ethnic makeup, yet criticised for its overweening state power and the political laissez-faire of its people. And it may be that we don't need the hierarchical Singapore model to develop our 'system brain'. Universities might argue, for instance, that growing principals is at least part of their core business. Most university education faculties here have educational leadership centres with long shelves of leadership literature. They offer qualifications in leadership, publish educational resources for leaders, hold conferences, do research, run seminars and newsletters, and deliver leadership development contracts let by the Ministry of Education. Is this good enough?

Not if you read between the lines of a plethora of recent reports and the astonishing response of primary principals, arms folded and feet aggressively apart, to the minister's proposal to beef up collaborative practice. The review of the Teachers' Council in 2012[30] made it plain that quality control, including over principal performance, was an issue for the whole system. Quality leadership apparently boils down to how well our 2500 self-managing boards oversee their principals' work. Isn't that a professional insult—non-professionals managing professionals' performances? Reports by ERO ensure that the appraisal processes happen. But too often it's tick-the-box. Who controls the appraisal processes? Who knows whether appraisers are doing a good job or a snow job? Back-scratching from peers is sometimes evident. The Ministry of Education doesn't have any reliable data about the quality of its principal leaders and the profession generally.

Most interesting in the McKinsey report is the third ingredient for a top-performing system: the connectors, the mediators, the go-betweens. They provide the hands-on support for schools, and share and integrate improvements across the system. They support community connections and grow the performance of school leaders. International experts, including the OECD's Andreas Schleicher, note that leadership excellence is 'sticky' in a competitive environment. By this they mean that our system tendency is for some schools to gather up expert teachers and learning managers, keep them and not share them (which is why some parents and principals are reluctant to see their 'best' teachers seconded to help out in other schools). The career pathway for principals is to migrate to wealthier communities and stay there. 'New Zealand will have to think much harder how it will actually shift knowledge around pockets of innovation,' Schleicher advised.[31]

The writers of the McKinsey report expressed some surprise at the importance of the mediating layer to system gains in student achievement. This echoes the understandings of researcher Cathy Wylie, who showed how government agencies in this country are unable to do anything more than build relationships based on reactive problem-solving on a school-by-school basis.[32] Wylie points out that if we were to redesign the way our system works today, perhaps we would not ask so much of school trustees and nor would we expect them to stand alone, disconnected from each other and from the community agencies that they ought to be working alongside. Boards need to be seen as part of a 'collective' critical to connecting communities and developing them.

The missing vital connection is the governance intermediary that acts as a catalyst for co-design thinking, collaborative working, and collective impact approaches.

Principal power

New Zealand's dilemma of system leadership and poor settings for working together can be seen in the National Standards story. While principals are well organised, they don't always speak with one voice. Some see the big picture; others only work on the practical day-to-day. Initially, some primary and intermediate principals saw monsters lurking in the murky politics of the National Standards policy ('*Why* do we need the standards again?') and felt 'bullied' into doing something they didn't believe in. The response of some principals at the point of implementation was, unbelievably, to return documents unopened to the Ministry of Education. Others felt overwhelmed by the avalanche of sometimes competing information that accompanied the policy's introduction. Calls from the principals for a limited 'trial' were widely seen as delaying tactics. More embarrassing, the Ministry of Education had fumbled the pass. No one picked up responsibility for building the professional capacity of primary principals to understand standards-based assessment or become data literate. Instead, principals felt professionally disengaged, pedagogically compromised and philosophically challenged by the clearly changing purpose of schooling.[33]

On the other hand, I've spoken with some principals who were bellbirds for the policy, singing of increased debate within the sector about the issues of underachievement among Māori and Pasifika students; of exciting professional growth; and of validation of their years of work under the schooling improvement banner.

There is a tendency for principals to equate their professional discussions with public debates. Their statements sink under the weight of complicated, often incoherent or contradictory views and philosophies. Public opinion, on the other hand, is often formed in soundbites. The neat media label for National Standards is 'controversial', but few could articulate why. Professional voices smother that vague yet substantial stakeholder: the public interest in a public education system.

Principals sit on the school board as both trustee and executive employee. That's an awkward fence to be sitting on. School leaders in this country spend more time on administrative tasks and less time on professional learning and professional leadership than many of their international peers.[34] Voilà—the case of the Expanded Job Description—which over the last quarter-century has inflated the principal's job and, paradoxically, held her at weak accountability for school outcomes and no accountability at all for system outcomes.

The most important decision a board will make is appointing the principal. Consider the market environment of principal appointment and management. Boards can choose to get the support of a 'board advisor' as they make this most important decision—or not. (It costs money.) There may be governance or HR expertise on the board—or not. (It's less likely in working-class neighbourhoods.) The pool of applicants can be high quality—or not. (High-decile and low-decile schools must compete for quality applicants.) Anyone can apply. Unlike in Singapore, principalship in New Zealand does not come with an obligatory certificate, although there are opportunities for principals, prospective principals and middle managers to get accredited leadership training.[35] Once appointed, principals can choose to access materials to help them in their role—or not. (The Ministry of Education's website for educational leaders has extensive 'guides' on how principals could manage their school, but few prescriptions.) Principals are accountable to boards through annual performance reviews, subject to quality benchmarks—or not. (These are too often conducted by colleagues who are seemingly unaware of the professional conflict of interest and signed off by boards unused to the role of employer.)

Principals hold prestige as well as financial and social power. They can be leaders in their communities on all sorts of issues, not just academic ones. When a principal expresses a point of view, parents do listen. The communication instruments principals use are the school newsletter, the parent–teacher meeting, the board as an amplifier, the school website and social media. The messages resonate around the community—to grandparents, neighbours, local newspapers and notables like local MPs. When principals ask their communities to act, things happen. Policymakers therefore understand how tricky it is to implement education policy, especially policy opposed by principals. As Simon Smelt has written:

> Those involved don't simply follow instructions, nor are they simply passive in the face of an imposed change or perceived threat. They react and adapt in the light of their own context and understanding and goals. One could say that 'play is ongoing' and that, for example, a new policy will result in another round of play in response.[36]

Or, as Brian Annan describes it: 'We liberated educators to take control in their own communities, and now we can't take it off them.'[37]

The leadership field is full of constructs that suggest how leaders should work: servant leadership, shared leadership, authentic leadership, ethical leadership, collective leadership, professional leadership, transactional or transformational leadership, and more. Whatever the practice, principal leadership is privatised; that is, our cadre of principals are dispersed across the system, individualised to each board and forced to be inward-looking. Their skills and talents are utilised exclusively for the benefit of the school to which they are appointed and the community they serve. That can be as widely or narrowly defined as the principal chooses.

Principals receive training on professional leadership, and more comprehensively on the key relationship with a board. No one 'owns' leadership over a principal's professional growth in governance. There are no quality standards for good governance. The NZSTA encourages boards to exercise leadership in their role, but that is supposed to be a finely balanced one between board and principal powers. When the principal–board relationship is imbalanced and dysfunctional, students miss out because there is no effective leadership for the school anymore.

Whether the principal is an expert or a mug, the only way for the public to differentiate is to use social category markers. So, the higher the decile and size of the school, the more credible the principal must be —unless some scandal proves otherwise.

Problem-solving power

Educational inequality persists because power rests with those who have positions to protect. Auckland has 32% of the country's decile 1 schools, but these schools enrol 60% of the country's most disadvantaged students. The profile of disadvantage has ethnic, social and economic dimensions. Yet efforts to address system inequalities are often stymied by professional gatekeeping. To attract top Māori and Pasifika graduates to educational roles has always been an issue. And now there's a demographic imperative for changing the nature of the teacher workforce. Training graduates specifically for the very different cultural context of teaching in low-decile communities has seldom featured top of the agendas of those who guard entry to the profession, not to mention the disruptive impact of new technologies on teacher practices. Few initiatives are as ambitious as the Teach First NZ attempt to reduce educational inequalities via teacher recruitment and pedagogies for cultural empowerment.

In its first summer, Teach First NZ attracted high-flyers to an intensive summer training at the University of Auckland and then placed them in secondary schools in stressed Auckland and Northland communities. They would work with real students in authentic classrooms, attend intensive weekend and holiday seminars, and be thoroughly immersed in the social, cultural and cognitive dimensions of reducing disadvantage. It was, and is, a big call.

But as represented by union interests and some academics,[38] the Teach First NZ initiative apparently has a hidden agenda. The 'quality' baseline for teacher training, fixed in philosophy and practice, is fiercely protected by the universities. This creates an invisible barrier to innovation in initial teacher education. Despite nods to the poor and disempowered, orienting existing systems of teacher education to the task of addressing educational disparities was not in the then Teachers' Council brief.

Yet student and teacher demographics are changing. The children of the baby blip are superdiverse and are coming through Auckland's primary schools now. Secondary schools, on the other hand, are feeling the effects of a demographic dip. The dip passes through the expensive post-war baby boomer suburbs first (Takapuna, Howick, central Auckland). Empty spaces in their schools are filled by commuter students. When the student population in rich suburbs shrinks, it is schools in poorer communities that must make teachers redundant. The number of teachers leaving teaching is presently low.[39] The profession is ossified as a rock-solid layer of tenured teachers bed longer in the working groove. Teachers unwilling to retire will gum up the teacher labour market until 2019, when a larger birth cohort moves into secondary schooling. By default these teachers exacerbate the hollowing-out of lower-decile secondary schools' rolls by preventing a new and fresh generation of teachers from entering the profession in the highest-need settings.

There is a point at which ethnicity moves from being a *quantitative* measure of a school—a count of how many students of each ethnicity are at the school—to take on a *qualitative* description of the culture and values of a school. That point is not fixed. At some point the weight of numbers shifts traditional middle-class New Zealand schooling to a new set of cultural values and social practices. South Auckland schools no longer look like the kind of school in public policy assumptions, because they are no longer even multicultural in nature. Their most distinguishing feature is a distinctive, brown, urban youth culture and lifestyle where the unmeasurables of cultural vibrancy and social disadvantage are closely related to the learning going on in the classroom. These schools face issues of school governance, school leadership, teacher quality, resourcing and delivery over and above the individual economic and social circumstances of the students or of their neighbourhoods. And getting teachers into these schools requires a different set of assumptions underpinning how you train teachers and how they should practice. These schools need circuit-breakers, not reinforcements to the status quo. When the baby boomers retire, the next generation of teachers must not mirror the present one. Thankfully, the new Education Council of New Zealand's remit includes independently championing policy-making that enables shift.

Independent evaluation from the New Zealand Council for Education Research showed how positively principals, colleagues, participants and students received the Teach First NZ pilot.[40] But for these students to continue to get access to enthusiastic and energetic new teachers, an outdated teachers' collective employment agreement, creaky legislation and inflexible union and academic attitudes must not stand in the way. The union went to the courts to stop the placement of Teach First NZ participants in schools.

Problem-solving cannot rest only with those who have positions to protect. Transformation necessarily involves innovation and disruption to the status quo.

Investing in educational success

Why do some schools continue to fail year after year? The definition of school failure is vague, and failing schools are almost always connected with failing communities. How satisfying, though, to ask that question from a vantage point of privilege. Labelling failure doesn't get disadvantaged children very far. Sharing what makes schools successful is a far more empowering idea.

In early 2014 the New Zealand government announced it liked the idea of shared and layered expertise, and so it planned to invest in a new kind of leadership. The Investing in Educational Success policy encourages schools to cluster together in deliberately structured Communities of Learning (CoLs) to collaborate on measurable improvements in student achievement. It initially appealed for the 'career structure' it suggested, for promoting excellence in teaching and leadership and keeping it close to the classroom. The policy at least returns us to the notion of a public national education system; that all schools need to serve any and all children, with the highest quality leadership and teaching support possible. Failure is not acceptable. That ought to take us to the polar opposite of the market model and the competitive frame.

However, the apparently splendid initiative carries a fire risk: it puts on an overlay without addressing the suitability of the fibre underneath. The principal is a system pivot. It can be 'a colossal waste of time and money,' suggested professor Viviane Robinson of the University of Auckland, when you cluster up leaders who have competitive mindsets, conflicts of interest and unclear mandates.[41] As the Ōtara, Māngere and Manurewa schooling improvement projects showed, principals operating in a culture of competition are not easily persuaded to collaborate. Even when they do, their commitment is entirely voluntary and lasts only as long as the principal feels okay about sharing data and operating with external scrutiny. It is by no means certain that the hardest-to-shift and most isolationist schools will actually benefit from the government's investment—and it may be that the schools who will benefit most will be those already comfortable with inquiry and collegial operation. As we noted earlier about the continuum of working together, collaboration commits you to action *even when your shorter-term interests aren't met.*

The minister reassured the New Zealand School Trustees Association that the new policy would not change system settings. But for well-meaning and dedicated parents with little or no experience in trusteeship to take on complex responsibilities for setting strategic direction, employment, managing finances and property, monitoring student achievement, and overseeing businesses with a large staff and assets worth millions of dollars—that's a big ask in itself. The market model depends heavily on the mindset of schools, principals and boards about their individual interests. Moving to a network model requires those interests to become shared. Even when boards and principals cope with the complexity of their own governance, the experience of South Auckland is that co-operating clusters fall apart without a strong facilitative mechanism—that is, a backbone joining up all interests. The new policy fails to change any of the macro settings that might shape network operation. It doesn't insert the intermediary layer that the McKinsey report showed was so vital. The mindset needed is the opposite of the one the market model encourages.

The minister's reassurance of no change to the governance model appeased the New Zealand School Trustees Association. You could choose whether or not to join in. 'Participation [in the Investing in Educational Achievement policy] does not in any way reduce or affect the current powers or autonomy of boards and/or principals,' soothed the president.[42] In a sector characterised by deep suspicion of government policies and erratic leadership alive with conflicts of interest, cop-out is easy. Those uncertain in their professional practice; the schools with something embarrassing to hide; those who encounter uncomfortable data; those with hubris or a non-collaborative streak, can simply not join in, or bully others into working to their interests. The new investment may still fail the poorest, most disadvantaged communities. Failure becomes endemic.

To compete or collaborate? It's a real-world tension. The needle on the continuum of collaboration still hovers uncertainly over the morning-tea-once-a-term end of the scale. Governance in New Zealand is stuck. The model, in all its iterations, is old hat. To turn around persistent, long-term school dysfunctions, the first thing South Auckland needs is School Governance 2.0. Only legislative shift can deliver that. What political party will own next-century policy?

The McKinsey report highlighted the role of intermediaries in rapidly improving systems.[43] What international experts are signalling to us is that something is missing in the way we govern schooling here. The intermediary role isn't located anywhere in our education legislation. Staged, structural governance shift could come in the form of local missions-in-the-middle—say, Network Education Commissions (or similar title). Whether they could be based on the community-of-interest or school clusters that already exist may be negotiable. Intermediary entities wouldn't wave boards away, but they ought to change the relationships boards have with each other, with their principals and with the national settings for education. Local-level commissions could be supported by a centrally provided budget which keeps them as small, innovative, nimble and adaptable connectors to the stakeholder interests within prioritised communities. This kind of investment is demonstrably more likely to work towards shifts in practice and results than flinging resources over a dysfunctional market like chocolate hail over vegetables.

There are many ways to expand on this intermediary idea. Shaping the structure, role and actions of a Network Education Commission is certainly the work of a task force with a very clear understanding of community empowerment work. Such a mechanism would operate with the distinctiveness of local communities in mind and with genuine transformation as its ambitious outcome.

6

The lost decile point

Why decile shouldn't matter, but does

It is simply impossible to have an island of educational excellence in a sea of community indifference.
—Ernest L. Boyer, Carnegie Foundation[1]

For anyone who cares about the education of their children, choosing a school has become an incredibly important business. With our Kiwi 'fair go' sensibility, we feel a vague and inexplicable sense of discomfort at why a school's decile matters so much. Once, decile was a tool for compensation, for making up for the deficits of families and communities. This idea is powerfully attractive; it fits into the 'fair go' ethos that used to be embedded in our culture. Unfortunately, today it has a much more powerful meaning related to social cachet and class. Decile has become a carrier of prestige and distinction. Decile sells newspapers and magazines and houses. In Auckland at least, our conversations about home and happiness factor in the local school's decile. School decile is central to our personal decision-making because decile underpins our class aspirations and our search for social and economic advancement. So any shift in decile policy is front-page news.

I once spoke to a group of Auckland's future leaders from well-educated business backgrounds about education in South Auckland. They were surprised to discover that decile is not a measure of quality and that a school cannot change its decile simply by working harder or better. Decile is merely shorthand for the socio-economic status of communities, not for how well a school delivers education. No matter how often educators and policymakers point this out, this blind spot about the nature of decile persists in the wider public domain. Other messages about decile are far more powerful.

Education in Auckland has become what economists call a *positional good*—that is, something you value because everybody else desires it.[2] A positional good is finite: not everyone can have it. In the big societal rush to be part of the middle class, even if you are doing better than your parents did, it doesn't automatically mean you are doing well by your children if you just send them to your neighbourhood school. You compare your children to other people's children in your social sphere. 'It's not what you know, but who you know,' says Bourdieu, the French intellectual who argued that economics alone don't explain poverty.[3] His theory of social capital hints at a universe where the top jobs go to the posh people who go to the most elite schools. School as a positional good is a variation on Veblen's theory about luxury goods that we discussed earlier in relation to early childhood learning: the more exclusive and elite the service, the more desired it becomes.

Resourcing schools

Policymakers know that how resources are distributed is about power, politics and class. Decile was designed and implemented in the early nineties as a response to 'need'. Don Brash's famous Orewa speech in 2004 took the narrative in a new direction.[4] Brash no doubt intended to be provocative, to grab the political agenda and set up an alternative story to the (Labour-led) government narrative of the day—'Closing the Gaps'. His message still resonates: 'We are all New Zealanders.' Despite Brash's staid delivery, the speech, titled 'Nationhood', had a riveting effect on the electorate. His key message so appealed that it prompted a 17-point surge for his party in the polls.[5] The public debate exposed an unlovely underbelly in our race relations and quickly degenerated into a question that goes to the heart of our sense of collective *us*: 'Are Māori getting more than their fair share?'[6] The agenda gained traction and turned into a campaign. So-called 'race-based funding' came under sustained attack. Campaigners publicly calculated that removing 'race' from schools' funding would redistribute \$6 million across the system.[7] The orchestrated media onslaught—now reminiscent of the tactics highlighted in Nicky Hager's book *Dirty Politics*—gave the centre-left government of the day such a huge fright that it prompted a reversal in the Closing the Gaps policy, which had only just started hitting its straps. The opposition scored an astonishing victory as officials were instructed to scour policy across all sectors, everywhere, to remove any reference to race. Government wiped ethnicity from the decile calculation.

So decile is no estimate of the proportion of students in your child's class who will be white, black or brown. 'Multicultural' once used to mean Māori and Pasifika. Mai Chen, through her *Superdiversity Stocktake* report,[8] has extended the meaning of multicultural to encompass the full range of immigrants to the city. Less than half of the children in Auckland's 538 schools are New Zealand European/Pākehā children.[9] The biggest Auckland schools are high-decile schools, but these schools don't fit the Euro-centric model of New Zealanders. Almost all will display somewhere the many different flags representing the students' countries of origin. Even greater diversity is educated in the 150 mid-decile schools of Auckland.

Yet Auckland's diversity hides an ugly reality. The huge social shift in New Zealand's largest city means schools are separated out like oil and water. North Shore and central/eastern Auckland schools are largely decile 8, 9 or 10. The schools in Māngere and Ōtara are almost exclusively low-decile, mono-cultural and brown. Of the 53,000 Pasifika students in Auckland, seven out of ten attend a decile 1–3 school.[10] Eighty-eight Auckland schools have rolls of 50% or more Pasifika students,[11] most of those in the Māngere–Ōtāhuhu and Ōtara–Papatoetoe local board areas. New Zealand's largest city has segregated suburbs and segregated schools.

This self-evident segregation in Auckland—and the link between housing and schooling[12]—is an elephant in the policy room. The ethnic divide that the decile ratings apparently describe has been obvious for at least 15 years.[13] Segregation of schools has been a public conversation in the US for decades. We have almost ignored it as a public policy conversation in our largest city.

So how do schools get their decile numbers? A decile number starts with the New Zealand Census, a reckoning that occurs every five years (apart from the hiccup of an earthquake). Counting people is a place-based activity. The base unit for the census is the local area 'meshblock'.[14] New Zealand is divided into neighbourhoods of a hundred or so people. We all live in a meshblock-sized pixel, bundled up with other meshblocks into an 'area unit'. Zooming out, as on Google Maps, area units become suburbs, suburbs become local boards, and local boards become wards of the Auckland Council to create a screenshot of the city.

Meshblock details matter—our dwelling type, how long we've been here, how many of us live here, how many bedrooms we have, our ethnicity, our jobs and our incomes, our qualifications—because they are the foundation for measures like the socio-economic deprivation index, a widely used social research tool originally developed for the health sector.[15] It measures 'need' and then puts 'need' on a scale of 1–10. The higher the meshblock score, the needier the people are who live there. It is a place-based measure, not about individuals. Similarly, school decile measures the deprivation of the poorest 20% of New Zealand's neighbourhoods and how many of the school's families live in that neighbourhood. Officials test the addresses of students on the roll against the meshblock rating for five 'factors'—household income, occupation, household crowding, educational qualifications of parents and dependence on income support. But it is important to remember that only one-fifth of neighbourhoods have any statistical significance for decile. Only deprivation counts; not wealth. Confusingly, school decile ratings have a scale that runs in the opposite direction to the deprivation index. That is, a low-decile school reflects a community with *high* levels of deprivation; a high-decile school reflects a community with *low* levels of social deprivation. This is unfortunate. Perhaps this high–low, rich–poor muddle made decile easy to misunderstand at first. It did not take long, however, for the public to work out the positional advantages that school decile number bestowed.

A high-decile school in Howick might have families who are beneficiaries, but because they live in a small group of flats in an otherwise up-market street, the meshblock won't feature in the bottom band of household income. The principal of a school in Manurewa has a meshblock in her zone where new and more expensive houses with water views are being constructed. The proportion of her students with addresses in this meshblock is nil, so the meshblock doesn't count even though it is in her school's zone. Ethnicity doesn't count. And even more confusing: though 'decile' means 10%, only about 5% of students attend decile 1 schools and 15% attend decile 10 schools.[16] The lived reality of schools, students and communities becomes invisible in the decile calculation. *All* of the counting is about a paper definition of deprivation in communities. Decile is not about the school or the quality of learning that goes on inside it. It's about neighbourhoods. Decile ties the social networks of neighbourhoods to the school—these social networks are a form of capital that reproduces inequality.[17]

Decile funding salves our conscience about poverty. But is it really true that poor schools get huge top-ups from the government? All schools get operational funding from the Crown which arrives as cash in the bank. It covers a lot of a school's fixed costs, like heating, lighting and cleaning bills; paying for administration staff and school librarians; boards of trustee payments; and so on. Schools don't have to specifically account for how this money is spent (except by following the rules of good public service management). However, nationally only 10% of school funding that arrives as money in the bank is in the form of 'top-up' for disadvantage, and this is not evenly distributed, as the table below suggests:[18]

Decile	Total operational funding ($)
1	145,312
2	141,676
3	129,319
4	124,287
5	130,806
6	135,286
7	113,819
8	143,415
9	132,333
10	166,763
No decile	2,406

Figure 2: Total operational funding for schools according to decile in 2014, in thousands of dollars

The table reveals some things, and hides others. Although 10% of schools sit in each decile, higher-decile schools tend to be larger. Wherever there is school choice in a community, the higher-decile school sucks students out of neighbourhoods and grows its roll. This explains why the table shows decile 10 schools with more funding than decile 7, 8 and 9 schools. Post-election 2014, decile funding was re-jigged. After eight years, around 784 schools moved up one or more deciles and 800 schools moved down, indicating a perceptible shift in the socio-economic profiles of school communities. The lowest decile schools get up to $1000 more per student, we are told in the media. That's deception. The dollars abate rapidly. Decile 1 has three categories: on 2015 figures, decile 1A schools get $905.81 per student; decile 1B $842.11; decile 1C $731.30. Take six steps down the list to decile 2F and the funding is less than half of the decile 1A rate.

Operational money is housekeeping. And there's no doubt about it: New Zealand taxpayers get good value from the flexibility of school operational funding. New Zealand sits very low on the corruption index, so the hazards of devolution—fraud, mismanagement and principals' perks—are (mostly) contained. Remarkably, we rarely find the kind of blatantly wasteful allocations often associated with public sector expenditure in other countries. Schools have become very creative in managing their money. Nevertheless, major capital and school staffing expenditure has *not* been delegated to school boards.

All public schools are staffed on exactly the same formula no matter their ethnicity or decile makeup. The formula comes partly from teachers' agreements with government, for example for student–teacher ratios, and partly on historical agreements regarding curriculum delivery, for example for technology classes in intermediate schools. The staffing formula for schools applies across the country. The calculation for teachers is complex but resolutely par across high- and low-decile schools. To stress the point, poverty and disadvantage are not included in the calculation for teachers in the school.[19]

It was not always so. Prior to the 1989 reforms to education, schools in Māngere and Ōtara enjoyed extra support from governments, partly because of a benevolent Department of Education, partly because of powerful political interests, partly because of the area's extraordinary social history. In a 1981 review report entitled *Tomorrow May Be Too Late*,[20] eminent educator Dr Peter Ramsay publicly confirmed that the former Department of Education was granting substantial aid in the form of additional staffing and extra finance to schools in those suburbs. In the case of primary schools, all received staffing at 15–20% above their roll entitlement. For secondary schools, staffing was more 'discretionary' and ad hoc. Ramsay's report concluded that additional staffing was a perfectly legitimate recognition of the particular challenges in those two suburbs; the issues were 'almost without parallel in New Zealand,' he said. He built the case for an 'eligibility formula' for additional staffing for these schools, based on such broad criteria as new entrant attainment, the levels of 'health and hygiene' of students, their English-speaking skills and their ethnic composition. However, Dr Ramsay found schools did not use that extra resourcing well: he expressly called for aligning the extra staffing to student achievement. Hold that thought.

Unfortunately, urgency is not a characteristic of bureaucracies. The juggernaut of reform took over. Post-1989 the schools in Māngere and Ōtara were no longer the departmental special cases they had been. Place-based staffing was wiped: teacher entitlements were reduced to a formula redistributed 'fairly' across all schools.

Although state schools get most of their money from the government, nothing stops them raising money from other sources. The most obvious fundraising, of course, is parent contributions in the form of voluntary fees; but other fundraising may be philanthropic or commercial in nature. Understanding community contributions to school funds is complicated, not least because of the way in which schools present their financial reports—but it is critical in showing how social and cultural capital widens social inequalities.

So how much do schools raise each year? At the end of every summer newspapers run cliché items about the cost of going back to school. The extraordinary costs of uniforms and stationery, plus invoices for standard fees/donations can be worked up into a topical interactive story that encourages commenter views on the newspaper's website or on talkback radio.[21] The Education Act is clear: every child between the ages of 5 and 19 years who is not an international student 'is entitled to free enrolment and free education at any state school'. Free means no fees for getting into the ballot or teaching the curriculum. Exceptions include a 'take home' component (for subjects like art or technology) and any extra-curricular activities, like sport.

Of course schools set fees according to their estimate of parent capacity and willingness to pay.[22] There is no scientific method. As in any market, principals compare fees charged—sorry, donations requested—by surrounding schools and advise their boards accordingly. The suggestion that principals might have an eye to a rate that dissuades less affluent families from applying is difficult to confirm.[23] There is plenty of anecdotal reference to the subtle and not-so-subtle pressures on parents to front up with money (for example, requiring payment with the enrolment application). Equally apparent is the absence of any fee in some of the lowest decile schools because the effort to collect it is uneconomical. There's an accounting line called 'school donations' in schools' accounts, which the Ministry of Education tots up. Six years ago, reports quoted $98.4 million—up from $75 million in 2008.[24] Family First, a national lobby group, claimed that schools actually raised $266 million, the largest amounts from secondary schools in Auckland. (Which school raised the most? Auckland Grammar. It raised $8.7 million over six years.)[25]

But there's something of the green-eyed monster here. Shouldn't we expect parents to put skin in the game? What parent would deny her children the latest technology in every classroom, pods of tablets and well-equipped music suites if he or she could afford it? Why shouldn't the parents at Remuera Primary School support its Development Trust, with its $5 million target to ensure 'a significant and ongoing income stream for the school'?[26] State schools that match expectations of private schooling are surely to be applauded—aren't they? These questions are the stuff of talkback radio. They are perennial, because they are not solvable without tackling context.

So let's take some contextual examples. The following is to do with equal opportunity and participation in secondary school sports. First of all, imagine if you will the $20,000 it costs to kit out a school's sports teams. Compare what happens in three schools:

School A is high-decile. Its school teams and representatives get fitted out by parents paying directly for the uniforms. This is not a 'donation'—it's the price of participation, and the family pays.

School B, mid-decile, asks parents to pay, but only half do so. This school spends $10,000 of its funding on sports uniforms. The other half is received from parents. So it looks like School B is receiving $10,000 more from parents than School A.

Low-decile School C pays for sports uniforms. It applies for a Lottery grant to cover that cost. It looks like it is receiving $20,000 more than School A—if its application is successful. If not, of course, it has spent $20,000 that high-decile School A has not.

Consider, too, what kinds of sports are available to students. Cycling requires gear that students from most low-decile communities can't afford. Rowing fees can run into thousands of dollars. A school that collects fees via a 'club trust' can charge costs at whatever rate parents are willing to contribute—and it will not appear on the school's books. In effect, the sport becomes a privately funded part of the state school's curriculum.

Now consider how other fundraising efforts can distort the apparent income a school receives. School D raises $500,000 towards a new gymnasium, a large sum of which is donated by a single philanthropic trust. School E raises a quarter of a million dollars for its 1st XV to tour Argentina. School F raises sponsorships for sports scholarships and sports coaching. All of these activities can be reported differently in the school accounts—so it's difficult to quantify the advantage that school decile actually delivers.

Finally, let's refer to the *New Zealand Herald* exposé of schools' spending on the premier schoolboy rugby 1st XV competition in Auckland.[27] Five schools—Auckland Grammar, King's College, Mount Albert Grammar, Sacred Heart College and Saint Kentigern College—collectively spend more than $400,000 on their 1st XV rugby teams. The chief executive of College Sport, the body that runs the premier competition, is reportedly worried that young players believe that 'the only pathway to top level rugby is via a school with a significant rugby budget'. South Auckland has apparently become the talent pool from which richer schools lure the most promising players away from their home secondary school, impoverishing the competition. The effect of the widened resource gap becomes self-fulfilling. Sports offer powerful prestige, and prestige gathers resources to itself.

There is an undeniable social dimension to school success, linked to Putnam's now-famous theory of 'social capital'.[28] On enrolment evenings, prospects at high-decile schools get shortbread and professional presentations in flash new buildings; at low-decile schools, they get the best foot forward. High-decile schools take the school band to Europe with no fundraising at all; low-decile schools take the school band to Waihi after doing the Countdown stocktake. High-decile schools pay a drama coach to support the school production; low-decile schools find a volunteer. High-decile parents pay for extra maths coaching; low-decile parents can't. Students in high-decile schools BYOD (bring their own devices); students in low-decile schools don't.[29] Donations and fundraisers are a jumble of counted and uncounted contributions from parents and the community towards the education of the children. In 2011 these sources represented 7% of all revenue that schools got in New Zealand.[30] But only a PhD in forensic accounting would dare to tackle a comparison between schools.

Our schooling system is globally attractive. International students represent only 2% of the total revenue for schools across the country—but that's still big dollars. International students are good business not only for schools, but for communities too. The nearly 7000 overseas students who came to Auckland schools in 2015 paid millions in tuition fees and brought foreign exchange into our economy and vibrancy into our communities. But the spread of this economic good fortune is not even. Around 54% of all international students in schools end up in Auckland[31]—at least, certain parts of it. The higher the school's decile, the more likely it is to attract international student income. Significantly, only about 3% of fee-paying students end up in decile 1, 2 and 3 schools.

The considerable heft that these students add to a school's budget and the total economy in a community is as welcome as an Olympic medallist on homecoming day. Schools like Macleans College charge tuition of $18,000 per student (for school year 2016) plus various other fees (for considering the application, textbook bonds, homestay fees, stationery, etc.). The approximately 275 full-time equivalent students at that school gross $4.95 million in income (the Crown gets a chunk in GST and levies). This one school's international fee income exceeds the total income acquired this way by all decile 1, 2 and 3 secondary schools in the country combined. Macleans College enhances its educational offering with this income to the advantage of students in its zone whose families already have high social capital. The Howick/Bucklands Beach/Botany community earns $2.7 million in homestay income from this school alone.[32] The school is a neighbourhood generator of economic prosperity—wealth which doesn't spill over to nearby poor communities.

In a devolved education system, local solutions to local problems constitute splendid flexibility, but all priorities have to be juggled. Following the global financial crisis, over 90% of state and state-integrated schools had at least enough current assets to cover their short-term debts,[33] and by 2012 the proportion was even higher.[34] Still, school budgets tighten, as they do for all businesses, within economic and electoral cycles. Decile makes little difference. This tells us two things: that most school boards and principals manage their finances carefully and responsibly, and a few are challenged in financial management for all sorts of reasons, possibly little to do with wealth or poverty.

Nevertheless, claims of system underfunding are as likely from high-decile schools as low-decile ones, from political point-scorers and self-promoters.

Low-decile schools have invisible costs that high-decile schools often don't have to meet. To list the ways those invisible costs arise is pointless; every programme that a low-decile school runs—for example, a breakfast club programme or homework support sessions—can be tit-for-tat balanced by a corresponding expectation in a high-decile school for classroom equipment and resources matching those in the private sector. Like the sugar treat that becomes a normal part of everyday life, fundraising ratchets up the impression that schools are underfunded or unfairly treated.

The qualitative difference in high- and low-decile schools, of course, is that teaching and learning begins with access to social fundamentals like healthy diets, warm and stable homes, and functional and supportive families. When these family and community resources can be assumed, schools can focus on delivering achievement that is on a par with quality education services all over the world. And there's plenty of evidence that many Auckland schools do so. But policymakers can no longer assume common social and community baselines.

The only conclusion that we can reach about school resourcing is that inequalities are not simply addressed by dollops of money from government. *How* resourcing arrives in schools (as cash, as teacher entitlements, as family social capital, as social expectation, as programme or initiative resourcing, and so on) appears as important as *how much* arrives. Schools need resources delivered differently (such as Social Workers in Schools) as well as differentially (to do with the share of resources).

Why school deciles fail to address inequality

There's a dimension of decile that takes us into the sociology of communities. For the most entertaining description of New Zealand communities, go no further than marketing specialists Caldwell and Brown,[35] who ascribe tribal stereotypes to suburbs. These stereotypes appeal not because of their scientific truth but because of their sweeping concordance with our general understandings of ourselves as a city and a nation. On the North Shore we are apparently highly competitive, ambitious and achievement driven; we like league tables, competitive grading, streamed classes and knowing how our children sit relative to the rest of the class and the country. In Grey Lynn we look for progressive schools where it's okay to be arty and multicultural, but excellence in academic and cultural pursuits is important. In round-vowelled Remuera, what school one went to defines the rest of one's life. In Ōtara, family and community are paramount; there is pressure to 'do the right thing' and uphold appearances, and church-based schools with a sense of belonging and support are preferred. In Papatoetoe, on the other hand, we prefer the local state school. Other places reflect other stereotypes (the Balclutha heartlanders, the Raglan free spirits, the avant-garde of Cuba Street). The point Caldwell and Brown make is that schooling is part of the brand of a place.

Decile, in the spirit of a brand, has become a social marker, a label co-opted by media, parents and the public for very different purposes than those for which it was first designed. Decile sells magazines and real estate. Schools carry weighty cachet and attract advantage as their decile star rises. Decile helps us to answer the urgent public question: Where are Auckland's best schools?[36] Indeed, the big Auckland angst about education drives some parents to rort the system, requiring some oversubscribed schools to publicly respond with strategies for confirming home addresses. The agonies of choosing a school are reflected in discussions on social media. School 'quality' in a market is no different to buying a T-shirt at the mall or in the high street at Newmarket—the T-shirts might *be* identical but you don't *feel* identical when you try them on. Convictions trump evidence. Do parents believe children will get a better education at a higher-decile school? Yes, we do.

The social stakes on educational choice are so high that the intense competition between secondary schools is now seeping down to the primary level on the assumption that good grades at primary school will deliver your child to a secondary school of your choice.[37] All of this undermines the very schools that decile is supposed to help. The minister of education recognises sector anxieties about the label.[38] So should she dump it?

Atelaite has successfully completed her first year as a student in the Bachelor of Health Science programme at the University of Auckland. A recent student of Tangaroa College, she is a delightful guest speaker at a function hosted by Counties Manukau Health for Pasifika winners of scholarships for tertiary studies in health. She narrates for her sympathetic and appreciative Pacific audience her scary experience as a brown face in a university lecture theatre full of white and Asian faces. She describes reading *Metro* (magazine) in the library in her last year of school. She looks at the rankings given to all of the schools in Auckland. 'TC was dead last,' she says, with pregnant pause. 'But I knew that we were not the deadbeat school that the magazine made out. I was so angry! I picked up that magazine and tore it up.' Her face is full of the emotion of the moment. 'My biology teacher threw me out of the library.' Her audience laughs. 'Sure, I should not have torn it up. But that magazine should not be labelling us as failures, making us feel as though we don't count.' Her point rings a bell. The audience cheers. Atelaite's achievements and her ambition to make something of her life are invisible in the data that *Metro* provides. She intuitively spots that the words 'decile' and 'ranking' have become twinned by the media, and her audience knows it too.

Ranking sells magazines and newspapers. *Metro*'s annual series on secondary schools ('The Best Schools in Auckland') always gets front-page billing. Advertising (a picture of private school blazers) provides a commercial incentive for the magazine to continue to offer this annual advertorial as a 'public service'. Marketing 101: advertising is not just information. Schools define the students they have and who they want to appeal to for enrolments when they place an ad here.

League tables are publicly appealing because they speak to public anxieties about the merits of state schools. *Metro* arrived at school rankings in 2012 by calculating the merit and excellence passes at NCEA Level 2 and weighting them with decile to arrive at a 'score'. On the surface, this looks as though it might take into account the social deprivation in low-decile schools. And perhaps it does. Ethnicity, gender and social class are arguably also indications of student success. But that's not the story *Metro* wants to tell its audience. League tables are attractive—yet I haven't seen a league table that specifically reflects the achievements of Māori or Pasifika students.

The 2013 *Metro* analysis examined the 'leaving qualifications' of students, the proportion of school leavers who had no qualifications when they left, and the proportions who had qualified at NCEA Level 1, 2 or 3. Again, the ethnicity and gender stories inside the data were absent. That year, the league tables were very complex. As a rough guide to the value of pass rates as a proportion of students, *Metro* calculated the drop-out rates of students from Year 9 to 13. Transience is more a feature of some communities than others. Perhaps it is unreasonable to expect that in a system that is supposed to encourage kids to look at their options, we critique schools where students choose to take up out-of-school learning or are driven out by increasingly unaffordable housing.

That this data point accompanies the *Metro* league table, however, is a worthy expansion of the simplified table that merely records NCEA pass rates. Nevertheless, it is the conclusion of the article that is most telling about the social and commercial tensions in league tables:

> Seriously, asking about the best school in Auckland is asking the wrong question. There are many very good schools . . . Look for one that engages well with its families, and that knows the value of attracting and keeping good teachers. Where the tone of the place seems right for your child, where you are confident they will be safe and where you think they will thrive. Our analysis should give you good grounds for comparison. We also hope it helps with the questions you need to ask.[39]

Perhaps ironically, the 2014 and 2015 editions still had that 'wrong' question on the cover: 'The Best Schools in Auckland'. Still, the conversation has shifted to recognise, as Hamlet might advise Horatio, that there are more things on heaven and earth than are dreamed of in a single figure. 'League table' is no longer central to the discussion about secondary schools. Now, it's all about the choosing.

School choice is electorally appealing. It gives parents the right to choose—at public expense—the school their child attends. Myths accompany this idea. The first is that the discipline of the educational market will make schools perform better. The theory is that schools will diversify to create a market niche for themselves, offer higher quality programmes to meet the 'stratified social purchasing power of different consumer groups',[40] and more quickly adopt new ideas. There's been no hard evidence anywhere in the world that it works this way, not even with charter schools.[41]

The second myth is that you can compare schools with businesses; if businesses don't cut it in the market, they exit. 'Failing' schools ought to be closed too. In real life, it's very difficult to close schools. As successive ministers of education have discovered, closing a school when a 'community'—that is, principal and board—doesn't want it closed is a tough exercise. When a *network* of schools fails, as in Māngere and Ōtara in the 1990s, it is politically and socially uncomfortable. Closure inevitably applies to schools in poor neighbourhoods, not rich ones. And you can't close 40 schools in a poor suburb, even the worst half of them. These children are least able to afford to commute and least likely to be acceptable to neighbouring communities. The market cannot make the schools *and their network* functional again; so who must fix them?

The third myth of school choice is that the market of schools encourages parents to make rational choices based on such things as quality, convenience and price. In fact, school choice is emotionally loaded. Housing and class are the unspoken assumptions behind choice in education. It's not facts that matter, but the emotive content of messages about schools. Community perceptions, preconceptions, or, dare we name it, prejudice—these are social calculations to defend one's social position.[42] Decile has become a tool to help you choose your child's school and to define your class.

The policy options associated with freedom to choose and equality of opportunity are poles apart. Freedom to choose will trump equality of opportunity, because middle-class parents invoke their *right* to make decisions in their children's interests or their *right* to choose on a matter as important as education.[43] This is a new phenomenon: parents have not always had this right. Think of giving a small child a desired toy. Taking the toy away without a tantrum is a matter of extremely careful negotiation or distraction. Ministers past and present are understandably reluctant to take choice away.

The peculiar zoning of some schools in Auckland is an historical artefact of the great shift to schooling choice in the 1990s. The removal of zoning regulations resulted in a competitive and venal scramble. Schools could decide for themselves how they would prepare an enrolment scheme and which parts of their community would be included (although they did need the secretary of education to agree that they had an overcrowding problem). Professor Chris

Lubienski of the University of Illinois, visiting New Zealand on a Fulbright scholarship, found schools had intentionally skewed enrolment zones to improve their decile ratings.[44] This was a way for schools to protect and enhance their market positions. Some anonymous principals even admitted gerrymandering the system to maximise the intake of students from higher-income areas.[45] None had the absolute right to attend their local school. The results were chaotic, even blatantly unfair. The manipulation was such that schools like Glendowie College could exclude Madeline Avenue, a street of state housing right next to its fence line that was locally notorious for its social problems. Tensions about this exclusion boiled over into local newspapers.[46] (As a pointed aside, Housing New Zealand recognised that this street sat in the midst of other expensive real estate, so it sold all the houses to a private developer, who removed them and renamed the street Mount Taylor Drive. Glendowie College later rezoned to include the new houses, responding to middle-class demand—and did so exactly in line with the political permissions). Did competition make schools better and give parents more choice? Schools, not parents, ended up with the choices. They could set entry conditions, reportedly including such subjective criteria as 'student attitude to education'. By 2002 the pressure on parents to enrol in favoured secondary schools in Auckland extended to newspaper reports of bribes offered to principals,[47] or parents using temporary or falsified home addresses to suggest their child lived in-zone.[48]

Grammar zones are real estate bonanzas. Heaven help anyone who tries to cut out families currently in the zone of favoured schools in order to make the zone 'fairer' for others. In effect, zones are a done deal, set in concrete by the vested interests of real estate. In 2014 Aucklanders in the twin grammar school zones for Auckland Grammar and Epsom Girls were upset about the proposal from two other Auckland schools, One Tree Hill College and Selwyn College, to include them in their zones too. Their fear was that this might lead the elite grammar schools to shrink their school zones, thereby excluding their children—and reducing their property values.[49] As a society, we've adopted the positional mindset that social advantage should be preserved because we've paid money for it through our real estate choices.

Sadly, it is somewhat naive to expect that school zones have been drawn up in the spirit of the law. Schools are built on 'reputation' constructed from the social capital of families in communities. Social psychologists use the term *internal narratives* to describe motivations for how people act. The system incentivises boards and principals to be responsible for the kids in their school, not for the health and wellbeing of the entire network of schools in their area. Principals are being measured on their own school's results, and this is always easier to show with middle-class students. A board has to ensure that 'all students can attend a reasonably convenient school while ensuring other schools don't experience enrolment problems'.[50] So a principal's internal narrative might go like this: 'I believe in public education, so I will enrol whoever comes in the door.' Or: 'My professional credibility is on the line if my school does not succeed with students who may require more educational effort.' Or: 'My board would not want their children to sit alongside others from that part of town.' Or: 'I don't want *my* children to sit alongside difficult others. Someone else can deal with them.'

Which of these narratives is most likely? Professor Martin Thrupp of Waikato University and visiting Fulbright scholar Chris Lubienski describe two sides of the same issue: the 'inconvenient truth' about the middle-class mindsets of education sector professionals. Teachers and principals of South Auckland schools who live in middle-class suburbs send their own children to middle-class schools. When principals move from low-decile to high-decile schools, they are congratulated (the movement is rarely the other way). They adopt selective and sometimes unethical practices in a public education system—like cherry-picking enrolments.[51] When student numbers in their own zones drop, middle-class schools raid students from the schools of the south and hide it by 'accepting out-of-zone applications'. Former principal Bali Haque publicly admitted that the system encourages such behaviour.[52] The behaviour entrenches disparities in the social status quo.[53]

The ease with which principals and teachers express concern about access for the disadvantaged, yet fail to see how their actions perpetuate the widening divide between rich and poor, is perhaps more noticeable to those outside the system than to those within it. As the Education Review Office pointed out,[54] the more than anecdotal failure of many schools to welcome students with special needs is only another facet of the same narrative for decile—one that serves school choice and maintains disadvantage rather than compensating for it. It is a fundamental human right, not a gift of the market, for every child to have quality schooling. Every school has to be a good school, not just those that parents 'choose'.[55]

Real estate enthralls Aucklanders. Housing stories dominate the *New Zealand Herald*. We drool over dream homes or those from which we can make capital gains and rental income. In the cafés and restaurants of Auckland, we discuss schools and real estate as if they are the same thing. And in one sense they are. Schools, like our homes, are about our aspirations to be well-off, or at least middle class.

Property reports in Auckland now include the deciles of all schools in the home's area. Says Quotable Value Ltd: 'With access to a range of online property information and valuation services, including your home's value, local area sales, weather and school zone information for each property, you will be able to make more informed choices.' The term 'top schools' suggests a marketing hierarchy of preference, like 'top shops' or 'top movies'. The logic is repeatedly reinforced: the higher the school decile, the better the school zone and the pricier the home. This is not just an Auckland phenomenon, of course, but there has been an inexorable shift that has resulted in concentrated pockets of poverty and poor housing in parts of the city. Even high quality schools in these pockets struggle to attract students as parents aspire after something 'better'.

Despite the clear link in real estate marketing to schooling, the ratcheting up of investment in housing in New Zealand is a demand-side factor not even mentioned in the Productivity Commission's *Housing Affordability Inquiry*.[56] Home-buyers exercise school choice via their cheque-books every time they consider a school zone as a factor in their purchasing decision.[57] A school's decile has become a self-fulfilling prophecy—property prices go up next to desirable schools, so only higher-income families can afford to buy into the area and decile goes up even further. It's a version of the Matthew effect, where the rich get richer, and the poor miss out. Housing thus becomes a driver for the polarisation of Auckland's schools. The reality is that even if real-estate buyers don't have children, they are likely to prefer investing in areas with high-decile schools simply because of the long-term maintenance of value a home in that area represents. This phenomenon has been studied elsewhere as an expression of re-segregation in urban America.[58]

Decile also poses an ethical dilemma. Schools need a mechanism to redress disadvantage, but the mechanism is so loaded with meaning that it damages schools with the 'low decile' label.[59] The introduction of an equity formula was once welcomed by school principals and boards. It recognised the consequences of the social environment for school outcomes. According to former secondary principal Ann Dunphy, the decile descriptor 'represented an impersonal mathematical measure of community resources'. It meant principals no longer had to deal with the offensive question: How many Māori and Pacific Islanders go to your school?[60] But sometimes policies don't end up helping, but hurting.[61] The Germans have this wonderful word for it: *Verschlimmbesserung*.

Decile has such strong populist appeal that it no longer matters what the evidence tells us. In 2012 the Education Review Office announced it would no longer publish the school's decile rating with its reports, arguing that it was irrelevant to the quality of a school. The media response was to claim this was about secreting public information away. Misrepresentation, misreported data and nonsense conclusions are the cake-crumbs of everyday science. For as long as decile exists as a government tool, it will be discoverable. Simply suppressing decile does not seem a satisfactory answer.

Decile funding is actually a very restricted view of the possible policy responses to community and family disadvantage that many children in South Auckland face. It's a view restricted to the agency of schools to make change and assumes that schools, like Herculean heroes, can shift the problem of students leaving school with few or no qualifications. It suggests that, with a little bit of decile funding, schools ought to be able to make a difference.

The opportunity in decile funding was to better shape good practice. The reality of decile has been to fund occasionally brilliant school initiatives, determined by evidence about what works and what doesn't—and to otherwise support mediocre spray-and-hope efforts. This *modus operandi* was inadequate when Peter Ramsay wrote his report about South Auckland[62] and is still inadequate for the goals the government has set for the system. It is not fixed by funding that continues to depend on the market as a force for wise and targeted spending of educational resources.

Decile funding is an operational subsidy, the size of which was pulled out of some fiscal envelope in Wellington long ago—as if to say, this is how much you've got to spend, now go away and make it work. The rationale for decile would never get past a hawk-eyed Treasury official these days. Why? The 2008 Key government's ten-point plan for Better Public Services was a reform agenda intended to go wider than the reforms of the 1980s. Back then the atomised agencies of government, once a single unwieldy bureaucratic orchestra, formed their own chamber groups. Unfortunately that made 'whole of government' as challenging to play as a Mahler symphony. Better Public Services was intended to re-harmonise the public service into a new slimline modernity that actually supported government priorities. Consistent with the political de-stigmatising of policies that risk backlash, though, the reforms were as bland as a shopping mall and as universally popular. The Key government expected the state sector to be 'innovative, efficient, and focused'.[63] His government directed the traffic towards priority outcomes—which although closely linked to the social disadvantages inherent in Māori and Pasifika communities, initially mentioned Māori and Pasifika student outcomes scarcely at all. Māori and Pasifika communities are invisible in the construction of decile. That's a policy problem.

The current school funding regime doesn't address other policy problems either. Onshore oil rigs and offshore oil rigs both produce oil. But the costs associated with getting the oil out are very different. Now that substantive evidence is emerging (from the National Standards) that students arrive at school with significantly different levels of basic skills, how do you justify staffing schools with no distinction between the schools that accept kids with skills at the expected standard and those with kids that need extra resources to get them to the system target? Within each year's cohort of approximately 60,000 students, almost 7000 are at a high risk of not achieving NCEA Level 2. And there's one group of five-year-olds, about 600 children each year, three-quarters of whom Treasury confidently expects won't achieve NCEA Level 2 or equivalent.[64] If we know all this at age five, an investment approach must surely dictate differential *staffing* for schools that serve these students.

Decile is now embedded in public policy as a discriminator in the delivery of certain services. Programmes like Social Workers in Schools are allocated to schools within specified decile bands. School nurses are assigned this way too. The depth to which decile has become embedded in policy thinking is illustrated by the tension between its supposed lack of connection to academic outcomes and decile's use as a means of comparison in public data about student achievement. When agencies like the New Zealand Qualifications Authority report their qualifications data according to decile, you immediately understand that of course a high-decile school is going to get better NCEA results than a low-decile school. So decile ranking becomes the tool by which you get a seemingly objective indication of comparable quality across schools. The problem with this is that everyone recognises class and ethnicity go hand in hand, and perceptions of ethnicity are as likely to determine school desirability as actual statistics about the ethnic mix of a school's catchment or even its academic results.

Decile has shifted from being a descriptor of a community's poverty to a creator of positional advantage. School decile, like the tuatara, is a remnant of the past. Decile persists in public policy for two reasons: because the externalities of education as a positional good are not as well understood as the 'equity argument' for additional funding; and because middle-class aspirations are powerful. Rejigging decile will be a significant challenge for any minister. Since we've already established that decile is *not* a measure of ethnicity, funding via decile becomes curiously irrelevant to the task at hand; it's merely a kind of secondhand response to the hand-wringing about poverty and system outcomes for Māori and Pasifika students. Decile is problem-oriented rather than solution-focused.

How to transform decile into investment

What could policymakers do instead? At the time of writing, school resourcing is in the policy-redevelopment pot. Policymakers are faced with a number of choices, some of which are less palatable to the sector than others.

The first temptation might be to play about with the technical formulae for calculating decile. Tinkering is attractive because it is a relatively simple solution. But it doesn't remove decile as a positional tool, nor does it tackle the ghettoisation of parts of Auckland or the real causes of achievement disadvantage. Even if you changed the way the indicators were calculated and combined, this becomes a mere rearrangement of the status quo.

A version of this tinkering approach—a suggestion from principals and teacher unions to more meaningfully consider the socio-economic profile of communities[65]—reduces dependence on a single number as a funding tool. Sure, uncoupling decile as a marker for *all* schools makes sense. Decile is relative to the base 20% of socio-economically deprived neighbourhoods, therefore any marker above the 20th percentile is theoretically irrelevant. Policy could shift to simply removing any label for schools above the relevant percentile. This really represents a status quo approach.

Other policy possibilities, five of them briefly discussed here, include:

(1) Connecting funding to statistical risk factors.

This currently appears to be the preferred policy direction. The New Zealand Treasury's analysis of children at risk of poor outcomes suggests that a penny spent now saves a penny later.[66] There are five caveats, though. Attaching funding, as in a voucher, to high-risk children carries the danger of stigmatising them. Secondly, matching dollars to individuals inside schools is both impractical and possibly unethical, especially when numbers may vary widely. Schools with few such students may find new reasons not to bother enrolling them since the compensation won't be enough to reward them for their trouble. Schools with lots of high-risk students, especially small schools, have woes enough in self-management without adding new burdens of accountability to their budgets. Thirdly, a child's risks are deeply connected to intergenerational circumstances, and without attention to whole-of-family/whānau approaches, the investment will inevitably fall short of its purpose. Fourth, attaching funding to student risk generated by factors not in the control of the school suggests a broadening of the purpose of schooling beyond educational achievement. Finally, and perhaps most importantly, making schools central to wraparound services makes sense within a community, but the corollary must be a strengthened suite of administrative support services to the school, not just for the individual. This is because disadvantage is often concentrated. When you have a school where 100% of the new entrants would fall below the expected standard at first assessment, you have to take a global view of the supports needed. Resourcing policy must consider how schools in highly stressed communities (especially small ones) must manage the presence of security (health and safety), psychologists, teacher aides and more than their fair share of special needs staff, cultural advisors, community liaison, police, rampant parents on P, and Child, Youth and Family officials. School principals report that they are constantly firefighting in addition to their regular responsibilities to consult on charter, prepare budgets, define the learning direction, manage appraisal, and heave aboard trustees bewildered by their responsibilities. In September 2016 targeted funding of exactly this kind was touted as a test run for the replacement of decile.[67]

(2) Connecting funding to student achievement.

Peter Ramsay's famous suggestion back in the early 1980s to create an 'eligibility formula' for schools in South Auckland explicitly connected funding to student achievement. His report was, at that time, fully endorsed by teacher unions. The education system is now awash with data and primary schools are learning to make (better) judgements about the achievements of their students based on the National Standards. The danger for this data is it becomes single-use evidence on which to rank schools. The opportunity in the data is that it allows for more targeted interventions to improve student outcomes—that is, to pay out on the basis of recognised need. However, today the education sector would react with horror to Ramsay's suggestion, seeing embedded within it 'pay for performance'.

There are less scary narratives. To use a Waikato dairy analogy, it is far easier to make butter from full-cream milk than from skim milk. Yet skim milk is still a valuable product. If a school could show that new entrants have had poor early childhood education experiences, that children fit the Ministry of Social Development's vulnerable children's profile (as described in the Treasury paper above) and require intensive support to get them to the National Standard by the end of Year 1 or Year 2, then schools ought to have access to more teachers, more expertise and more targeted resources to invest in educational basics. At other transition points in the system (from primary to intermediate, from intermediate to secondary), modern data management techniques enable the pinpointing of need: it is no longer a secret which students require most support as they progress through the education system.

Connecting funding to need has to be finely balanced for two reasons: the administrative burden of defining need; and the risk of unintended consequences. No one wants to return to the days where school resourcing depended on the principal's capacity to make a 'special case' or to pull strings. Reportedly there was once an almost obsessive view in the New Zealand Treasury that the high-minded mandarins of the old Department of Education had allowed certain schools and principals to feather their nests way beyond affordability and natural justice. Political advocacy and discretionary pots of money for this or that purpose meant that some schools and groups of children regularly 'missed out' on additional support (guess which ones?). The Treasury view then was that school funding entitlements ought to be data-driven and transparently delivered. Decile became a useful Treasury defence against constant pleas for special assistance, a Teflon-coated policy impervious to all other calls for help. Decile funding had blanket application, putting special circumstances beyond the reach of the politicians. The lesson from this is that the data on which any decision for extra resourcing is made must be simple to collect, verifiable and valid, and linked to whatever the government of the day's priority goal for public education is.

Secondly, there are risks of unintended consequences or distorting signals. Would schools manipulate data to get more money? It won't be long before the achievement data of all public schools is genuinely and usefully in the public domain; the technology is nearly there. System attitudes to public accountability may take some further time to catch up. Gaming the system is a hazard to professional ethics and reputation all over the world. In America, where standardised tests are everything, schools now face such serious consequences from poor test scores that they use sleights of hand such as classifying students as disabled or putting them into so-called 'special education' programmes so that they become exempt from state tests and so on.[68] Over recent times, various American school districts and states have been rocked by school cheating scandals.[69] Delivering resources only on the basis of tests, however delivered, is a one-eyed view of the disadvantages children face in getting to success in learning. Fortunately we don't have standardised tests in New Zealand (for a variety of excellent reasons). Our version of data-gathering is National Standards. Driving *everything* to student achievement data may create such rigidities in the system that we lose sight of the cultural and social purposes for schooling and, ironically, increase the pressures on schools to exclude students from enrolment (see the following chapter) or from their data.

(3) Connecting funding to social rejuvenation and neighbourhood renewal.

In Philadelphia the city was grappling with a dysfunctional network of inner-city schools in distressed neighbourhoods. As the state took over the city's schools and signed away the 'worst-performers' into privately managed charters, a partnership with a local university for a new kind of public school looked far more promising. Pennsylvania State University needed to renovate its increasingly ghettoised surroundings and reconnect with its community. It had resources that could be applied to urban renewal. It was ideologically committed to public education. So it set up a partnership that included unions, city officials and education officers, as well as the community. The eventual success of Penn Alexander School was pivotal to the neighbourhood's resurrection as a desirable place to live and work. In the space of 13 years, housing prices in Penn Alexander School's area quadrupled.[70]

Auckland has its own version of neighbourhood renewal projects. Both the Tāmaki Transformation Project (a partnership delivered through the Tāmaki Redevelopment Company, whose joint shareholders are the Crown and the Auckland Council) and the Southern Initiative (led by the Auckland Council) take a place-based view of transformation. Underpinning these projects is the understanding that school, system and community resources can work together to create a bigger impact. Unfortunately, resources for transformation are too often locked away in discrete boxes. If policymakers assessed the total amount of decile funding that came to the schools involved in these projects and *enhanced* that pool with other targeted resources that helped to shift educational outcomes, what might the total resource pool look like? By adding compensatory funding to a bigger pool specifically targeted at *both* community and educational outcomes, the school would have greater flexibility and additional commitment to apply to its core business: making sure students succeed.

Given that the problems of neighbourhoods impact deeply on schools, and the resources of schools can add much to neighbourhoods, by viewing the decile resource not as compensation for poverty but as part of a bigger package of services designed to collectively lift the whole neighbourhood from its disadvantage, the school itself becomes both a leader and participant in an effort to make a difference across the community and its networks. In effect, discretionary decile funding becomes part of a bigger effort which both encourages and obliges schools to cluster up, become more engaged with their communities and empower each other.

This is not a new idea. Teenagers in low-decile areas have particular health needs, and now we fund nurses for their schools. Social workers are assigned to work in low-decile schools. In the Tāmaki transformation effort, schools already pool discretionary funds for collective work. This is how 'full-service' schools work as vehicles for community empowerment. Most community-connected initiatives involve contractual arrangements of some description. All of them make a connection between investment and outcome—and could demonstrably contribute to gains in student achievement.

This ought not to be a step too far, given that the cluster approach is already being applied to the sector. The disadvantage is that the market model for schooling makes this a less useful option than it might otherwise be. Shifting from the market to a network approach would have to be a prerequisite for this to work properly.

(4) Full-service schools policy and circuit-breaking leadership.

Technically, even though decile funding is there to compensate for the general social disadvantages that apply to the neighbourhoods in which the children live, you generally can't spend that money on community development or adult learning. A school gets funding for *the teaching and learning of children* enrolled at the school. This makes it theoretically iffy for schools to spend their money on feeding children breakfast, for example. School funding is not for feeding the body, it's for feeding the mind. But it's a circular argument: If it's the parents' responsibility to feed the children, the school should sheet the responsibility for breakfasts back to the parents. But if children still arrive at school tired, hungry and grumpy, and the school gets measured on how well the kids are doing at school, and a breakfast programme demonstrably helps kids to do well, wouldn't every principal want a breakfast-in-schools programme to help the school's scores improve?

Is parent education a legitimate spending of decile funding? There comes a point when a parent engagement initiative morphs into an adult education programme with an intergenerational approach, as argued in an earlier chapter. We referred then to the full-service school idea. Instead of looking at decile funding as a top-up for disadvantage encountered by the school, a full-service school reorients itself to families and community to advance children's learning—the return on investment, if you like, that schools like Victory Primary School in Nelson and successful Kura Kaupapa Māori have become the model for. Such collaborations, fairly difficult to manage without mediating support, begin with the idea that families must access education as intergenerational circuit-breakers. By targeting resources to holistic learning needs, we more clearly connect to the broader suite of public service goals and obtain much better value for money for government as a result.

The full-service school could be greatly enhanced by rethinking the contribution the decile component of a school's funding could make to the services available in a community. The details of this, it seems to me, need to be part of a negotiation process at the community level. In the urban context, no one institution ought to 'own' the full-service idea. It's the package of services that a community is able to access that is key, as well as the combined effect those services have on the social and cultural wellbeing of, say, Clendon or south Ōtara. Good schools add value not just to students but to their communities too. A mediated negotiation process about the full suite of resources available and the outcomes currently being delivered would, of itself, deliver the 'community development and engagement' from which schools are so often isolated. However, under the present governance model, the definition of 'community' means something very different for a school (parents and caregivers) than it does for a neighbourhood. The evidence is overwhelming: when schools purposefully connect to communities, they can be circuit-breakers in the cycle of poverty and disadvantage.

The obstacle is the schooling model that tightly measures a narrow set of student outcomes and makes that the product for the market.

(5) Weaving high-quality professional practice through targeted cluster resourcing.

As chapter three described, we already know *how* to improve teaching and learning. How can policymakers make low-decile schools the epitome of professional challenge and personal growth? It must become possible for teachers to believe that it is exciting when you go to a school in a high-need community to work on worthwhile and stimulating learning initiatives and projects. Transforming these schools will require them to have privileged access to extra staffing and external supports that kick-start change. In a nutshell, decile funding could be bundled into a shared pool of expert teachers over and above the current staffing entitlements all schools get.

The policy option here is not merely an adjustment to school staffing. These 'expert teachers' could be located via an intermediary that aids a cluster of schools serving high-need and at-risk students; a sharp departure from the school-as-the-employer model. The home for professional expertise that schools can tap into, flexibly available to work alongside the teachers already employed in schools, takes the Investing in Educational Achievement policy out of the complications of the market model and offers a bridging process to a more networked administrative model. It establishes an intermediary entity—the missing system ingredient referred to in our previous chapter.

This book is not the place to explore these policy options in detail. They are here only to show that decile is not the only response possible to the challenge of resourcing schools serving the highest-need communities. In sum, decile funding arrived at a time when public policy could not conceive of schools as anything other than self-managing islands. Decile now entrenches only the status quo: and that's not transformation.

7

Who's not here is a community issue

Managing for outcomes

The weather, the radio said, was only local.

You've got to be there to learn. Attendance is a ticket to becoming hooked in to learning. We know that students absent from school for 15 days at Year 8 and late for another 15 are less than half as likely to pass their NCEA literacy and numeracy credits three years later than those students who attend school regularly and on time.[1] Truancy is more than a symptom of student disengagement, of educational and social failure. The realities of school attendance in South Auckland offer lessons in how public policy has failed to respond to the realities of neighbourhood. The quest for social transformation in the south has to include community empowerment to support every kid being in school, on time and prepared for learning, from day one of their school career.

Why every day 29,000 students are not in school[2]

New Zealand mothers are generally not Tiger Moms[3]—even in the wealthiest places, families condone days out of school. It seems we are just—*ahem*—casual about the legal requirement to be present every single day school is open. Families take off for visits to Australia or Fiji at random times during the year. On any school day you may reasonably expect to find a school-age person, possibly in the care of an adult, out and about in your local shopping mall. On some regional festive occasions—for example, for the ASB Polyfest in Auckland or for the Mystery Creek National Agricultural Fieldays in the Waikato—schools avoid being 'open for instruction' simply because otherwise absenteeism is absurd.

There are, of course, good reasons why students might not be in school every day. Your child may be sick, representing the school for cultural or sporting events, be overseas, caught up with a bereavement, or subject to force majeure (like a flood, closed road, snow-in, vehicle breakdown, fire or accident). There might even be exceptional family circumstances accompanying such sensitive matters as family violence, a court hearing, or a medical or dental appointment—and you would be justified in keeping your child away from school. On average, justified absences run at about 6% a day.

You might be surprised at what goes unjustified and unexplained, though.[4] Even with a note, absence during whitebaiting season, lambing season, fruitpicking season or any other agricultural or sporting priority is unjustified. If you are sitting your driver's licence test in school hours—unjustified. If you take the kids away on holiday somewhere, even with a note you're condoning their truancy. Sleeping in or recovering from a weekend hangover is not an excuse. Nor is going shopping on sale day, or taking the day off because it's a birthday or Chinese New Year. Babysitting is unjustified, unless there is an exceptional family circumstance. Waiting at home for the plumber to call—unjustified. And if your child is staying away from home and hasn't got any transport to school—well, you'll just have to be better organised. Even being away for a ballet or music exam is a no-no, although the school's policy may allow the principal discretion to waive attendance for any of these kinds of circumstances. An absence that is condoned by parents may be treated as a 'justified absence' in the data gathered by schools, but may still be outside the legal requirement of compulsory school attendance during term time. 'I feel churlish objecting to absence for a holiday overseas with a parent,' says one principal, 'especially when it seems to be a pattern with so many of the parents—including those on my board.'

Unjustified absence rates are much higher in low-decile schools. Why? The anecdotes accumulate as I visit schools all over Manukau. Thirteen-year-old Karina didn't go to school because she was 'sick'—in reality, she was protecting her little sister from her dad, who worked shift duties and was home during the day. Twelve-year-old Joseph was away because his teeth hurt, but no one took him to the dental clinic. Fourteen-year-old Karla declined to return to school because she was being bullied. Eleven-year-old Sita didn't come to school because he was too tired; he'd been at a church camp all weekend and had to get up at 5 am for before-school seminary. Twelve-year-old Vaine stayed home because someone had to look after her diabetic grandparent that day. Sharona and her sister only had two school uniforms between them—on washing day they stayed home. Rena grew out of her school blouse so she wore a jersey every day she was there, hot or cold, to hide the poor fit—and on very hot days, she found an excuse to stay home. Uniform is often cited as an element in absenteeism. Six-year-old Hosannah from Manurewa didn't start school at five because his mum didn't have a uniform for him. Community wardens reported in a Manurewa study that it was all very well to march the older kids to school when they found them lurking on the streets during school hours, but it was disheartening to have them turned away at the gate for incorrect uniform.[5] Health issues feature, too—infectious diseases like scabies are distressingly common in Auckland, as are respiratory illnesses, especially in winter. Housing is another factor—students must move between relatives and houses as rents become less and less affordable.

Middle-class kids start the school year on day one. For most secondary schools, enrolment takes place in term two or three of the previous year, but every January there's a scramble in South Auckland and other high-need areas to get enrolments finalised. Hundreds of students sign up late, and enrolments continue to dribble in for weeks after the official start date. The principal of one Māngere secondary school reported that his school enrols as many as 100 students in the last week of January.[6] A Manurewa primary principal claimed nearly 10% of his roll is not there on the first day. Principals are forced into undignified public calls to get families to commit to their children's schooling.[7] Blame cheaper airfares once the holidays have finished. Families frequently send children back on one-way tickets to Fiji, Samoa, Tonga, the Cook Islands and across to Australia to spend time with family during holiday time. The return to New Zealand at the close of the summer is prioritised on cost rather than timeliness. Blame poverty. The start of the school year is an expensive time for families, especially if new school uniforms, stationery and other items have to be bought. Blame lack of social capital; punctuality and being reliably present are lifetime habits modelled and formed from an early age. Friendships and groups in school are set on the first day, and a late-arriving child finds it harder to fit in. At secondary school popular subjects and classes become 'full' and the student late to enrol has fewer choices. How much harder to become engaged and stay engaged in learning when you've missed out on the scene-setting lessons! A student two weeks late starting school in Year 11 may miss out on up to 50 lessons—20% of the first term—perhaps the crucial ones explaining the requirements for NCEA. Many low-decile schools haven't confirmed the roll until week three or four.

If it's not okay to be late starting, it's also not okay to be late to school every day. Blame cultural expectations. We all live in a world maxed-out for time. We run from one meeting to the next, trying to squeeze one more task out of the day than the clock actually permits, or to finish one more conversation in order not to seem rude as we rush to the next. In Japan time has a precise and fixed meaning. In America they use the term 'tardiness'—it's a cultural offence to be late for an appointment or a meeting. Latinos and South Aucklanders have something in common: being present at the appointed hour is a flexible agreement. This isn't an excuse for arriving to school late, but it may explain it. When schools mark a student present or absent on the roll it could mean they were late, but not very; absent, but only part of the time; or justifiably absent, like for exam leave, and so in effect present. The Ministry of Education advises that persistent lateness is now to be described as 'intermittent absence'. Secondary students skip school more than primary school students. At primary school, younger children stay home more frequently than older children. Perhaps in a society that accepts homeschooling, compulsory attendance is not a line worth holding. Indeed, for some it doesn't feel like the state has given them a golden opportunity to learn. In any given week, 10.2% of New Zealand's school population is away, 4% of them for unjustifiable reasons[8]—which equates to some 29,000 kids wagging school on any given day.[9]

The policy bedrock for attendance is that self-managing schools should, well, manage it. But attendance is a multi-layered issue. Non-enrolment, truancy, unjustified absence, intermittent unjustified absence, absenteeism, transience, turnover, suspensions, exclusions, expulsions and exemptions are the myriad terms for compliance with the law and the consequences of absence. Patterns of school attendance are multi-dimensional. If we want a full-attendance outcome, we need to look at the issues as we would a statue—'in the round'.

How the market failed those hardest to reach

The fury of school de-zoning and the competition of the early 90s hid problems of attendance. School boards were supposed to take 'all reasonable steps' to make sure kids turned up. To see the patterns of attendance as they really were in South Auckland, the education system needed more sophisticated tools than individual teachers marking rolls, school managers chasing up waggers and school boards receiving occasional reports from the principal. None took responsibility for children not on their schools' books. Apparently, attendance for Māori students was particularly poor, although who could tell? There wasn't any robust data collection across schools. Most trustees were not Māori and no one asked questions about exclusionary enrolment practices.

Alarmist headlines about the truancy problems in South Auckland began to feature regularly in the *Manukau Courier*. 'Schools Helpless As Truancy Soars,' shouted the local newspaper in September 1991. In May 1992, it claimed 'Hundreds Go Hooky', even as the *New Zealand Herald* ('The Missing 3000')[10] was highlighting for a larger audience the inadequacies of the new system and its effects across the community. Who had control or legal responsibility?

More than one principal tells me that to follow up on an absentee takes more money, time and energy than the school could reasonably set aside. Prioritising attendance just leaves less funding and time to educate the ones who do turn up. 'Gone up north' is a pretty vague indication for a busy school manager to follow up on. Students who don't re-enrol in an intermediate or a high school—

well, they could have gone anywhere. Besides, they are unlikely to be the cream of a school's prospective enrolments. Prosecutions for non-attendance are a bureaucratic nightmare, not part of your training as a principal or teacher, costly for the school and unlikely to succeed anyway. Legal diligence is no enhancer of your school's crucial reputation in the community.

The belief that schools alone could be and should be responsible for dealing with attendance persisted among policymakers for a long time. Five years after the market reforms and the operation of school choice politics, a study by the Ministry of Education about the attendance issue zoomed in on schools and their attendance systems.[11] Clearly, some schools had better systems for managing absence than others. The study authors concluded that 'some schools are not tackling the problem at all while others are barely coping'. The underlying assumption was that if schools did their job well or *worked together* (a policy proposition somewhat at odds with the competitive market setting), the problems could be reduced. The research unit concluded that if the ministry went looking for good practice and wrote it up, then they could share it with the other schools and all would be better.

But the newspaper headlines about crowds of students playing hookey on the streets made politicians take notice. Having made schools responsible for attendance, MPs found it difficult to contemplate how to make the system as a whole play to their priorities. A 1994 parliamentary inquiry into children in education at risk through truancy and behavioural problems pointed out the obvious: truancy seemed to be widespread in some communities.[12] Politics is the ability to make a decision, while power is the ability to do things. To merely quote the ministry's summary about what schools needed to do was one thing; politicians made more impact when they scolded officials. At the very least, they said, the Ministry of Education needed to set a universal definition of truancy so that reliable recording, collection and reporting of data could occur.

Paying for no-shows is economic and social inefficiency. At what point does a no-show count as no longer enrolled? The official magic number is 20 days. Schools faced a moral hazard: the system held perverse incentives for schools to apply the 20-day rule in ways designed to avoid financial penalty. So the ministry designed a specialist service for the 20-day rule called the Non-Enrolled Truancy Service (NETS). Schools were supposed to ring the ministry if they'd 'exhausted all efforts' to get someone to turn up for 20 days, and then NETS was supposed to sort it out. Confusingly, NETS was *not* a service for dealing with those 'who only go to school sometimes'. It was for the permanent absentees who had walked away from the system altogether, confounding the system's duty to give children an education.

From a desk in Wellington it's hard to work out the exact issues behind non-enrolment in South Auckland. Life's tough for some kids. Some have disorganised families. Some just never get enrolled at all, possibly because their families have arrived in Auckland as migrants, legally or illegally. Housing issues keep transience high. Some families decide to go overseas or to another part of the country, and then end up not going, or going for only a short period of time, and they don't get their act together on the return to Auckland. Some students are expelled and never get to the next school. Some have health issues, including mental health. Some enrol in the correspondence school (now Te Aho o te Kura Pounamu) but do no learning. Some get exemptions to go to work and end up not doing that. And some are out from sheer disillusionment with life and school. Twenty days is a reactive rule. Even with the NETS service in place, policymakers could not resolve problems of system management. Enrolment across 2700 schools with a paper-based system was inefficient to administer. Inaccuracies dogged the work of the NETS attendance officers who had to find those kids on the ground. It was obvious that the system needed modern technologies.

How many students in South Auckland are not enrolled in school? This is a remarkably difficult question to answer, even today. By the end of 2005 the Ministry of Education was sufficiently organised to be able to quantify non-enrolment. That year, NETS snared 558 young people aged 6 to 15.[13] The ministry had records for a further 516 who had 'legal exemptions' to be out of school. That was over 1000 young people swimming around in the moats outside the education keeps of South Auckland. But the Achievement in Multicultural High Schools's Alternative Education programme (a backstop for the most difficult kids in the system) reported that of 14 consecutive enrolments from out of system in 2005, still only 60% were known to NETS.[14] In 2006 the Counties Manukau District Health Board dug deeper into community networks.[15] Informal sources such as Māori wardens, friends and peers, youth workers, transitions service providers, health personnel and police will all be aware of individuals out of system. But they won't necessarily have processes in place to turn that knowledge into data for the Ministry of Education or action with schools. The stories of this outside-schools workforce might be anecdotal, but 'informed guesstimates' from transparent calculations suggested, if nothing else, that a significant problem existed then—and may even continue to this day.

Surveys of absence rates are now a regular part of Ministry of Education data-collection.[16] The surveys provide a basic understanding about the justified, unjustified and intermittently unjustified absentees. Secondary school students bunk school more than primary kids. Higher-decile schools have lower unjustified absence rates. Frequent truants are most likely to be Māori or Pasifika. There are unjustified absence 'hot spots'—schools and communities where there are particularly high levels of truancy. Since the minister of education has been clear that improving student achievement means getting the official absence rates down, attendance has become a priority.

Although the ministry set out to lower absence rates, the trends go stubbornly in the wrong direction.[17] Auckland's unjustified absence statistics look less alarming than in the far north, Gisborne or Kawerau. Nevertheless, rates of 4.3% in Papakura and 4.7% in Manukau (compared to 3% across Auckland) indicate a major problem. Some principals cannot believe it is as low as this. Either there is inaccurate data management or there are hotspots that only locals know about. In any event, shift those percentages to numbers and the scale of the problem looks entirely different in South Auckland than it does in other parts of the country.

The education sector itself did not, still does not and will never have the capacity to determine the true extent of non-enrolment, nor does it have the resources to address the most challenging attendance issues. There are overlapping circles of influence over the legal requirement for young people to be at school. The work of YouthLaw Aotearoa, district health boards and social services agencies will be just as important in addressing the underlying causes of poor attendance and its consequences as the work of schools will be. But collective impact is diminished because we don't manage data for outcomes and nor do we empower communities, as the following case studies show.

Manurewa: a community case study

Manurewa has 32 schools with a combined roll of over 16,000 students. Many of them disengage from school earlier than students from other suburbs (71.1% of them stay at school until they are 17, compared to the Auckland average of 85.2%). Less than a third of Manurewa students leave school with University Entrance,[18] compared with 57% across the whole city. Local politicians like to support local schools. However at the turn of the millenium the problem of truancy was of such anecdotal concern to the Manurewa Local Board that at its November 2000 meeting it set aside $10,000 of community funding to explore the particular local dynamics.[19]

There's a school of thought that says that local government shouldn't be worrying about things that are the responsibility of central government. Think again. Break-ins, street violence, shoplifting and car conversion are all crimes connected to youths out and about with no purpose. Police statistics for 2000 showed that Clendon police were dealing with approximately 1200 offenders a year, and teenagers aged between 14–16 were responsible for a third of all burglaries in the Counties Manukau policing district. There were 596 arrests of youths involved in burglary that year. Non-attendance at school is most certainly a community issue, and the Manurewa Local Board wanted to do something about it.

A highly respected community development worker employed by the Manukau City Council led the charge. How did John Durham go about it? He surveyed students and gathered data from the District Truancy Service (DTS). He led focus groups with significant players in the community, including the Manurewa Marae, and feedback sessions with local school principals and police youth officers. Although John made a genuine effort to look at the local picture in the round, when we met over a coffee at the council cafeteria one day, he expressed his frustration about the muddle of the data. The best information that the community could come up with—one of the two secondary schools declined to participate!—was 'indicative truancy rates', which showed that the problem was greater than national rates suggested but still hazily inexact. Council officials used the term 'keyhole' to describe John's report. The Clendon community network was blunt in its feedback 'that Principals and Boards [need to] take notice of what the children are saying about school (in many cases it is the school not the children that is the problem)'.[20]

The report reflected a genuine sense of community dissatisfaction about how non-attendance was being managed. 'Truancy is a community problem, and the community at large needs to take ownership of it,' wrote John.

The Manurewa Local Board was further disempowered, however, by the inability of government officials to discuss policy design around truancy services with communities. District Truancy Services were the Ministry of Education's response to the truancy landscape, and the ministry could work with schools but not with communities. The Manukau City Council's community development team believed in the power of networking and was the glue for many kinds of network actions. Unfortunately, the Ministry of Education and its schools could not effectively connect to it. My tribute to John Durham, as I write this, is to honour his prescience about the importance of taking a whole-of-community approach and his efforts to include all voices. John unexpectedly passed away just as the Manurewa Local Board's truancy work was about to enter a new phase.

The arrival of DTS was a policy admission that schools couldn't address the question of attendance by themselves. At first, DTS was contracted out to providers in selected areas. In Manurewa, Finlayson Park School successfully bid for a local contract in concert with the Manurewa Principals' Association. Later the ministry expanded DTS across the country so that all schools could ring someone to do the running around after absentees. It sort of worked. 'Sort of' because some schools used the service and others didn't (mostly, it turns out, the higher-decile schools didn't).[21] 'Sort of' because there was a dedicated backstop for schools. 'Sort of' because a connection with the community was being crafted. It certainly didn't make it easy for anyone other than the schools to kick-start action or leverage their own resources into the problem. In effect, schools became the gatekeepers of referrals. Despite ongoing political rhetoric about their importance, communities were effectively shut out.

In Manurewa in 2003, attendance became a strand of the Manurewa Enhancement Initiative (MEI), a Ministry of Education-funded working-together exercise for all the schools in the area. The paper-based enrolment records of 31 Manurewa and neighbouring schools were thoroughly combed to understand the patterns of attendance in the suburb. Nothing of such scale had been done before. The findings were enlightening but strictly not for publication. Was absenteeism a particular problem in the area? Yes, it was. Were there groups of students with better attendance than others? Yes, there were. Peak attendance was at Year 6 (the end of primary school). Māori and Pasifika students had a consistently lower attendance rate than others. Attendance rates decreased as you went down the decile scale. Young children were far more likely to be away than their older siblings. Some classrooms had better attendance rates than others. Transience was an issue, especially for Years 1–3 children from the poorest areas.

Principals concluded that parental or community attitudes were at fault: parents needed to recognise how important regular attendance was, especially in the early years,[22] and the impact of transience on learning. So the consortium of schools embarked on a community education campaign ('One School Is Cool') which included pamphlets, posters and various other targeted 'projects'. Though all this was deemed successful, it's difficult to tell what difference it made. The Manurewa principals might usefully have explored the links between transience and housing and education—but of course, that is way beyond the scope of action the education sector could lead.[23] They might also have empowered community leaders in defining the campaign. They didn't because they couldn't; it was never in their brief or within their resources.

The Ministry of Education still relies heavily on in-school management of attendance issues. Over time, its advice to schools has become more sophisticated,[24] and now most schools, including those in Manurewa, are using electronic attendance registers (eAR) that help them to analyse data much more efficiently. Ministry advisory documents invite school boards and principals to ask questions such as: 'What is your data telling you and what are the stories behind this data?'; 'What are the roots of persistent unjustified absence in your school?'; 'Does attendance at your school match the national average and/or meet Māori and Pasifika targets?'[25] These are in-house questions. Though these are public schools, attendance data is still not public information. Data is highly relevant to quality community problem-solving. Yet to this day there is no reliable mechanism for school data to be pulled together so that the community can see network attendance trends and address emerging problems as they happen.

The best guess (from the patchy data available) is that in Manurewa truancy levels are still running about 5% above the national average[26] and that schools are dissatisfied with the truancy services available to them. Collating and sharing data is a task that requires resources. Schools operate in a low-trust environment. Their first instinct is to ask what motivates others in using their data. School principals and their boards seek veto rights on anything that might impact on the reputation of the school in the community.

Community questions are different to those suggested by the Ministry of Education and the low-trust ones asked by schools. Yet there is no agreed-upon forum in which questions can be safely prepared, shared and discussed. Does school attendance in our suburb match the national average and/or meet Māori and Pasifika attendance targets? Is the trend an improving one? Can we see the (matching) trend in youth crime statistics? Can we collectively do something about it? The mediating layer between schools and between schools and communities—the vital connections that facilitate cross-school, cross-sector sharing and feedback—are missing from the system.[27] Solutions proposed are led by the microclimates of individual stakeholders with limited powers. The bigger picture is unseen, the community disempowered.

Connecting communities in policy and practice

The Ōtara truancy service was once just two people: Pat and Mihi. They knew the families in their area, lived there and were part of their community. When I first met them in April 2000 they worked on their own out of Te Puke o Tara, the community centre on Bairds Road, as one of 170 DTS contracts then operating around the country. They shared a single fixed phone line and a tiny office, its chief virtue its central location. Early every morning they received phone calls from schools, after which they went out trawling for truants.

Pat and Mihi had to work out for themselves whether they were meeting ministry or school expectations. After a few years, the Ministry of Education cut the 170 providers around the country to 70—it was more administratively convenient for the ministry to engage fewer, bigger providers. Pat was still part of the service in Ōtara, but now he was working under a governance and management structure provided by the Ōtara Boards Forum (OBF). This 'district' contract with the ministry extended across to Māngere, Papatoetoe and parts of Manurewa. The contract emphasised good management and 'output'. It was a numbers game. How many referrals were made this week? How many cases were 'closed' or issues resolved? Each truancy service around the country, an island of effort in an uncharted ocean, was expected to develop its own database and systems to manage the work. There was no money in the contract for training and support for the truancy officers. The contract did not reward collaborative or collective effort to look at the problem 'in the round'. The contract did not empower the truancy officers to build relationships across the community for better wraparound—although they tried to work closely with students and their families.

Over a period of ten years the OBF officers developed a deep and sophisticated understanding of attendance issues in their community. They built up data that helped them to assess who was wagging, which local families needed support and which schools valued their service. They had access to information that is often classed as 'private', unavailable to state agencies, but which is part of local knowledge. The officers understood the dynamics of local families in ways that many of the teachers and principals, who did not live in the suburb, could not. 'We are not authority figures, like police, with powers to remove children from home or to prosecute,' contract manager Bill Takerei noted. 'We're about relationships with families that are focused on positive things like getting your kids organised and at school every day.'

Local knowledge meant the officers knew where the truants hung out. At Hunters Corner in Papatoetoe they piloted a shopping area initiative designed in partnership with police, Māori and Pacific wardens, Manukau City Council officials and their town centre ambassadors and multi-agency youth offending teams.[28] The operation included the distribution of a booklet for businesses on how to deal with truants, an 0508 TRUANT phone service line for reporting truants, and a training session run by the police for wardens and truancy officers. This initiative was successful enough to be expanded. But much of this was over and above the outputs directly required by the OBF's contract with the ministry.

In 2009 DTS were again reviewed. At first, the review seemed to be about looking for best practice among the various community services. Fortunately the reviewers were far smarter than that. They recognised providers as experts about their patch. But they also zoomed out from the local picture and took in the bigger scenario, especially the ministry's management of the service. The ministry's management was 'ad hoc', they said. The ministry had a plethora of initiatives addressing the attendance issue, and schools were operating seven (yes, *seven*) different student management systems that did not always speak to one another. Administrative efficiency could not be improved without better overall planning and management. Said the reviewers to the ministry, reflect harder on your role:

> The nature of the issues surrounding truancy is such that any meaningful response requires collaboration across a wide range of agencies on a day-to-day basis. This requires truancy management services to maintain an effective array of networks. The effectiveness of these networks is an element of success because it

> helps identify opportunities to leverage off, or assist, the work of others; and it reduces the risk of [services] pursuing initiatives that cut across the work of others.[29]

Multiple agencies trying to address attendance could look like collaboration or on-the-ground confusion. To illustrate: government pumps up police numbers in the Counties Manukau district. Neighbourhood Policing Teams (NPTs) are not intended to be a permanent feature of police operations,[30] and now there are three NPTs in Ōtara, each taking a different approach. Bill Takerei, the manager of the OBF's attendance service, ticks each of them off. *Tactic one: be proactive.* The gung-ho police team decides to work directly with schools. The schools decide this is a good idea and ring the police instead of the appropriate attendance service for every missing student. This is a sledgehammer approach; a cop visit to the family home is not an entry-level action, especially if the absence turns out to have a reasonable explanation. *Tactic two: pass it on.* The NPTs are far too busy and refer everything to the attendance service. *Tactic three*: *a mix of the above two approaches.* You are never quite sure what will happen next. Lack of clear policy turns into a competition about who gets the brownie points: the attendance service for its contracted outputs or the NPTs for their key performance indicators. Is it sustainable for the police to become the de facto truancy service? Of course not.

No one disputes that police and attendance services had to work together. On the ground, though, it just looks like the police and education ministers need to share lunch.

In 2011 the Ministry of Education took a new tack. It offered the OBF a new pilot contract for an 'integrated' service which connected the NETS and truancy services. The pilot gave schools a designated attendance advisor. Note the shift in language. The full spectrum of non-attendance and its kaleidoscope of bits—unjustified absence, intermittent wagging, non-enrolment, suspension, expulsion or exclusion—could be wrapped into a single proactive effort between the service, the schools, the community and other agency services like police and the CYF service. The pilot showed what is possible when you get a new database and a properly resourced co-ordinator to hold the service together.

And then other communities around the country tested models for an interagency 'war on wagging'. The organisation ROCK ON (Reduce Our Community Kids Offending Now—how we love project acronyms) is the escalation of effort, a *third-tier* response, when schools and the attendance service haven't been able to break a pattern of absenteeism. From the outside, it looks smart: key officials from the police, school attendance officers, school managers and social welfare services like CYF meet regularly to establish new levels of in-the-round effort for the hardest-to-reach families.

But community capacity-building is not an output the Ministry of Education wanted to buy. The attendance service in South Auckland was put back into the policy crucible. The ministry reduced still further the number of contracts it would hold across the country, so that one provider would cover 'Area 2', a euphemism for a peculiar geographical invention of the Ministry of Education—very large, with services decoupled from neighbourhoods. Wellington-based administrative requirements took priority over community boundaries (such as Auckland's local board areas, the operating districts of police or health boards). The contract, put out to competitive tender, was now worth a considerable sum of money. However, the tone of the service promised yet more of *dealing to* rather than *working with* communities. These suburbs in South Auckland were New Zealand's largest and poorest; would this new contract fix the attendance issues there?[31] Would there be better public services, as the prime minister promised?

Like the weather, we should expect attendance issues to be very local, but decisions made in Wellington on service coverage seem to ignore community capacities. Change is inevitable. The white-hot fuel that forged the Ōtara boards together in the first place, a heady mixture of community outrage and commitment to collective action, burned out. It's understandable that Ōtara board chairs and their place-focused forum didn't want to be responsible for governing an attendance service for the whole of South Auckland—their own schools are their priority. The OBF's swan song is more than symbolic. A collaboration of school boards starting out as an innovation in collective governance ended up as a petered-out promise. Government sought collaboration but service delivery is competition. The tendering process failed to nurture local capacity. The measures of contract success were poorly aligned to how communities think and work, and models of operation were imposed and measured in limited terms. The impossible-to-measure attributes of community cohesion, local network leadership and strong connections are rarely in a contract's key performance indicators. It's difficult to see how large-scale attendance contracts covering multiple local areas would improve the capacity of communities to self-monitor the participation of children and their families in learning. By March 2014 the signs were not promising.[32] The ten years of institutional knowledge and community credibility built up by the OBF through its attendance efforts, the jobs that the service gave local people: all were now gone. The legacy was some community bitterness that, once again, a new 'service' would arrive, wash the stones of Ōtara clean and then leave at the whim of a government agency's contracting arm. Where is the long-term commitment to community empowerment and development in that?

Attendance and social dysfunction

In 2011 more than 1400 young people were kicked out of school. There is significant community support for the dismissal of disruptive children. Bloggers, columnists and editorial writers erupted on the news of a Paeroa primary school that 'took a stand' on a disruptive student against the wishes of Ministry of Education officials.[33] According to the law, a board has the absolute right to 'control the management of the school as it thinks fit'. Not unreasonably, most parents are unwilling to have their children sit alongside bad influences. It is sheer hell for other students and teachers to have in the classroom a damaged thug who constantly disrupts learning for others. Many principals and boards don't consider themselves as upholders of public education but as protectors of other children's welfare. It appears that a violent 10-year-old with a pattern of interrupted schooling has no rights. Says the principal of one elite boys' school: 'Look, these are the rules and if you don't like them, you don't have to come here.'[34]

YouthLaw Aotearoa called on policymakers to set up a review body for board of trustee decisions to suspend, exclude or expel students.[35] It argued that such tribunals have been operating in the UK for some years. This suggestion certainly addresses the symptom of parent boards responding randomly to the rights of other people's children to a quality public education. But it doesn't address the basic problem of how a public education system balances competing interests.

Where do booted-out students go? Sharlene, an Alternative Education student kicked out of her local secondary school, told me that finding another school took about six weeks, lots of meetings and disappointment when people said 'No'. She felt 'stink like a reject'. She missed her previous school's guidance counsellor's support. Alternative Education (AE) is the system's backstop for those who drop out or are excluded from mainstream schools. As its name suggests, it offers a 'non-traditional' form of secondary schooling for the most 'at risk' in the system. These are tough kids to teach. The AE units require highly skilled teachers and individualised programmes for learning. It is not optional, nor is it meant to be sweet—AE must dance to the same tune as mainstream schools. Any school that volunteers to be a sponsor of AE expects impacts on its bottom-line data on student achievement. That some schools support AE units speaks volumes about their commitment to do the best for every child in the community. The Education Review Office assessed AE's successful outcome rate at 37%,[36] where successes constituted getting a job, enrolling in a course or returning to a regular school. To expect that they could achieve national qualifications too is a huge leap of faith. These young people also end up in youth justice residences. Youth justice researcher Alison Sutherland reported her conversations with 25 young people who ended up in one.[37] She concluded that school wasn't the cause of their offending, but negative experiences at school, compounded by a tsunami of incidents in their lives, inevitably propelled them towards truancy and dropping out.

Principal Youth Court judge Andrew Becroft looks to education as the best chance for a 'king hit' to reduce youth offending.[38] He reported that about 35% of young offenders before the Youth Court aren't at school, and that the research shows that 'better than psychological intervention, better than counselling, better than most things is attendance at school.' But schools find his message uncomfortable. 'A problem pupil removed is a problem solved for that school but not for our communities,' he told a conference of school trustees in 2012.[39] 'It's simply relocated.' As the judge well knows, the education system retains no safeguard for the right to be at a public school.

Conduct problems at school show up early and have far-reaching implications.[40] Māori students are three times more likely than Pākehā to be excluded from school, and Pasifika twice as likely. Students from South Auckland are four times more likely to be excluded than those from the North Shore.[41] One of the most robust and pervasive findings in the literature on problem behaviours is that these children will come from homes that are multiply disadvantaged. Their families may be dysfunctional, poor, unemployed or transient, afflicted by a sweep of social, economic and cultural limitations. It's no surprise then, that in the absence of respectful, loving relationships in their own homes, these children fail to meet standards at school, become disenchanted, disengage and then disappear. An expert group's estimate that '15–20% of Māori tamariki and taiohi will exhibit conduct problems sufficient to merit attention' is tragic for South Auckland, where the largest concentration of young Māori people in New Zealand live. But this is not just an ethnic issue. Non-attendance at school is merely a symptom of a wider social challenge related to the social and economic circumstances of families and communities. There's a clear link between attendance at Year 8 and achievement of literacy and numeracy credits in NCEA.[42] Attendance is a community challenge that matters.

The good news is that youth crime does appear to be steadily falling in New Zealand. The latest public data represents a significant improvement from the situation in 1996, when unregulated marketisation of schools first resulted in out-of-control school attendance issues. According to the Ministry of Justice, police dealings with children (the child apprehension rate) peaked in 1996 at 543 people in 10,000, dropped to 336 in 2008[43] and dropped further again in 2011.[44] The youth apprehension rate (14–16 years) also peaked in 1996; the number of children and young people charged in court is now the lowest it has been in 20 years.[45] Does this represent a reduction in incidents?

Diversionary measures, such as a ticking-off or a police Youth Aid alternative action, have clearly had an effect. Cumulatively, by improving their strategies for dealing with youth misdemeanours and with more overt ministry monitoring of levels of suspensions and expulsions, it is likely that schools have also contributed to this improvement. But the bad news is that there is a core of 'persistent' offenders who appear in the Youth Court, and who are probably responsible for 40–60% of offences. According to the former principal Youth Court judge, every Western country asks the same question: 'How to influence aggressive, impulsive, non-enrolled teenage boys (disproportionately Māori), often alcohol- and/or drug-dependent, who have conduct disorders and who come from disadvantaged and dysfunctional families with anti-social friends?'[46] The latest answer seems to be to reform the roles of the state and CYF in the care of the most vulnerable children. Activist social reformer the late Celia Lashlie would probably have agreed.[47]

Policy design and managing for outcomes

This chapter has followed the school attendance policy-making flow and its impacts in South Auckland. The first policy response to truancy was to blame schools and to highlight 'best practice'. When that proved inadequate, policymakers designed District Truancy and Non-Enrolled Truancy services, originally local, later packaged into more manageable (from a Wellington point of view) output contracts. Along the way, policymakers looked for improved data management inside schools. Then 'efficiency' drove a total re-think of the service approach.

These are all outsider solutions to a complex inside-the-community problem, driven by the contracting requirements of the state and the priorities of the Ministry of Education. Not one of these responses allowed communities to take collective responsibility for problem-solving. The 'end-users' were not involved in policy design.

It sounds so simple, so basic—to be 'managing for outcomes'. Yet impact depends on policymakers placing a value not only on expert knowledge but also on knowledge that comes from the community itself. Shared public knowledge is crucial. Policy can't just be theoretical. It must be grounded in the on-the-scene action. What this means for South Auckland is that policymakers need to be aware of—more than that, understand and be guided by—what is going on at the flax-roots. To shape a different future, policymakers must consult more widely, not just with those with interests to protect (such as truancy contract holders) but also with those who have influence in the present, those for whom and with whom a vision can be realised. Communities need to be able to act on their own behalf.

There are many techniques for doing so. Unfortunately, community development approaches that invite principals, boards, social services and local government advisors to work together have often felt more like red tape than improvements. What's needed is resource attached to community facilitation, governance and power over the resources.

Watch how communities work, and then design solutions from what you observe, advises Fred Dust of IDEO, a global design firm.[48] 'Design thinking' is the latest policy term for collaboratively inquiring around shared problems. It's a deliberate process that involves exploring new choices and alternative solutions together. It will involve in-the-field research that asks new, more insightful questions and gets closer to the lives of those involved in making education fit-for-purpose for all communities. Design thinking, like product development, uses prototypes to see whether an idea is viable and evolves it to a workable model that is scalable and efficient. This kind of work requires missions-in-the-middle with local credibility, and educators and social development experts, to work together in ways that are new. If the mayor of Auckland, the ministers of social development, police and justice, and the minister of education (and by extension schools) committed to an agreement to work together on attendance (perhaps through a special-purpose governance arrangement), the collaboration would require mature leadership, pooled resources and a mediating organisation with powerful leverage.

Budgets are the most closely guarded possessions of organisations. Aligning them across the silos of government agencies is a huge matter. The opportunity to improve results and reduce waste and over-spending, especially for the most vulnerable children, is undoubtedly embedded in the idea of Children's Teams or the Ministry of Social Development's Community Investment Strategy. In practice, 'design thinking' for student attendance in school would create some of the discomforts that Nabokov describes in the epigraph to this book. The conclusion of this chapter is that only a focused, community-linked intermediary operating within a next-generation school governance model could facilitate shift.

Part 3: What Is Education For?

Why do we want kids to go to school? This is an important question because transformation in South Auckland rests on our collective understanding about the system's purpose. The next two chapters take what appear to be opposite views about the purpose of schooling. Is it about a job? Is it about wellbeing? These two chapters explore the huge assumptions behind why we care so much about educational outcomes—and why that adds to the complexity of South Auckland.

8

Of talent and potential, pathways and pipelines

Or: learning that will get you a job

Youth joblessness is a 'wicked' problem that sits alongside some of the other wicked problems discussed elsewhere in this book—that is, intractable, pernicious and persistent problems resistant to solutions.[1] Kiwis understand that it is not okay to begin your career on the unemployment benefit or as part of an underground economy of drugs, prostitution, fencing and petty crime. Fixing youth unemployment is a power play of competing agendas. Our fixes depend on our understanding of the roots of the problem. 'Causal stories' for youth unemployment vary. They could be:

(1) the economy and globalisation; or
(2) the victims and their laziness, fecklessness or lack of moral fibre; or
(3) the schools, the curriculum and the teachers; or
(4) the rapidly changing labour market and youth employability in it; or
(5) employers and their practices; or
(6) inequality and low social capital; or
(7) the benefit system; or
(8) social disintegration.

Fixes vary, too: Prime the jobs pump for economic doldrums. To strengthen social connectedness, give youth mentoring a whirl. To modernise a public education system 'in crisis', reform qualifications. To strengthen the connection between learning and the workplace, sharpen careers counselling and work readiness programmes. To realign lifestyle carrots and sticks, reform benefits. To rebalance incomes and inequities, reform the tax system. And at the extreme end of policy options, give them old-time religion and boot camps.[2] Politicians and policymakers describe the problem, its cause and solution, in apparently rational ways with statistics and other data to back up their view—but each according to their underlying philosophy about how the world ought to work. Most wickedly, in plumping for any one of these solutions, new dimensions of the problem pop up in unexpected places. The solution becomes the problem becomes the solution in a never-ending Escher staircase of cause and effect.

There are many metaphors to describe that transition time between age 16 (still in school) and the destination (a job). These metaphors frame our thinking and shape our stories. The metaphors may involve 'journeys' and 'navigations', moving towards 'horizons' and climbing 'mountains' and crossing 'bridges', negotiating 'minefields' and 'playing fields', following 'star paths' and 'road maps', going up 'ladders' and down 'snakes', climbing up 'stairways' and traversing 'staging points', going down 'pipelines', following 'tracks', making a 'passage' into adulthood, undergoing a 'metamorphosis' or following the 'steps of Tāne (poutama)' in an ever-upward 'quest' for knowledge. These metaphors represent movement and change and carry multiple cultural and social meanings. We use them to tell stories about the problem and the proposed solutions.

We must journey back if we want to journey forward. 'Me haere whakamuri kia haere whakamua', as the saying goes. The 1994 Prime Ministerial Task Force on Employment took a special interest in youth disengagement and unemployment.[3] It found a confusion of policies across the employment, social services and education portfolios. The resulting youth employment strategy, a top-down government effort implemented two years later, reorganised 'incentives' like bright cones at roadworks, so that school-to-work pathways were better marked. Curriculum and assessment changes in senior secondary schools got the green light; government raised the school leaving age, raised eligibility for unemployment benefits to age 18, and set up case-managed job-seeker assistance. Yet as the 20th century closed and the new millennium opened, there was no noticeable dent in the manifest issues facing young people in Manukau. One in five students was still leaving school with almost nothing to show for his or her time there. Youth unemployment was unacceptably high. And the point of raising the school leaving age was . . .?

There is extensive research about what happens to young people when they end up NEET (not in education, employment or training).[4] Unemployment scars young people for the future. Skills acquired at school atrophy. Habits of commitment to work wither away. If you are unemployed as a young person, you are much more likely to be unemployed when you're older. You have less chance to accumulate capital (so you are therefore less likely to become a home owner or have savings), you are more likely to be involved in crime and you are much more likely to have mental health issues or be affected by substance abuse. Those are *personal* consequences.

It carries a price for the community too. In the late 1990s a consortium of Manukau's civic leaders (the Manukau Employment Consortium) led by Dr Jack MacDonald of the Manukau Institute of Technology commissioned some research from Ernst and Young,[5] modelled on an Australian study.[6] By weighing up things like benefit payments, health consequences, foregone productivity and so on, the cost per unemployed youth in Manukau in 1997 was calculated at $58,760 per annum.

But it was too early to turn on the lights. Statistics New Zealand only started collecting accurate information about NEETs in 2004. The situation by then did not look as bleak—real effort had gone into case-managing young people into 'positive destinations', some through community-led initiatives, and by that time youth unemployment was trending down. This was only a temporary fix, however. During the financial panic of 2008 and 2009, youth unemployment soared again.[7] Year on year, in sedimentary layers, the NEETs in Auckland accumulated so by 2012 there were some 29,000 15–24-year-old Aucklanders doing . . . well, mostly nothing.[8] Aside from the social dysfunctions, there are economic costs. Fifteen years after the first study, Dr Gail Pacheco of AUT University reported her calculations of lost productivity costs and the *direct* impact on the taxpayer purse by using a much more conservative set of assumptions:[9] an estimated $28,981 per young person per year in Auckland.

It's a global bomb. Why should Auckland be any different? In a world where 'work' is being redefined, education policy, youth employment and economic development sit in a single policy crucible, fired by the modern search for 'productivity'.

Bridges and youth mentoring

Bridges are everywhere in our lives, offering a spanning solution to reaching one piece of land from another: the Auckland Harbour Bridge; the Manukau Harbour Bridge; those rickety, breathtaking crossings of Peter Jackson movies. We use the bridge metaphor for joining what is otherwise divided; for gaps and differences. The bridging metaphor is the choice of those who want to open the world to those 'from the other side'. When you use the bridge metaphor, you are defining the problem as an issue of two worlds—that is, family, school, care and nurture on one side of the bridge, and economic and social responsibilities on the other.

Youth mentoring is a response to the problem of two worlds and is deeply involved in building relationships and community. Mentoring (from the Greek character Mentor, who tutored and watched out for the young Telemachus) matches a more experienced person with a younger, less experienced mentee to positive ends. More rarely, mentoring works in small bonded groups, developing a cohesive, relationship-based set of responses to life's challenges and goals. One summary suggests various aspects of the process:

> helping, coaching, tutoring, counselling, sponsoring, role modelling, befriending, bonding, trusting, mutual learning, direction setting, progress chasing, sharing experience, providing respite, sharing a laugh, widening horizons, building resilience, showing ropes, informal apprenticeships, providing openings . . .[10]

How youth mentoring grew momentum in this country illustrates the art and science of community problem-solving. The initiative grew from isolated outbreaks of a good idea, to groups working alongside each other in free association, to a formal acknowledgement of the importance of coherence, to getting consensus that youth mentoring has a part to play in addressing the problem of youth disengagement and failure to reach destinations. Youth mentoring has successfully become a collective noun: a community-led 'movement' illustrating community governance at work, with some nurturing from central government. The process that validated this idea is worth examining.

Youth mentoring was 'emerging practice' in New Zealand in the 1990s. Scouts New Zealand, GirlGuiding New Zealand, the Boys' Brigade, the Girls' Brigade, the YMCA—all had splendid histories with youth development as their starting point. They are out-of-school activities. Only once unemployment became a feature of our labour market did in-school youth support begin to get more attention. From an Australian idea, Rotary clubs introduced peer support to New Zealand schools in the 1980s with considerable success.[11] No one imposed peer support; rather, schools of all socio-economic profiles embraced it and made it a cornerstone of their pastoral care delivery. It could operate in-house, had a champion in the school guidance network, and had ready-made external support. Perfect—as far as it went.

As school segregation increased in Auckland during the 1990s, the supports that the left-behinds once received migrated too. Initially, youth mentoring in Auckland had a Band-Aid look. Principals in distressed communities resorted to personal connections to bring in the external learning supports needed; so, for example, the Rotary club of Penrose began a partnership with Penrose High School to mentor their at-risk students. Famously, a Fletcher Challenge company executive,[12] having watched a TV programme about the plight of South Auckland schools, approached Tangaroa College with an offer of help, which turned into a mentoring-style programme with company executives and students. On arriving in South Auckland I discovered other isolated outbreaks of the mentoring idea: the Manukau youth employment consortium had introduced a programme at Ōtāhuhu College (offering an external provider to manage the programme); Project K was refining the one-on-one youth mentoring model in partnership with schools; Big Brothers Big Sisters was operating in Dannevirke, and Big Buddy and MATES—now well-known programmes operating in the 'youth development and support' space—were beginning operations in Auckland.

Now picture this scatter plot of activist organisations. There is no connecting thread. There is no viable 'roll-out plan' for youth mentoring. Initiatives depend on cheerleaders and serendipity. Under the gentle heat of a slow burner, a loose network of enthusiasts bubbles up in Auckland; they coalesce to share experiments and build expertise. The Auckland Youth Mentoring Association's activities become gradually refined into a purposeful series of workshops and seminars, attracting interest from scores of different programmes and leaders operating in the region. Initiatives pop into the limelight in show-and-tell meetings. A muddle of programme purpose and practice is obvious. Some programmes are about self-esteem and emotional wellbeing; some about leadership; some about building faith and culture and identity; some about crime prevention; and a fair few are about educational achievement. Getting programmes up and running takes both enthusiasm and management know-how. A gathering in Dunedin attempted to set the stage for a national umbrella organisation to supply help and support to youth mentoring organisations. A year later, a conference in Blenheim attracted sufficient enthusiasts to put together a kick-starter 'executive' group for a national association. (That effort sank into a quicksand of constitution, equity matters and parochialism.) Philanthropic funding was limited and programme outcomes unreported; and so government interest was light. Although the problems of youth disengagement in Auckland were urgent and significant, activities were being run on thin soup and fresh air.

I was interested in the broader sweep of options for young people. All of these small programmes and individual efforts seemed worthy. Of the dozen initiatives operating across Auckland, how did young people or their schools access them? How did they add value? How did they get funded? Did they deliver—especially for the Māori and Pasifika youth of the city? Someone needed to midwife services that measurably transformed opportunity for young people on a larger scale, raised quality standards and co-ordinated efforts. Auckland needed a more robust organising model.

Ten years ago a Churchill Fellowship report by Robin Cox, who had visited the US and Canada, recommended a special-purpose trust to advance mentoring activity in New Zealand.[13] Such a trust, led by a core group of highly skilled and professionally credible people based in Auckland, announced itself by hosting a conference with a cross-country invitation list. The trust was deliberately designed to fill the classic intermediary role; that is, it was not a competitor in the provider market, but a resource holder, facilitator and advocate. Central government agencies could see how useful this was, to work with a 'peak body' that can read the whole landscape—too often, providers can only see their piece of it. The emergent trust gathered sufficient funding to employ a manager whose strengths in defining mission and strategy enabled it to grow in credibility and confidence. By hosting biennial conferences with growing participation, strengthening its expertise and connecting to researchers, hosting local workshops and communicating clearly its 'network' focus, the trust finally got a national mandate to play a leadership role for the movement and became the New Zealand Youth Mentoring Network.[14]

Academic interest lends weight to community-led action. The network facilitated an innovative partnership between the University of Auckland and the Great Potentials Foundation to develop a Stage II youth mentoring paper which combines theory, research and practice. Most youth mentoring programme managers now see the sense in participating in the network and having an advocacy organisation that offers a credible programme of work and asks evaluative questions.[15] More recently, the Vulnerable Children Act 2014 gave the network the ministerial fillip it needed. As for the young mentees themselves: in the newsletters and annual reports of many youth mentoring organisations, the stories of young people attest to the value of the mentoring experience.[16]

The New Zealand Youth Mentoring Network is a structural response to a process need. Today there are over two-dozen organisations operating specialist youth mentoring programmes in the Auckland area alone.[17] Youth mentoring and youth work often overlap. Possibly hundreds of youth workers operate in the Auckland area. The story of the Youth Mentoring Network sketches this book's point about community governance: for ideas to be transmitted, refined and improved as part of a shared effort to make a difference, you need a catalyst and connecting structure. Competing organisations can't be neutral. When you have an independent co-ordinator, everyone can access flax-roots knowledge that usefully informs central policy-making.

Still, youth mentoring does not offer a 'solution' to youth unemployment. It won't create a single extra job. It is all very well to build bridges, but without jobs, young people are faced with bridges to nowhere.

Voyaging

What teachers know about the journeys and destinations of their students is coloured by their own experiences of the world—which are not always shared with their students. Bear with me here while I ask you to imagine Kupe, the first discoverer of Aotearoa. He is the master navigator on the vaka taurua, the double-hulled voyaging canoe; his skills include knowledge of the stars, the clouds, the waves, the birds, the islands and the weather. He is without instruments or maps. The way he thinks about the journey is determined by his ability to read and interpret the different sets of environmental cues that measure his progress.[18] Powerful mental constructions accompany this knowledge. When we use a Polynesian navigational metaphor like the star path, we must understand it in relation to the Polynesian experience of the whole voyaging process. A navigator on a European sailing ship travelled the same oceans with sextant and astrolabe, charts and mathematical calculations. In Captain Cook's time, navigation was no more safe and predictable than for Kupe before him. For both Polynesian and European travellers, the journey's departure and arrival points may have been the same. The same stars, the same waters. But the science and technologies underpinning their journeys echoed the knowledge bases and world-views of those on board. The metaphors don't describe a shared experience of uncertain and ambiguous journeys.

In my last year of teaching I was assigned a 'Communications English' class, a Year 12 group of students. The school had separated this class from the mainstream and I was to deliver an experimental programme. These students had already failed in the academic classes. They immediately recognised Communications English as a 'reject' course. 'Humph,' said Melinda, only more rudely. 'We're not good enough to pass the other stuff.' Then, in response to my face of dismay: 'Oh, sorry Miss!'

It should have been my apology. The class was small by the standards of the school and many of the students were 'challenging'. Released from having to prepare them for a pointless end-of-year exam, I searched for valid, creditable activities that would reward their efforts. Accumulating credits was, at first, rewarding enough. As the year progressed, I came to understand that actually the credits were a bonus with only short-term meaning. Credits were, to them, simply a second-rate reward mechanism. These students were expecting to leave school soon, and as far as they could tell a credit in English would count for nothing in the workplace. In some vague way I understood we were talking past each other. Middle-class me wanted them to succeed for the sake of success and because success would open up their world; but *they* only wanted to bother if it got them something concrete in return, like a job. One by one during the course of the year my students left. Sometimes the school knew about this departure, sometimes we just guessed. Big-man Jayce got a job as a builder's labourer. Melinda got a cleaning job with her sister. Joanna got pregnant. These students were all passive resistors to learning and disillusioned with school. They could only imagine something better once released from its rules. I couldn't see how the English I was delivering, a collection of random unit standards, worthy and achievable, would be of value to them. My job as the teacher was to prepare these young people to compete in a tight job market as compliant, preferably semi-skilled workers. I made an effort to incorporate ideas and experiences from their lives into the lessons. But middle-class me had only a shallow experience of contemporary working-class life and the reality of youth joblessness, and my training as an English teacher never included any sense of direct job preparation. I, too, felt a failure.

Transition programmes in schools were initially an 'employment strategy'. They were supposed to make students as work-ready as possible, employable and better able to make wise choices about their future. The rhetoric was too convenient. In reality, those programmes became a sideline for the academically challenged, leaving mainstream learning untouched. A school that will get you a job? Yeah, right.

The value of local knowledge

What should good transitions actually look like for young people in South Auckland? Young people don't actively seek out unemployment as a lifestyle; it happens to them as a consequence of their total life and educational experiences. That's noticeable in community development work. Local government leaders set up the Mayor's Taskforce for Jobs as an expression of their own dismay at the effects of joblessness in their backyards. The enthusiasm for a nil-youth-unemployment approach was catching. Of course, in Otorohanga you can name every NEET and every employer. Still, knowing where the jobs are or how to go looking for one in the urban jungle of Manukau—that's valuable local knowledge. A major 'Jobs Jolt' policy package released by the fifth Labour government in August 2003[19] helped set up a Manukau project with a case-managed approach for ensuring young people reached a 'safe destination'. Service design was heavily influenced by youth development and mentoring philosophy.

I was part of the project's service design. We theorised four possible client groups: those who were 'secure', with families able to help them make the shift; those who had in-built 'resilience', who would make it anyway; those 'in risk', too deep into drugs and alcohol, with mental health issues or family violence matters for non-experts to resolve; and those 'at risk', unnoticed and unaddressed. This last group would be the new service priority.

Initially, the service ran as a pilot with six schools serving Māngere and Ōtara students. It placed 'brokers' alongside the school's pastoral care team but also worked with school leavers on their destination. Crucially, the brokers were not teachers or part of the school's staff. The purpose of the brokers could not be confused with the school's curriculum priority; they were there to meet the *community*'s strategic objectives for youth employment (through the Mayor's Taskforce for Jobs)—and to build the local knowledge about the jobs landscape which schools could never build for themselves.

There are advantages in working with schools as community partners. Schools are permanent, long-term institutions, much more stable than the community organisations that surround them. Schools have personal information about students, their qualifications and strengths, their families. They know (or ought to know) when a student is ready to leave or has 'left', and brokers located there could apply immediate support. Brokers could also build connections into the local labour market, following up the peripatetic drifter no longer on the roll, and maintaining the relationships required to open doors for students, as well-connected families do. The data showed extraordinary success for the pilot. The brokers filled a niche.

Yet a broker one day tells me how uncomfortable he is feeling. A class-size group of students at one school has been identified as not achieving credits or gaining academic value from the school programme. The school wishes to move these 16 students on, so that it can concentrate on those who are gaining credits. 'I've contacted the families,' he said. Yes, that was in his job description. 'But they are upset.' One of those young people—let's call him Pita—has almost no credits, no choices and no idea what to do next. We consider the competing perspectives facing him. Pita's *mates* are his most important support; and some of them are still at school. The *school* sees Pita as disruptive—he has already opted out in spirit and is unlikely to gain any more credits; resources and teacher time are being wasted. The *family* optimistically thinks that Pita should stay at school to get at least some qualification. The *community* does not want youth like Pita wandering the streets, joining gangs, going on the dole or disrupting other students' learning opportunities. Prospective *employers* will see that he has a poor attendance record, no credits, poor literacy and numeracy, and is generally unmotivated—why should he be taken on? His *church* helped Pita to prepare a career plan, but didn't foresee him being asked to leave school early. Only the private *training provider* is pleased—Pita is a potential client. What is the broker meant to do? Should he empower Pita to make his own decision? Challenge the school? Persuade the families that this is 'all for the best'? Find him a supermarket job? Just enrol him in a course and claim him as a 'successful placement'?[20]

These are everyday dilemmas, never satisfactorily resolved. Wicked problems are often like crossword puzzles: one or two out-of-place letters and the whole solution falls apart. A pilot project has a limited life. Over four years, the brokerage service worked with nearly 1200 'at risk' young people like Pita. The Ministry of Social Development then moved the service into a national youth services framework. Outputs delivery and central policy design and implementation diverted the service from its original community-developed philosophy. Youth Service became part of welfare reform.[21] The service's clientele shifted to the NEETs, young parents and beneficiaries. The service is no longer visibly a community-designed partnership with schools to support the vulnerable into a safe destination. It's a government-designed rescue service instead.

There is a coda. Under the banner of the Mayor's Taskforce for Jobs and with the significant support of the Tindall Foundation and other charities, Auckland Council has reimagined a jobs brokerage service as a council programme called Youth Connections. It's a partnership with local boards that complements the work of central government departments, and brokers ('youth connectors') are either council employees or employees of community contractors. The service fills an important gap and delivers heartwarming human-interest stories about students placed in work.[22] It's hard to tell whether it's effective or efficient. The service depends heavily on the existence of actual jobs or training opportunities. To hurry things along, in April 2014 the Auckland Council launched the Mayoral Youth Employment Traction Plan to boost the involvement of businesses (through an employers' pledge) in the project and the conduct of targeted job festivals, with a co-ordinating hub at the office of its economic development organisation in downtown Auckland. These are worthwhile efforts. The traction plan 'manages' the challenge at the interface. But it doesn't re-engineer the process of transition or transform the landscape.

Poutamatia

> **Poutama.** 1. (noun) the stepped pattern of tukutuku panels and woven mats, symbolising genealogies and also the various levels of learning and intellectual achievement. Some say they represent the steps which Tāne-o-te-wānanga ascended to the topmost realm in his quest for superior knowledge and religion.—Māori Dictionary Online

The Tertiary Education Commission uses Tāne's quest for the three baskets of knowledge (worldly things; spiritual things; evil things) to describe the four discernible paths that young people take into post-school learning:[23]

(1) going straight from school to university and then out into the workplace;
(2) going straight from school into training, often workplace based;
(3) taking a gap year or more;
(4) intermittently enrolling with multiple tertiary providers over multiple years.

The first two of these paths represents positive outcomes from school. The last two represent economic 'inefficiency', both for the learner and for the community.

Inefficiency looms large in Auckland. Public confirmation is difficult to obtain, but anecdotally 80% of University of Auckland students who come straight from school come from just 10 schools in Auckland. A major research initiative to understand why (known as the Starpath Project)[24] appears to have triggered significant improvements in NCEA outcomes in the lowest-decile schools of the city,[25] but apparently this still hasn't seriously impacted on the university's overall enrolment profile.

The second inefficiency is in the findings that between 15% and 30% of young people take breaks before and during tertiary education, depending on age and ethnicity.[26] They are disproportionately Māori and Pasifika. They are more likely to enrol in foundation and 'intervention' programmes and are less likely to progress to higher levels.

But policymakers have yanked up school pass-levels. Now NCEA Level 2 is a 'productivity marker'. There's been a 9.6% increase in school-leavers with NCEA Level 2 between 2009 and 2014.[27] The qualification is the desired 'efficiency' that sits within Auckland's economy—and how schools measurably contribute to the city's wellbeing. But is NCEA Level 2 enough to deliver equity in outcomes in Auckland and skilled South Aucklanders into the labour market?

Running in the background are the tired old arguments about pass and fail, 'vocational' and 'academic' tracks in secondary education. The apparent marker of school success is *university* enrolment. An apprentice plumber needs elementary physics to qualify as a tradesman, and a prospective nurse needs to have credits in basic chemistry and biology to begin study. These vocational pathways are not university ones, but they do require learning and skills at a level higher than ever before.

University Entrance requires a certain number of credits in university-approved (that is, academic) subjects at Level 3.[28] School leaders will tell you that communicating this to families with no history of tertiary learning has always been a challenge. Students who start behind need a serious heave-up to reach even ordinary goals. A careers teacher tells me that her mostly Pasifika students finish Year 13, 'but every year [she] meet[s] parents who are surprised and disappointed to find that their child is not eligible to enrol at university'. The 'I Have A Dream' Charitable Trust mentoring programme in Mt Roskill offered a view on how schools organise their curriculum.Young people face subject cul-de-sacs, the programme leader warned in 2013. 'Sometimes schools set [subject] entry criteria to exclude students they don't believe will succeed.'[29] He observed that teachers' expectations of students become self-fulfilling prophecies—and academic literature backs him up.[30] His trust connects disadvantage to the way schools operate in the belief that the whole point of secondary education is to get a qualification, and the purpose of the qualification is to go to *university* and then to get a job. Schools 'cheat' young people out of a future by tracking them into options that don't lead there. The assumption again is that there is only one pathway—going directly to university—that counts as success. (This is somewhat deflating for teachers who routinely offer 'catch-up' time during school holidays and extra tuition for students to ensure they achieve at whatever they attempt.)

Families apply competing social aspirations to vocational pathways. High-decile and private schools will market themselves for prestigious diplomas (such as the International Baccalaureate and, oddly, the Cambridge qualification). But in a world where everything is a market, even qualifications, schools in South Auckland must grapple with the needs of students *not* destined for university, even though their value as educational institutions is publicly benchmarked in the league tables against university-entrance achievement. The NCEA qualification lets these schools expand the range of options they can offer and gives students more opportunities to succeed. It's too easy to get alarmist and elitist about credits in barista services, child-minding, fork-lift driving and drivers' licences, even though they dovetail into jobs and family income, and empower and encourage young people to gain new social capital. Encouraging students to go straight from school into further learning is a more efficient use of public resources than letting them fail.

But will it be true that the more that low-decile schools succeed with their students in meeting the NCEA Level 2 target, the less desirable the qualification they deliver becomes? 'Is this a rise in genuine achievement, or simply a rise in credentials?' asks the *New Zealand Listener* cynically.[31] 'It's the expectation of the system!' explodes the minister of education. 'The qualification isn't the problem,' she says. 'No matter what we do, it seems we will never be good enough,' says one low-decile secondary principal in despair. 'We work extremely hard to do the very best by the students we get—even the ones that no one else wants.' Admits a local deputy principal: 'While the universities are calling for kids who have physics, chemistry and maths, it is unrealistic to prepare some of our students for university study.' Says another principal, 'We want them to succeed, yet we have to be practical: they are more likely to get NCEA Level 2 in other areas—and NCEA Level 2 is what we are being measured for.'

Knowledge and skills are important currency.[32] However, rising rates of NCEA achievement may not actually open up doors for South Auckland students, even as they enter post-secondary training or study. Maybe high qualifications are not *causal* to economic success.[33] If this were so, countries and regions with highly educated workforces would have high-growth economies—and Spain, Portugal, the UK and the US have large numbers of unemployed graduates. Something else is at work. Where is the equity in a qualifications market where the target, NCEA Level 2, becomes socially devalued because it has become too common-garden? The goalposts simply shift when the market replaces the local qualification with an international one. Inequalities widen.

Poutamatia describes the ultimate learning prize. It isn't learning to read, achieving at the National Standard or getting NCEA Level 2. These are indicators that young people are stepping up; but not indicators that poverty has been beaten, social prejudices removed, or spiritual and temporal wellbeing attained, or that one has graduated with a passport for a job. All the knowledge of the world may be distilled into qualifications. But we over-estimate their importance if we see them as the singular goal.

Pipelines and learning to earn

New Zealand faces a shortage of skills in the engineering and construction sectors. Employers who want to train up skilled technicians and tradespeople look favourably on students who have completed a pre-apprenticeship course, now set at NCEA Level 2. Although students may gain an apprenticeship without NCEA Level 2, they are much less likely to finish it than those who have. Now that the government has introduced Vocational Pathways awards at Level 2 (for specific combinations of credits), offers of apprenticeships will get tightly linked to achievement of those awards. Pre-apprenticeship programmes are the equivalent of the first year of a four-year apprenticeship and will become increasingly valuable endorsements—and in many instances, more financially rewarding than the university path. However, the schools sector and the community are struggling to get a grip on this new integrated vocational/academic environment.

You can get NCEA Levels 1 and 2 at places other than school. Many private training providers have carved out a foundation learning niche so that senior secondary and post-secondary learning now overlap. Secondary schools have become providers in a competitive market at the interface between secondary and tertiary learning. The government's target for NCEA Level 2 has become a *time*-linked target, not a place-linked one. Eighteen-year-olds have an open opportunity to get NCEA Level 2 or its equivalent via school, a school partner or a private trainer—they are 'finishing schools' for those who miss the target at 16 or 17 while at school. This profusion of services requires careful navigation.

If you see transition as a single-purpose economic flow that is about manufacturing talent, then a tighter metaphor fits: the pipeline. A pipeline is linear and functional. It involves input and output. There may be a single fat pipeline or multiple pipelines that operate side by side. The metaphor is useful in two respects. *Leakage* refers to the inevitable losses as South Auckland students enter the system at five or six years old, move from primary to intermediate or middle schools; to secondary schools and the qualifications levels; and then from the beginning of tertiary study to completion. *Staging* refers to the multiple valves in the pipeline. Nothing tells us more about a system's effectiveness than a measure of the proportion of students who begin and exit at the next checkpoint, and the next and the next, with the requisite standards or qualifications. Skills pipelines are meant to deliver three things: the 'basics' of reading, writing, counting and coping in the world; the 'generics' that we can use from one job to another and which make us employable; and the 'technical' skills in which we specialise. In a world of work changing so fast that even the most modern curriculum has to be flexible and adaptable, all three things count. The end result can be poured as precious liquid into the economy.

The world of work and the world of schools are now dangerously different. Workplaces want integrated skills. Most secondary schools teach discrete skills. Everything in the workplace has become digitised, every process from the production line to the service desk, from the farm to the consumer. If education is to serve employment, then the connections we draw between the worlds of education and work are vital. But making pipelines relevant is more than matching businesses to schools. To illustrate, the maths taught in schools and the use of maths in the workplace have been the subject of an Australian study sponsored by the chief scientist.[34] It is hardly surprising that many teachers ('6000 approaching or beyond retirement age') will not have encountered in their workplaces the language, the use of and the planning for e-commerce, big data and data analytics, cloud computing, collaborative intelligences, digital economies, cyber-citizenship and haptic technologies. The nearest that schools have gotten to integrated workplace-focused learning is the academy approach. That may not be enough.

When they were first established, *sports academies* were a 'motivational hook'[35] that accompanied the rise in the school leaving age and gained prominence through the sporting success of schools such as Aranui High School (established in 1999 with an emphasis on rugby and league), Raglan High School and its surfing academy, and golf and outdoor education academies elsewhere. They responded to the growing concerns about the disengagement of young men in particular. And central to their success was a shift to relationship-based pedagogy.

However, they constituted ad hoc development outside mainstream educational policy, and over time any school could put the academy label on a thinly disguised version of the traditional school timetable as a marketing tool.

Trades academies were initially a variation of the sports academy idea and could be adapted to other 'subject areas' (Onehunga High School developed a business academy in 2003 with its accounting and economics staff, private sponsorship from philanthropist Tony Falkenstein and the support of the University of Auckland Business School). The label applied to a school-within-a-school approach where students are offered a programme with a career theme, with a curriculum arranged so that students learn as a group. There may or may not be a specific link with an employer or tertiary institution.

Services academies, which began in 2008, had more formal policy backing and funding. They too were designed to keep young people staying for longer, like prospects to a web page. The target: mainly young men with 'average to limited success at school'. The attraction: heavy emphasis on outdoor education and physical fitness alongside literacy and numeracy basics, and a potential career in the military. The premium: active support from the New Zealand

Defence Force in the design and delivery of the programme. An ERO evaluation of 16 of these academies in 2011, after about three years of operation, showed considerable success.[36] For the students, many with hairy records of engagement with their schools, their time in the academies 'turned this around and helped them to identify and demonstrate their potential'. The ERO evaluation did not offer any data about the actual destinations of the students, but recommended better alignment to credit-gathering on the qualifications framework.

Trades academies became a National Party election promise as part of a trades and skills policy released by the leader in November 2008 at the Southern Cross Campus. More sprang up from February 2011 under the Youth Guarantee banner, offering training for careers in hospitality and tourism.[37] Like services academies, trades academies are based on a theory of partnership between schools, tertiary institutions, industry training organisations and employers. The government, looking for good wins under the Youth Guarantee policy, has funded many more trades academies since.

The Counties Manukau *health academies* project sits alongside these as one answer to the problem of the pipeline. Chief executive Geraint Martin of the Counties Manukau District Health Board blogs:

> In 2009, seated between the Honourable Bill English and Sir Stephen Tindall before a Prime Ministerial Job Summit, I had a conversation . . . about the fact that healthcare is one of the biggest providers of New Zealand jobs. That's certainly true of CMDHB—we are the biggest employer in Manukau City. Despite this, healthcare routinely imports a great deal of its workforce from overseas (myself included). Surely it makes better sense to enrich our local community with the education and jobs we can offer?[38]

In the Counties Manukau District Health Board (now Counties Manukau Health) service area, Māori and Pacific people are 16% and 23% of the population, make up a higher proportion of the in-patient mix than you might expect from the numbers, yet hold only 3.6% and 7.2% of nursing positions and proportionally even fewer medical positions.[39] Similar disparities can be found among midwives and jobs in allied health services. There are good reasons to look for a local health workforce—improved service quality, less risk, better access to healthcare and responsiveness to patient need, higher levels of service satisfaction, lower turnover rates, increasing job satisfaction and improved productivity and motivation.[40]

Unfortunately the existing talent pipeline outputs don't cut it: count the number of Māori and Pasifika children who enter schools in South Auckland; those who complete NCEA Level 1 (including credits in English, maths and science); those who complete NCEA Level 2, entitling them to enrolment in health sector training courses; those who complete NCEA Level 3 with the required credits for enrolment in professional programmes; and count those who complete the first year of post-school training, those who graduate and those who come back to work in Counties Manukau . . . it's too painful to dwell on the slim and slow drip at the end of the pipe. By one calculation,[41] fewer than 40 Māori students across the whole of Auckland were eligible to receive University Entrance in 2009. Not all of them would have taken science and maths at school.

Philanthropist Sir Stephen Tindall pledged a million dollars at the 2009 Prime Minister's Summit on Employment to support innovative training and employment initiatives 'for those communities that are most vulnerable to job losses in an economic downturn'.[42] The million dollars, combined with the championship efforts of the mayor of Manukau, the chief executive of Counties Manukau Health and various other 'stakeholders', resulted in projects to support prospective Māori midwives through their training and Manukau students into tertiary scholarships, and a health sciences academy within two partner schools with significant Māori and Pasifika rolls. The project added a final, crucial twist: those passing through these programmes are *guaranteed a job* at the end of the pipeline.

What the experiment has shown since is that science learning in secondary schools needs a new kind of cultural relevance. That's both pedagogy *and* connections to relevant opportunities for work. The pilot schools (Tangaroa College in Ōtara, and James Cook High School in Manurewa) exercised incredible partnership initiative to set up health sciences academies in their schools. An existing Year 10 careers awareness programme (Health Could B 4 U) was ramped up in the project schools to include face-to-face meetings with Māori and Pasifika health professionals about their career trajectories. Once enrolled in the health sciences academy at Year 11, students were offered work experience: day-long encounters at health science fairs; additional netbook and paper-based resources; peer tutoring and the promise of scholarships and celebratory events. Suddenly subjects like science, biology, chemistry and physics had purpose and glamour. Family involvement and commitment to students lifted student expectations. Inclusion of teachers and the principal's backing raised teachers' expectations of student capabilities. Absenteeism fell away, retention rates rose, and parent–teacher evenings buzzed with excitement as family got involved.[43] According to principal Ngaire Ashmore, the health sciences academy inside her school exerted significant influence on the way the school now thinks about its delivery, and the health board won the 2012 Equal Employment Opportunities Trust's supreme award.

And yet pipeline metaphors suggest that the problem is flow, not the terrain over which the pipeline must travel. The Counties Manukau Health board partnership with the Tindall Foundation has seen at least 15 midwives graduate into the workforce who might not have made it otherwise. Monitoring shows promising movement from the school academy, to tertiary scholarships, to health jobs in South Auckland. But this movement will never be smooth. Rina's story illustrates the bumpy social landscape. Rina arrived here with her family from Samoa when she was little. She began learning English when she started formal schooling. She attended Dawson Primary School and Clover Park Middle School before moving on to Tangaroa College. Rina's motivation, typical of Pacific Island students, is 'to honour my parents'. At the Equal Employment Opportunities Trust's AGM in 2013, Rina presented with confidence and grace her experience at the academy. The efforts of her school to understand in practice what a pipeline means and how that can translate into student achievement have been almost heroic. The efforts of the employer to motivate students, offer them possibilities and celebrate and reward their efforts have been equally outstanding. The idea of a purpose-designed learning pathway with a guaranteed job in the health sector at the end of it is appealing—but were clearly not central to her life. Rina feels overwhelmed. In 2014 I discover she is taking a gap year after the disappointment of receiving exam results that fell short of her dream. She fills her time with volunteer work for her church and family. Rina's peers are doing better. The problem with the pipeline metaphor is that it assumes a linear manufacturing process unencumbered by the branch lines, rocky relationships and cultural terrain that underpin real South Auckland lives.

Re-engineering the jagged edge

The Auckland Council quotes the 2012 finding that approximately a third of the 100,700 jobs held by young people were in two industries: retail, and accommodation and food services. Notoriously low-paid, these ought only to be staging posts to better-paid work. But are they?

Moving beyond these two industries requires higher-level skills. The hurdle into higher-level learning ('college readiness') and the line of sight into work has an extensive academic literature.[44] Interventions to fix the student (academic tutoring, youth mentoring, family inclusion) or fix what support the school offers (like careers counselling or study skills courses) all seem to work—sort of. More interesting approaches, however, dig deeper into *system* re-engineering. In many respects, career-led academies like the Counties Manukau District Health Board experiment are a step towards the highly successful German model of a career-linked curriculum and the emerging Pathways in Technology (P-Tech) high schools in America. The health science academies, with their targeted careers and employer sponsorship, are about a similar seamless workplace preparedness that those models apparently offer.

P-Tech high schools are industry-led partnerships for six-year high school and tertiary combinations, targeted to actual jobs in actual industries in local neighbourhoods for students in disadvantaged communities. This is a model that emphasises STEM subjects,[45] blends free public schooling with community colleges (equivalent to our institutes of technology), adds mentors from local businesses, adds practical workplace experiences and internships, and then feeds students directly into jobs. City or state economic development strategies have been the trigger for investment into these schools, particularly from employers, and there's a heavy emphasis on the middle skills so in demand by the global knowledge companies—jobs that need less than a university degree but more than a high school diploma, like basic-level software, electrical engineering and manufacturing technicians.

These initiatives operate at the secondary–tertiary interface—a 'jagged edge'.[46] When Dr Stuart Middleton at the Manukau Institute of Technology began his inquiry into the problem of youth disengagement here, he was well positioned to explore a secondary–tertiary partnership that, like the health sciences academies, fronted up to the raggedy line between secondary and tertiary schools and employment. His concept, the School of Secondary–Tertiary Studies, located on the MIT campus, arrived just as youth unemployment in South Auckland was about to peak. Local principals pledged support for it in anticipation of better solutions to their own dilemmas over their restless clientele. The government agreed to underwrite the project and modify the law to enable enrolment partnerships to work. The school has had some demonstrable success and added to the itch at the traditional secondary–tertiary interface. In form, the School of Secondary–Tertiary Studies is an 'early college high school'. Students simultaneously earn credits at secondary level and from a partnering tertiary institution without the high costs often associated with higher-level learning and within an almost adult learning environment. The point is to encourage young people to move through to tertiary studies purposefully and seamlessly, to keep study fees as low as possible and to up graduation rates in tertiary learning for those who have not traditionally opted for post-school education.

But seamlessness has challenges. Schools lose students to other educational institutions, the curriculum becomes more complex and schools must engage with tertiary institutions and the industry in deeper and more meaningful ways—and all of that change is uncomfortable. Despite outwardly successful pilots, there is still a whole-of-network inefficiency in senior secondary schooling right across Auckland, not to mention a lack of overall customer excitement in the offerings (exceptions proving the rule). No one has overall oversight of or responsibility for managing relationships with workplaces. Individual institutions operating at the interface can only act for themselves and within the partnerships they create. They are shackled by the professional rivalries that the market encourages. They must make their own assessments of what curricula to offer, sometimes without scientific analysis of where their students actually end up, what they are interested in, the realities of labour markets overturned by digital disruptions or city economic development aspirations that can only second-guess where the future of work actually lies. The capacity of secondary schools to purposefully link to labour market priorities is weak. Initiatives at individual schools fly high—such as the Microsoft classes at Avondale College, designed to provide a pathway into the digital technology industry[47]—but they don't yet constitute tight and managed pathways into work for every student in the city.

Although powerful educational leaders can be influencers for change, they can only reposition their own organisations, not redesign the system.

The Youth Guarantee policy put 16- and 17-year-olds into the spotlight. Since costs are a barrier to post-school engagement, the government buys fees-free places at tertiary institutions and private training establishments. These places, plus secondary–tertiary programmes like the growing number of academies within schools and the School of Secondary–Tertiary Studies, offer students choices. Not only can students now choose *where* they might study, they also have choices about *what* they can study. From a roll call of thousands of unit standards and achievement standards offered in our public schools, students have traditionally selected higgledy-piggledy pathways that might lead to a qualification for something, somewhere. Over the last five or six years, policymakers have sorted that jumble of diversified subject options into career directions called *Vocational Pathways*. Schools are invited to redesign their curriculum offerings around 'packages' of credits that align to these pathways, do not shut off future choices and offer direction to the choosers.

It's ironic: learning to earn has moved from its place as a second-rate track for students not good enough for academia to becoming central to government policy development. The pathways make no distinction between academic and vocational directions—even the most practical trades require an academic grounding at a much higher level than before. A couple of generations ago, secondary education abandoned the two-track structure of traditional grammar schools and technical high schools. Secondary schooling became 'broad-based'—unhitched from the labour market. Like a ship that needs slow and careful turning in a tight harbour space, secondary education is leaning in to the tack. Today, some secondary schools are moving back to offering differentiated pathways. But policymakers have perhaps underestimated how difficult the shift to pathways thinking is in practice.

So the drama of the pathways metaphor is in the government's expectation that learning in the senior secondary school must be workplace-focused. The pathway is visually described as a 360-degree set of options. It is a somewhat useful view: the starting point is a student standing in the middle, with six possible directions around a compass. Beneath her feet is NCEA Level 1, with its basic requirements. The designers have shaped six 'pathways', overlapping at the centre and fanning out to job horizons. Students who complete the requirements for a pathway at Level 2 will be able to earn awards and develop a 'profile' that helps them identify where to go next. The model is meant to encourage schools to tailor their programmes better to labour market opportunities and puts great store on workplace-based learning experiences ('meaningful and relevant learning close to the destination').[48] Government is clearly sending the message that it wants careers design and curriculum planning to come together as part of the 'provider package' for 16- to 19-year-olds.

However, this work is frustrated by the enormity of other shifts needed to make it all operate well. It would involve schools in a substantial redesign of the curriculum and their management layers and an intensive redevelopment of the connections to industry and employers that are a hallmark of academy success.[49] Schools that get kids a job must have 'connections'. But the possibility of the career academy model being applied in a 'wall-to-wall' approach matched to the Vocational Pathways—that is, enrolling *every* student into an academy-like pathway—can't become business as usual for schools. Seamlessness of services needs a connective layer.

I once counted over 30 different organisations in Auckland that work at the business–school interface, each with a 'connector' specialty that makes it valuable and unique, often targeted to careers in particular fields. The dearth of mechanics, electricians, computer technicians and practical engineers encourages larger businesses and well-organised associations to create their own 'talent acquisition pipelines'. These initiatives can show remarkable successes and tell wonderful human-interest stories. Yet each business and each school must develop and maintain a two-way bridge that involves a set of relationships which become exclusive to them.

Relationships are a competitive business. Gateway co-ordinators, located in schools and funded by the Tertiary Education Commission, generally establish and manage work placements through agreements. A large employer may be approached by perhaps a dozen co-ordinators. Well-organised high-decile schools close to the manufacturing heart of Auckland, should they choose to participate in work-based learning, have a natural edge over the lower-decile schools of the south and west in obtaining placements. Some schools work as a cluster; but even cluster operations are strangled by both a poor capacity to grow employer readiness and willingness to host learners (particularly Māori and Pasifika) and the culture of suspicion that not all schools and their students are getting a fair deal in access to placements. Aggregate data about Gateway outcomes is hard to find, and nothing useful is reported back to the business community to help them understand their contributions to the larger picture. Schools, too, have limited capacity to analyse and review the total impact of their efforts. What's the WIFM (What's in It for Me?) for a business in a relationship with schools? A bespoke talent acquisition pipeline has advantages for an employer—but it doesn't take workplace-linked learning to scale across Auckland, nor does it create the two-way bridge for genuine mutual advantage.

The Ministry of Education is working to set up networks of schools, tertiary education providers, employers and communities to develop new ways in which education can be offered.[50] These networks are supported by facilitators but don't come with the 'big picture' expertise on local labour market requirements, and still no one has the mandate or funding to grow the capacity of business and schools to work together. No one understands the sum total of all of the outcomes of people working in the school–business space. Auckland's Economic Development Strategy is all about connectedness. But until there is a robust governance structure for network-building, the city's strategy is unhitched from the work of the skills development experts.

Governance over the jagged edge

Youth unemployment as a problem is subject to the 'garbage can' model of decision-making.[51] It's one big mess of competing options and decision-makers with confused mandates, and it's unclear what the solution to the problem could be. Poorly understood and addressed problems drift into and out of the bin. Initiatives follow the ebb and flow of government policy for youth transitions services. The jumble of solutions to youth joblessness includes city projects, school curriculum redesign, strategies that talk about 'innovation' and pilots and 'design labs'. All of these 'fixes' suggest their own readings of the problem. Agencies rummage around in the bin for solutions that fix the problems immediately in front of them—but they are accountable only for their part of the problem.

There are bold targets for Auckland's economic growth, such as a 4% rise in GDP, more than twice New Zealand's average rate over the last 20 years. That suggests major structural change to an economy presently driven by real estate, consumption, infrastructure redevelopment and local services. Everyone concerned with making that economic miracle happen recognises the contribution secondary schools and their pools of potential talent could make to the city's productivity and growth ambitions. How should Auckland's labour market realities inform the design of viable pathway plans for the young people who will end up moving the economy forwards?

The Auckland Council proposes a 'game-changing' strategy comprising several work streams. The Mayor's Youth Employment Traction Plan promises that the council itself will model good employer practices by boosting numbers in its graduate and cadet programmes (to 70 young people each year) and hosting 'summits' to bring young people and business leaders together. Its flagship Youth Connections initiative links to a business leadership group to advance a 'shared economic agenda' for Auckland.[52] Actions include scaling up opportunities for young people to gain work experience, and 'developing and actively communicating a new employers pledge to give status and weight to this commitment'. It will encourage the Auckland Skills Steering Group (a vague multi-agency collective that includes 11 government agencies) to align its services and bring related activities under a single umbrella. This feels underwhelming.

Like the boy saving starfish on the beach, you can make a difference to that one, and that one, as you place young people into workplaces for pre-employment learning experiences. But it won't be nearly enough. The present structures for problem-solving in this city don't have a sufficiently broad mandate to be sustainably useful in driving large scale impacts. Not only is the whole-hearted public commitment of central government missing, there's no inclusive and cohesive oversight over this huge and complex task. In a nutshell, the jagged edge needs mission-driven governance.

It sounds retro: Auckland needs a fully independent youth skills and employment entity that provides oversight *over the whole school-to-work transition*, with the authority and capacity to stitch the jagged edge of secondary schooling, post-compulsory training and the employment market together, to work across the senior secondary and foundation tertiary spaces and be purpose-specific, innovative, inclusive and accountable to its public service and community shareholders.

One person's connector is another's authority figure, boss or gatekeeper. The mechanism could be a joint venture operation with major budget and oversight of the total government and local government contributions to this work. But that implies just more of the same. Better, Auckland deserves a purpose-specific entity that represents whole-of-community governance with an outside-in and inside-out view of the youth employment challenge, and weighty resources to effectively create impact. It would need to operate with the verve of a BizDojo or a Ministry of Awesome to collect up the stakeholders and connect learning to Auckland's Economic Development Strategy, Māori development agenda and the government's priorities, and then monitor outcomes. Central government and the council, employers, schools and tertiary institutions could be engaged at a governance level. But more importantly, the entity would need to be focused on the biggest prize: raising the productivity of Auckland's youth beyond the patches of social advantage that currently exist.

9

Have faith

Or: learning for the good of life and community

The public school has become the established church of secular society.
—Ivan Illich

The previous chapter explored the proposition that schools are there to get you a job. But schools are not just conveyor belts for qualifications. An education worth having delivers social justice and maximises democracy and personal freedom. These are often competing ideas. How can we reconcile them?

Karanga

A karanga, the formal welcome call by a Māori woman, invites one to engage with the heart and soul of community. This special part of New Zealand's culture is a growing feature of both civic life and school practice. For some, the karanga might amount to no more than an exchange of calls whose purpose is not much different to the welcome at your front door. The karanga has its parallels in Christian life in the bells and procession for the start of a mass or service; for Muslims in the call of the muezzin to prayer; in the calls for the dead in many cultures across the ages. The keening of a kuia as she calls visitors into the meeting place and the call in reply from another woman on behalf of the visitors are entry points to the important conversation that will follow—and offer something more spiritual than our predominantly secular selves would ordinarily respond to. This keening represents something that no book about education and learning, and especially one that takes South Auckland as its case study, should neglect. Transformation requires more than improvement in 'the numbers'. Transformation involves a deeper discomfort, one that touches the essence of our lives and who we are.

Secular schooling and powerful ideas

Our schools are supposed to be secular places. They became 'free, secular, compulsory' in 1877 with the implicit agreement that Irish Catholics, Anglican settlers, Scottish Protestants and whoever else happened along ought to be able to box along together in our public institutions, perhaps in ways they could not at home. It's almost accidental. At our official founding moment, we apparently spent only a few quick minutes considering the separation of church and state. Roman Catholic Bishop Jean-Baptiste François Pompallier, undoubtedly aware of the inside running of the Protestant Reverend Henry Williams to the hastily prepared proceedings at Waitangi in early February 1840, arrived with an entourage from the Hokianga. Upon observing the suggested document, he requested from Governor William Hobson a guarantee of religious freedom. The governor would have looked at the bewildering array of alliances under the canvas that summer's day, at the strange tattooed faces and unusual protocols, the scramble to remain in control of decision-making, and his obligation to get all these people to sign an already drafted piece of paper. Why quibble at Pompallier's request?[1] Hobson's career would not rest on securing the queen's religion; there were more important agreements to get. So our historic partnership began with a verbal commitment to religious neutrality, preserved in anecdote and the notes of the day.

Our first schools were mission schools, and highly successful they were, too, in bringing literacy to Māori and Pākehā settler children alike. The inevitable takeover of education by the state came with a commitment to continue Christian instruction. Bible in Schools is its remaining vestige.[2] The secular state is today a defining characteristic of New Zealand society. We don't have a state religion. The public separation of church from state comes with apparently declining private piety. Across the country, a shrinking number of people officially affiliate to any religion.[3] In the 2013 census, only Auckland bucked the downward trend.[4] We have a society that allows maximum personal freedom to worship whomever, whatever and however we choose. Religion is fine as a private interest, but we are uncomfortable whenever it appears in the public arena.

Secular societies are not necessarily *anti*-religious. Compare the United States, where public secularism is a principle of governance (but private religiosity blatantly stretches into the political arena) to the UK, where the role of the church is seamlessly bound with the constitution. Anglican bishops are in the House of Lords—but that doesn't mean English people are more religious than Americans. In Aotearoa, the church barely features in public life, and in the private domain we mostly drive in neutral too.

We relegate our sense of the sacred, the beautiful, anything lofty or spiritual in our lives, to certain abodes, places or events. In our art galleries, museums, marae, cathedrals and churches, we find representations of our deepest convictions. We enjoy being in our stunning landscapes; walking, climbing, holidaying. We recognise the Southern Alps and the Remarkables, the fjords, the seas, our wide-open spaces, for their grandeur, charm, quaintness or uniqueness. They appeal to our sense of wonder. We've made our appreciation of art, philosophy, architecture, nature and beauty a largely *personal* experience rather than the communal one associated with religion and tribal spirituality throughout the ages. Spiritual encounters become an explanation for the inexplicable expression of one's character or soul.

Our connection to our origins and the afterlife has become *cultural* as much as religious. 'Soul' is an old-fashioned word. We might patronise 'lost souls' as those with mental health issues. 'Soul music', rooted in the African American experience, has transmuted gospel and rhythm and blues into a modern, secular testimony which has crossed the Pacific and found a home here too. Music is not the only place for soul solidarity. In certain rather formulaic contexts, for instance, the opening prayer in parliament or a council meeting, or in hui or fono where collective decisions are being made, we express our oneness as a nation by appeals to something 'higher'. These ceremonies are like tailbones; vestigial reminders of our history. They are fiercely protected and have become culturally connected. A karakia is an acceptable beginning to any educational event, where a prayer in English may not be. 'Whakaaria Mai' is sung at civic events, where a hymn in English would not be. Is it because we are recognising the Treaty and partnership?

Perhaps one way of reading secularity in Aotearoa is to refer to the influence of the European Enlightenment on the education system here. Religious rivalries were surely in the tent at Waitangi, where Pompallier and Williams each sought to put a stake in the ground for their religions' futures in this land. Further south, Protestantism suffused the lives of the first settlers. Although the provincial councils were responsible for education, only the South Island provinces of Nelson, Canterbury and Otago had made adequate provision for public schooling before the 1870s, and the Scottish stronghold of Otago was by far the best organised and governed. It had direct links back to where Knox and Calvin had fought to free education from church control. Even though the University of Otago was established by laymen of strong Presbyterian conviction (one of the first chairs of the university was in theology), that conviction encompassed strong, well-governed local schools owned by the state. The free thinkers of Scotland rejected authority in the form of missives from churchmen 'on high', and believed in the power of reason and the ability of the people to make social change. Kiwis may trace their practical, make-do, no.8-wire streak to the Scottish Enlightenment. Our education system's free-wheeling leadership spins out from the Protestant values of do-it-yourself individuality and independence. We have a successful state schooling system precisely because the people who set it up possessed enterprise and adaptability free from the constraints of religious hierarchy and dogma.

Yet, as Gordon MacLauchlan argues, we are a passionless people.[5] Being down to earth as opposed to focused on the heavens, we are uncomfortable with outward expression of our most fundamental personal beliefs. The humanist Kiwi tradition focuses on the potential and abilities of people to solve earthly problems without divine intervention. We bypass the authority of the church. Many of us attend a church only for ceremonial occasions like weddings and funerals. We take responsibility for our own actions.[6] We can only blame ourselves for the ills of the world, and only we can do something about the wars, waste and wanton destruction of our environment, poverty and inequality, and human rights and social justice. The rampant secularism in our age is represented by populist contrarians like Bob Jones—who dismisses other views as 'hogwash'.[7] In our mild-mannered Kiwi way, no one firebombs the places of worship for other religions or attacks people in their homes or on the street because of their faith or lack of it—these would be isolated instances proving religious ignorance rather than entrenched fundamentalist beliefs. To emphasise our secular nature, on Sundays or Fridays our national pastime is . . . shopping.

Religion, or at least a belief in the powerful workings of gods, has always been an astonishing motivating force, anything but primitive, across human history. (How else can we explain why people would voyage back and forth across the vast Pacific and remain sane enough to build sustainable new communities on isolated islands at the bottom of the world?) Powerful ideas have a spiritual connection—even those that have led to the flattening of the world as we know it today. To dismiss the gods as merely crude explanation that ought to be supplanted by scientific analysis is to ignore the vast storehouses of literature and art, the deep reservoirs of cultural belief that shape our thinking and the evidence that people, everywhere, are more than the sum of their parts.

Sociologists have remarked on the sticky stuff that binds communities together, that helps us to establish our sense of place in the world and creates our identities. That glue is a set of ideas that we all share. However, they aren't always self-evident. The lack of overt commitment to ideas—political ideas, philosophical ones, religious ones or academic ones—is expressly reflective of the Kiwi lack of collective philosophical conviction. Hence the Occupy Auckland movement outlived its welcome in Aotea Square (enough is enough; we got the message). The intelligentsia grasps the message of Wilkinson and Pickett's *The Spirit Level*, but inequality as a driver for public policy has not breached the dyke of pragmatism in Kiwi politics. A big idea is too difficult to articulate in the soundbites on the electoral hustings.

So how do issues get on to the public policy stage in New Zealand? Most certainly not when they look like dogma or ideology. The articles of faith that underpin our educational policy in particular are embedded in the unspoken social consensus that we have a public education system which works fine 'for us', which tolerates diversities of religious and ideological opinion and whose values are immutable: free, secular and compulsory. And that's it. Public policy must tinker on the edge of this core position, even though we sense that perhaps it doesn't quite work well enough for a minority. We want everyone to succeed—'like us'.

No school is values-free. New Zealand's largely secular education system mandates values-based education and even supports teaching *about* religion. Once, in Wellington, UNESCO hosted a debate on values education between the nation's leading educational leaders. We showed a very practical orientation in response to these big ideas. The Quality Public Education Coalition hosted a similar forum, this time to launch a resource kit. In 2006 the New Zealand Principals' Federation commissioned a piece of research on values education, the point being to offer up good practice as a model for other schools in the delivery of a new curriculum.[8] The report's author came to no epic conclusion. She found that 'overtly religious' schools make religious studies a compulsory part of the curriculum and may even incorporate a curriculum strand for spiritual development. It turns out that values education in New Zealand is alive and well in state schools too and comes down to such practical examples as community service ('love thy neighbour'), environmental learning and peer support networks. The report concluded that it didn't seem to matter about the history of the school; whether from a church foundation or an enthusiastic leader, values education in New Zealand was 'evolutionary in nature' and often ended up being embedded into a school's practices even though it might have started as a stand-alone programme. Why did the Principals' Federation commission this study? The subtext seems to have been this: we back values education—as our various members define it.

The most interesting aspect of the Principals' Federation study was what wasn't in it. The commissioned work was to be practical in nature. Its central question: How did others 'do' values education? Nothing in the brief for this project put values learning into a larger philosophical context. References to Māori-led schooling, or the powerful ideas that lie behind cultural identity, or what constitutes successful learning and for what purpose, were not included. The assumption seems to have been that values can be made universal and that schools, secular ones in particular, need to be as open as possible to the diversity of opinions that exist among the parent population.

'You have your way, I have my way. As for the right way, it does not exist,' wrote Nietzsche. Moral relativism asserts that there is no universal moral law that applies to all people at all times in all places. Argues the New Zealand Foundation for Character Education: 'Neutrality in values in education is an unachievable aim. Schools must promote some moral values if they to work at all.'[9] Claiming to be an 'indigenous' response to the non-sectarian and non-doctrinaire framework of New Zealand's education system, the foundation advocates for a 'Cornerstone Values' approach (not a religious programme, a life skills programme, an add-on to the school curriculum or a class programme). It distinguishes between the development of values (concerned with the quality of students' thinking) and character (concerned with the quality of students' behaviours). The foundation's Cornerstone Values become 'an infusion that informs and directs everything that happens in a school'. This development of school culture was once annually rewarded with National Schools of Character awards. But moral relativism and the touchstones of New Zealanders' lives have not made it into public discussions about how turning all schools into 'schools of character' would deliver on system goals for student achievement.

Leading Māori academics and educators have made much of the underpinning values for Māori parents and children. Some have turned to the international concept of the good life, frequently framed as 'wellbeing', located in whānau and family. For most of a century, national wellbeing has been measured in terms of growth. Gross domestic product (GDP) is a clever compendium of numbers compressed to become a single symbol of progress, venerated as a sign of a country's wealth and therefore its attractiveness as a place to live and a sign of wellbeing. Among GDP's measurements are total economic output, a tally of export receipts, retail sales, spending on new infrastructure and so on. Improvement in the number equals gain in a nation's wealth, which equals improvement in quality of life. To get out of the economic mire, the economists and politicians tell us, we need to increase GDP.

Yes, but perhaps not quite. Whatever you think the good life is—say, an affordable house, a salary increase, nutritious food in the cupboard and time to spend with family and friends—governments across the globe now know that GDP isn't enough. While GDP tells us a lot about the economy, it says nothing of inequalities and nought about the other things in our lives that really matter.[10]

Wellbeing is complex. What matters to you may not matter to me. What counts as progress is more than a statistical question; it is also a philosophical one. The luminous works of Amartya Sen,[11] Martha Nussbaum[12] and others underpin an approach adopted by the United Nations Development Programme (now headed by our own Helen Clark) in 1990, which looks beyond GDP to a raft of other indicators that show how a society is advancing. The Human Development Index shows the 'richness of human life, rather than the richness of the economy in which human beings live, which is only a part of it,' says Amartya Sen. Statistics like life expectancy, educational achievement and per capita income contribute to a more rounded picture of how we are doing.

Former French president Nicolas Sarkozy commissioned a distinguished international panel of experts (known as the Stiglitz-Sen-Fitoussi Commission) to find alternative measures of economic performance and social progress.[13] The commission used a car metaphor to explain the nature of the shift required. Once, a car only had one instrument: a speedometer to show how fast one was travelling. A car's engine was expressed in horsepower. These were the things that mattered back in the day when people could barely imagine life without a horse. Today, we have a very complicated dashboard of instruments in our cars to tell us how fast we are travelling, how much fuel we are slurping, whether the brakes or the lights are working, when we have to replace the oil, whether all the seatbelts are fastened and so on. These instruments express our social priorities too. We have a seatbelt indicator because safety is important; the oil light is there because a poorly maintained car loses value. Similarly, we need to add to GDP a dashboard of other indicators that better indicate our own social progress and the things we value—although preferably not so complicated that we need a degree in statistics to understand it or make use of it. Wellbeing, therefore, becomes the totality of things that lead to a good life, including your human right and democratic freedom to live according to your religion and fundamental beliefs about the world. Human rights have become the new doctrine of our age.

What does wellbeing have to do with education? In the first decade of the 21st century, the government's *Social Report* series[14] took data already available (like early childhood enrolment rates, school qualifications and post-school graduation rates) as contributing measures to the big picture of New Zealand wellbeing. Later, the advocacy group Every Child Counts explored the factors contributing to Māori and Pasifika child poverty.[15] The children's commissioner and the former Families Commission (now Superu) also developed a suite of work on poverty and wellbeing.[16] The question of measures also exercised the New Zealand Treasury[17] and Statistics New Zealand. However, a shift in political mood has left us with public service targets as the key indicators of general social progress—and educational advancement too.

Although the international credibility of the brilliant minds who have worked on the global Human Development Index is undisputed, most educators in Aotearoa won't ever have heard of them or their work. Even suggesting a 'moral' basis on which to build educational excellence and economic power and sustainability has, to some Kiwi ears, an air of loony fringe. Difficult presentations from Mānuka Henare and others (from the Mira Szászy Research Centre at the University of Auckland's Business School) suggested forging a new Māori and Pasifika development index,[18] which ought to have triggered a whole new way of thinking about the place of education in meeting the wellbeing needs of Māori. Although the development index is such a powerful idea, few school leaders are grounded in the discipline of moral philosophy or would have the time or energy to understand its implications. How do you create legitimacy for a different way of seeing the world, illustrated by Māori academics and thinkers such as Mason Durie, Graham Hingangaroa Smith and others but ignored by the European lens and secular formation of today's educational leaders?

Entirely different worldviews underpin how we teach and learn. Our secular streak makes it particularly hard for Kiwi educators to get the point that Mānuka Henare makes about wellbeing as a cultural idea that applies to how we respond to educational need. To 'get' Mānuka Henare et al., you would need to respond with a pedagogy of cultural competence and socio-political consciousness. You would have some understanding of creation cycles; of the mauri of things—their life essence. You would have to 'get' tapu, the sacredness of some places, peoples, ideas. You would have to believe in the importance of reciprocity in relationships and economics. Mānuka Henare shows us that what Māori consider the good life and the freedom to live it includes concepts rarely found on the values list in school charters. Perhaps their general absence goes some way towards explaining why Māori express alienation from Western education. Is it unreasonable for these eminent academics to suggest that education for Māori may involve a rolling back of the usual secular assumptions? Or that the public service targets miss the point?

So how ought we to deal with things like whānaungatanga (kinship); manaakitanga (hospitality and generosity towards others); kotahitanga (unity and cohesion); and tiakitanga (custodianship of resources) if we want to make a difference of the transformational kind for Māori and Pasifika students?

The tensions of secular schooling

Churches are the basic organising principle for Pasifika communities in South Auckland. Draw a circle with a radius of a couple of kilometres on a map around the Ōtara Town Centre and count how many churches there are. The 30 or so on the map do not include those that don't advertise their presence in the web snapshot in Figure 3. The total community investment in spiritual development and religious connection flows into the politics of the suburb and the expectations the population has of its schools.

'Each day when we enter our school gates we are told to leave our faith and cultural identity at the gate and to follow the school's way of learning and curriculum. We are not told this directly, but it is hidden and invisible,' writes 18-year-old Auckland student Veisinia.[19] She continues:

> My church and faith play a huge role in my life and the way I see the world and my culture, identity, values and language is what defines me.

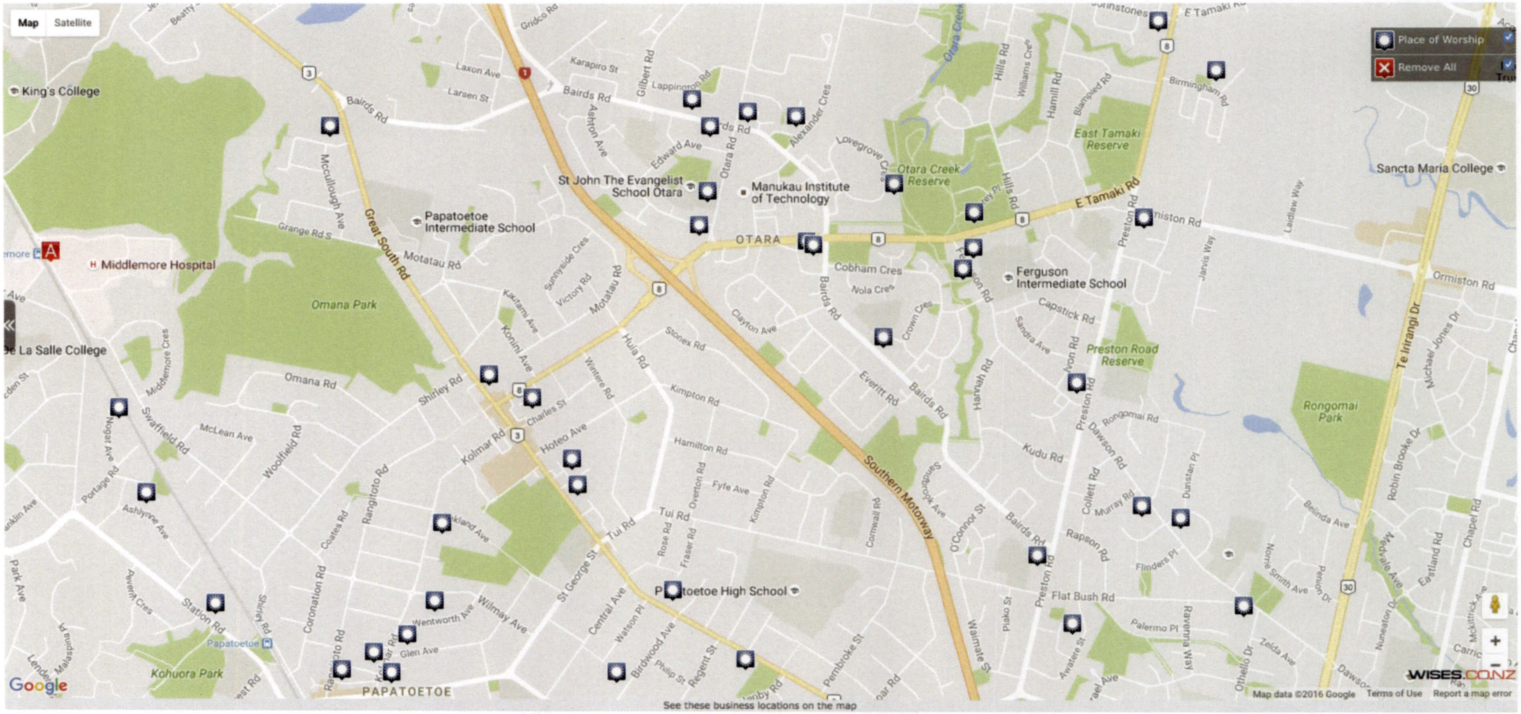

Figure 3: Places of worship near Ōtara Town Centre

> One religion cannot be promoted or endorsed by the education system because that would be unfair, but . . . it is clear that the majority of the Pacific Population are heavily involved in church and are Christian, and a way must be found to encompass this in our learning.

She was asked if she had heard of the Pasifika Education Plan 2013–17. She hadn't. But when she looked at it, one thing jumped out at her: the lack of reference to the faith of Pasifika families and the impact it has on their daily lives.

Vei's perspective runs directly counter to the secular thrust in New Zealand society. There are 266,000 Pacific people in New Zealand, half of them Samoan, and two-thirds of them living in Auckland. It's a young population, and those young people are New Zealand-born and schooled. Their non-secular lives seep into their learning lives. The speeches from head boys and girls at South Auckland public-school prizegivings thank the Lord, their parents and their teachers for the opportunities they have been given and the blessings they have received. Their parents want them to get a useful qualification and a good job, not only because they contribute to their families, but because it enhances their value to their church community too. These students offer respect to elders, commit to the wisdom of teachers and leaders, and read their Bibles. Vei is reflecting on the tensions in a public education system that must forget why it is secular in order to respond to the expectations of Pasifika families and communities, and then paradoxically receives outsider backlash to the presence of spirituality in schools.

The tensions ooze out into other aspects of educational delivery. They have been there for a long time, reflecting unspoken assumptions. Secondary education in New Zealand during the 1960s commonly featured a school day that began with an assembly. As the school accompanist, a privileged position, I had to be at my public secondary school on time every morning to play the requisite opening bars on the piano for the massed singing of the hymn of the day. I remember our principal Mr Morrison, resplendent in academic gown, conducting the whole school in vigorous renditions of 'Praise, My Soul, the King of Heaven', followed by a prayer and his school address. By the time I graduated as a teacher, the school assembly had become much more secular. Even though the secondary school assembly has evolved, unconscious references to spiritual or religious community remain in the use of karakia and waiata or other rituals, deliberate or spontaneous. In present-day South Auckland schools, the annual prizegiving ceremonies will diverge from the expectations of traditionalists in other parts of the city. Elsewhere you might find 'Good evening' or that nod to biculturalism, 'Kia ora'; here, we begin with a karakia and/or a mihi. The physical surroundings may include stage decorations, woven mats and tapa cloths that reflect the cultural backgrounds of the students, as well as flowers, photographs or school icons. As for the awarding of prizes, a march across the stage, a smile and a handshake may be accompanied by side-ceremonies—parents rush up to gift garlands, head-dresses, and money donations, for example, as well as the traditional applause or tautoko or haka. These ceremonies carry an irony. The tracings of Christian heritage, protocols that reference the dead and the living, and ceremonies that are moving for their emotional and spiritual content—they all sit uneasily in a system that theoretically demands secular approaches. You won't avoid any references to traditions, sacred or secular, by going to a state secondary school in South Auckland.

The secular and the cultural intersect at many other points. It's the First XV game. The players begin in a huddle. Is the huddle just a simple group hug that helps a sports team to focus for the game ahead? Heads bowed, the captain speaks. The team is searching for cohesion and a higher purpose. It cannot be surprising that the captain may lead the team in a pep talk, a prayer or a haka. Whatever the ritual, it will reflect tradition, perhaps secular but certainly not irreligious—and is deliberately designed to speak to the emotional or spiritual drives of the players. Rugby carries a lot of prestige and mana, and the rituals of this game are ingrained in our national psyche. Even in this most un-churchy of places, the rugby field, we search for something larger than ourselves that distinguishes us from any other sporting foe. These traditions go right to the heart of the person—or should that be 'soul'? 'We understand heart better than soul,' the coach of one South Auckland college First XV team explains to me. He adds, 'In high performance sport we spend a lot of time understanding the body, the food we must eat, the exercise we must do. We spend too little time understanding how the "heart" of a person operates, and too little time coaching to it.' Māori and Pasifika protégés need to dig deep when they play—and to help them do that, the coach works with those cultural and social connections that have meaning for them. He believes this must apply not only to their sport but to their academic studies too.

All around the world, nations endorse the idea that shared values build national cohesion. Education that cultivates the humanity of citizens and allows us to imagine how we might live alongside difference is important in moving people past racism and prejudice to a future together. The New Zealand national curriculum devotes space to values ('to be encouraged, modelled, and explored').[20] They are there precisely because politicians and policymakers realised that our diversity deserves attention, that chasms need bridges. Therefore, students in New Zealand are to be taught to value the following things: excellence; innovation, inquiry and curiosity; diversity in our different cultures, languages and heritages; equity, through fairness and social justice; community and participation for the common good; ecological sustainability, including care for the environment; integrity, which involves being honest, responsible and accountable and acting ethically; and respect for the human rights of themselves and others. And according to the curriculum: 'The specific ways in which these values find expression in an individual school will be guided by dialogue between the school and its community.'[21]

Not all young Pasifika people or their elders would share Vei's view about the need for greater spirituality in public schools. There does seem to be, however, an astonishing correlation between the academic successes of Māori and Pasifika students and the connections their schools draw with their spiritual and cultural lives. Church College of New Zealand, formerly a private co-educational secondary school located near Hamilton and sponsored by the Church of Jesus Christ of Latter-Day Saints, educated a large population of Polynesian and particularly Māori students (74% Māori in 2006), from the day of its opening in 1958 to the day of its closing in 2009. The comparatively high levels of achievement among the students at the college could not be simply sheeted home to its 'academic priority'. The college provided an environment that validated the religious and cultural values of the students, where their heritages were reaffirmed and normalised, and where even those from dysfunctional homes could find security and stability.[22] In its closing years, students from decile 3 Church College were gaining the basic NCEA Level 1 qualification at nearly double the rate of their counterparts in other schools of similar decile (88% compared to 45% in 2005) and at higher NCEA levels they also surpassed the achievement rates of similar schools.[23]

Other church-based schools achieve outstanding results for their Māori and Pasifika students too. At McAuley High School, a largely Pasifika Catholic secondary school for girls in South Auckland's Ōtāhuhu, NCEA results have been so notable that in 2013 *Metro* magazine's editor made an astonishing suggestion:

> If this country is really going to get serious about eliminating the long tail of failure in our schools, it's possible the single most valuable thing we could do is shoulder-tap the key Catholic educators and give them a free hand in low-decile schools that are not doing well.[24]

McAuley High School's decile is, of course, only the crudest measure of that school's student cohort. The value-add of a school's community is more than decile can tell us. Emeritus professor Ivan Snook of Massey University argues that it is unreasonable for all schools to be able to achieve what schools like Church College of New Zealand did, and what McAuley High School and De La Salle College do.[25] Simply transposing a Catholic principal into a secular state school might not have the effect that *Metro* suggests, unless the community itself wishes to become infused with Catholic values. And asking teachers to replicate what teachers at McAuley High School might be able to do is a sad misreading of the context in which teaching takes place.

Sociological studies of schools have long pointed to the costs of cultural adaptation. Back in 1979 a UK study suggested that student success can be at least partly sheeted home to the capacity of children to adapt to the (sometimes alien) cultural environment of schools. 'It is,' says Peter Woods, 'as if school consists of a number of invisible doors, and people change as they go through them from one context to another.'[26]

The coping experience he describes is exactly the experience of exchange students from all over the world who come to New Zealand to learn something different and in some way 'alien' from their own ways of learning. The experience has value; perhaps because it requires subtle adjustments to how you understand the world. However, the more different the learning milieu, the more challenging the experience. Many students don't have to go overseas to be a 'visitor' to the culture of the school. Woods' point was that schools don't set out to teach adaptability; they *assume* it happens by itself. Secular schools, or schools that fail to recognise culturally determined values and principles of wellbeing, may unconsciously require some students to adapt significantly more than others.

Russell Bishop[27] showed the importance of a 'culturally responsive' pedagogy of relations—that is, how in classrooms where culture counts and where teachers know the stories of students, *who* they really are, their cultural and social connections as well as their academic needs, students can succeed. The Education Review Office explored why a group of low-decile secondary schools seemed to get better NCEA results—and concluded that parent and whānau engagement had something to do with it.[28] A pedagogy that aspires to social justice and offers a rich multicultural curriculum which engages students of all ethnicities seems self-evident. Whatever the answer, relationships—a fuzzy word, but at the heart of learning—shape wellbeing.

Perhaps we don't have to desecularise schools. But we can't expect that schools in South Auckland must be clones of white middle-class aspirations.

Is our secular system even capable of responding to two worldviews, two sets of traditions, when one is so deeply connected to matters of the spirit? How does this become 'shared'? Closing the achievement gap clearly requires more than some of the simpler measures for acknowledging diversity (such as participation in kapa haka, Polyfest or Māori Language Week).

Even when values *seem* universal, we apply a cultural lens to our understanding of them. Part of the task of educating a Māori person is to shape the future leadership of Māoridom. But it would be wrong to assume that success for Māori students might automatically create mana for individuals and strength of character, since in Māoridom mana is not just personally held but is linked to the mana of others—whānau, hapu and iwi.[29] Accordingly, a school that wishes to build the mana of its Māori students and build its capacity for leadership must understand how to build that value *in association with* the student's whānau and hapu. That is challenging—and perhaps it is the difference between secular education and education infused with religious and cultural values.

You could, of course, take a rigorously scientific approach to building character. Compare the long values list in the New Zealand national curriculum (as described above) to the pithy character education core of the KIPP NYC charter schools in New York City.[30] Based on the work of psychologists who have classified the positive psychological traits of human beings,[31] they have arrived at a list that reflects the American way: grit, zest, gratitude, optimism, curiosity, social intelligence and self-control. In sum: 'Work hard. Be nice.' The American penchant for measurement is reflected in KIPP NYC's attempts to set up a grading scale for these traits. As well as the usual academic grade point average, students apparently get a character point average. The character traits gain immediate worth because they are being measured. They matter. Measuring character might sound fanciful to our ears, even obsessive. But it at least begins to address the question of what makes schooling more than just a free, secular and compulsory qualifications factory.

The curriculum assumes a powerful place in transformation efforts. But in discussions about social transformation, the school curriculum is barely mentioned as an agent of change. 'The *New Zealand Curriculum* is a statement of official policy relating to teaching and learning in English-medium New Zealand schools,' advises the Ministry of Education.[32] Its purpose is to 'set the direction' for student learning and to provide 'guidance for schools'. This benign language hides a sharper truth: while the curriculum is not a 'prescription', some things are required. Schools must use the curriculum to meet National Standards.

The single cohesive document we have now wasn't always so neatly packaged. We used to have syllabuses and guidelines and prescriptions of such a variety of vintages, covering a wide range of levels and subjects, that it could only be considered an ad hoc collection of instructions on what to teach New Zealand children. The major curriculum review of the 1980s was stopped in its tracks by the juggernaut of administrative reform. The breathless pace and huge scale of change swamped everything. As the education sector came to grips with managing from the bottom up, curriculum became impossible to impose in the old top-down, profession-led fashion. The curriculum work of the 1990s never made it past the draft stage. A curriculum stocktake in 2002 set out with the purpose 'to better support teachers and schools to achieve the high expectations set by national curriculum policy'.[33] Quite who owned those expectations and what they were supposed to lead to was never clear. There was a long and publicly invisible process of workshopping, consulting, focus-grouping, going on fact-finding missions and identifying political steerage points, which years later resulted in a final product.[34] The minister of education signed it off on the understanding that principals and teachers would implement it. In sum, a curriculum is a politically acceptable instrument that essentially shapes the process by which one generation of New Zealanders will pass on knowledge and skills to the next generation. The curriculum reflects our collective purpose for why we make kids go to school.

At least, that's the way it's supposed to work. It's a world-class, empowering document. But does the fact that the curriculum contains a statement of values constitute a message of entitlement to values learning? Is learning about values compulsory? How do we know that those values are actually being delivered?

Within the education sector, measurement is fiercely contested territory. The data of schooling—notably, the National Standards benchmarks and NCEA results—focus public attention and effort on how well the students are doing at school, *marks-wise*. National Standards set the benchmark for what constitutes good progress through the system. Like on the dashboard in the car, the benchmarks should be only one indicator of many; and NCEA the ultimate measurable target. What in the curriculum gets measured, and why, has been debated for as long as exams have existed. But the choices for students are immeasurably constrained by how we go about setting the targets, what we count and what we report. Having devolved decision-making down to schools, social wellbeing has been reduced to the delivery of education services in accordance with a charter with government, an activity which leaves the child and her family with limited agency, teachers to blame for any system failures and community stakeholders irrelevant. Education and its summative measure, NCEA Level 2, dangle alone like the baby and the stork, in mid-air and out of context.

But clearly education does have more than an economic purpose. Otherwise, why would we bother with a values statement in the curriculum?

Why values matter

What if what policymakers want is not the same as what families and communities want?

According to human capital theory, you give someone a pathway out of poverty when you educate him or her. You measure this by how much household incomes rise. Education, according to this thinking, is a tool for economic advancement. So that's why getting a qualification is so important. But let's also be clear: there's no guarantee that if we get 85% of school-leavers in South Auckland to NCEA Level 2, poverty will diminish or lives will be enhanced.

The evidence is that the *total* package of goals, of which NCEA is but one (intermediate) target, may contribute to economic progress and hence social progress. To paraphrase Mānuka Henare's point, human progress is not just whether you pass NCEA Level 2 but how you arrive there—and what you do next.

Without an understanding of the values contexts in which learning takes place, we are tempted to assume that transformation is possible just by getting to the measurable targets. The increasing economic importance of the success of Māori and Pasifika learners, in South Auckland in particular, means that policymakers must pay attention to non-economic values. Ka Hikitia, the Māori education strategy of this country, expresses the desire for all Māori children to be able to live as Māori. This implies that two worldviews and two sets of traditions can and must co-exist in our schools. The open question is: how?

Education is not immune from the signature idea of capitalism—the market, which has taken over our lives. Health is a market, early childhood education is a market, the environment is a market, schools are a market—we are living in an age of 'market triumphalism', says Harvard University philosopher Michael J. Sandel.[35] It sends the message that money can buy you anything, including a quality education, and anything can be traded. And if you can't value it, then it is worth nothing.

It may be a sweeping generalisation to suggest that South Auckland's communities too often walk away from engagement with schools because they don't feel like they can change anything about the way in which their schools are organised and led, and because the values that underpin them are alien and the measurable outputs irrelevant. When communities are invested in the broadest outcomes from education, they will find the energy to effect transformation. Empowering communities, therefore, is a critical element in shaping the future.

Empowering communities is core business for local government. So the final chapter explores the role of local government in educational transformation.

Part 4:
Governance for Transformation

10

City-making and learning

Weaving the work of others

Auckland is now both qualitatively and quantitatively different from what it was at the turn of the millennium. The city appears to have the pre-conditions for investment in social wellbeing that might be transformative.[1] There is recognition among city leaders, including those in the business community, that Auckland's skills deficits are a basic economic inefficiency and a brake on progress. It seems to have all of the prerequisites for action: a sense of urgency (from city planners) about the need for social change in the south; a mandate that sits inside the city's guiding vision document, the Auckland Plan; and planning commitment for the Southern Initiative, which focuses on economic and social infrastructure (although whether that survives a change in mayoral leadership is uncertain). There are influential champions and willing offstage support. The council has recently adopted a community empowerment approach to decisions that affect their communities.[2] From a local government perspective it seems that all that is now needed is robust oversight and strong accountability, realigned budgets to grease the wheels; and then transformation might begin.

If only it were that simple.

Central power, local politics

To have a sense of 'livability', a city must have good infrastructure. Infrastructure is not just assets like roads and bridges, water and waste treatment plants, airports and ports, parks and libraries and leisure services, housing stock and city plans. Although the Auckland Council has responsibility for community development and economic development, it has no direct control over the social infrastructure that supports that—in education, health, social services, justice. Cities are supposed to be getting smarter, but 'unless city leaders exercise influence over infrastructure, they can't create the path to smart cities,' says city advisor Greg Clark.[3] In early childhood centres, schools, tertiary institutions and other learning spaces, key actors have power over the learning 'infrastructure' of Auckland.

How do key actors work together? They need a mechanism for doing so.

There's one strand of political thought in this country which says that local bodies should have nothing at all to do with social services, including education: it is a Wellington responsibility.[4] The knights of this philosophy care only about the village within: local government should be about neighbourhood life and the administration of places. Rates are high enough as it is. The tradition of central management in this country is tightly guarded and publicly so. During the second Key government, the minister for the environment berated the Auckland Council for its Proposed Auckland Unitary Plan.[5] The minister of housing vowed to smash Auckland's city limits.[6] The minister of transport harried Auckland about its rail priorities. The minister of local government tried to remove the word 'social' from the role of councils.[7] Overbearing parenting seems a feature of the central government–local government relationship, running directly counter to the global thrust for taking decisions at the most local level possible. The 2009 Royal Commission on Auckland Governance was clear: the city's social support structure was ramshackle and rickety—uncoordinated, incoherent, full of service gaps and double-ups. Auckland needed a mechanism for addressing its significant social dysfunctions.[8] It recommended an Auckland social issues board to oversee social development.

Unfortunately this recommendation did not sit comfortably in Wellington. Instead, cabinet agreed to a watered-down Auckland Social Policy Forum,[9] to be sponsored and led by the minister of social development and the mayor. Great hopes were held for a 'cross-portfolio approach' that would see local and central government work collaboratively on Auckland's social issues. Those hopes were soon dashed. The 'forum' was poorly connected into a supercity still in set-up mode, and central government decision-makers stood back to watch. Projects were developed in the fledgling forum's name, but its membership, fluctuating and expanding to be 'representative', could only advise. Having overseen the development of a couple of isolated projects, the forum shrivelled away like a forgotten balloon within two years of the new city's arrival.

Place-based approaches to social change are not a new idea in this country. The 2010–2013 Social Sector Trials of the Ministry of Social Development had a focus on the issues for 12- to 18-year olds in disadvantaged, small communities *outside* of Auckland. They involved the Ministries of Education, Health, Justice and Social Development and the New Zealand Police working together to change the way that social services are delivered. The trials were meant to 'test' what happens when the government contracts a local facilitator, organisation or individual to co-ordinate resources and action. The point was to reduce truancy, youth offending and alcohol and drug abuse, and increase youth participation in education, training or employment. The trials were overseen by a joint-venture board of chief executives from the five partner agencies. After two years of operation, evaluators could report improved community collaboration, increased responsiveness to the issues the young people were facing, and a broader base of services aimed at young people at each trial location.[10] The trials garnered strong support from community stakeholders, perhaps because they were seen as a 'catalyst for change', although the actual evidence for the nature of that change was difficult to find.

The evaluation offered some lessons, however. High-level, even ministerial, support gave the trials pizzazz and profile, credibility and legitimacy. Clear governance and operational accountabilities helped. But offline it wasn't all rosy. Collaboration can sometimes feel threatening; contracting doesn't feel like partnership and issues around the power and control of resources remained. Were these admittedly small communities in control of their destiny? Peter McKinlay, in a 2013 Treasury paper that reflected on the local–central relationship in the delivery of social services,[11] expressed some surprise that local government was not considered as a co-ordinator in the six trial locations. Perhaps there are blind spots in the public service about the possibilities for innovation, he suggested. But central government's relationship with rural communities is very different from its relationship with South Auckland.

There are conflicting messages about what the government wants councils to do about social wellbeing and education in particular. On the one hand, there is significant pressure to 'stick to the knitting'. On the other, there are sound economic and philosophical reasons in favour of local government involvement in learning, linked to three well-understood ideas. The first is about social capital in communities.[12] The bonds of trust that build in communities are a must for any ambitious collaboration effort. The second relates to the Dewey argument that education underpins democracy and the economy—and that is why local councils invest in libraries, museums, zoological parks and the arts. The third idea is subsidiarity;[13] that is, decision-making happens best at the lowest tier possible. But ambivalent signals from the government about how it will engage with councils and communities on social issues, how communities can genuinely exercise control and how schools might be involved are unhelpful to Auckland's case for social transformation in the south. Ways of working together are still more theory than practice.

Scattered throughout the many visions, strategies and plans consulted on, adopted and published by the Auckland Council since its beginning, there are embedded references to learning, education and skills. This suggests a consensus that the council does have a role in education:

- planning for where early childhood services and schools should be on the map;
- providing informal and lifelong learning through cultural institutions such as galleries, museums, libraries and archives;
- advocating for local learning issues, via empowered local boards;
- facilitating connections;
- leading the city's economic development;
- partnering with central government and other stakeholders;
- being a catalyst for collective action; and
- co-ordinating joint effort.

So how does council action in education unfold from this list?

Uniquely, Auckland has an executive mayor. This role was deliberately created to allow the city to have strong and independent influence. The mayor is the voice of Auckland, surely its social champion. So what does mayoral leadership for education and skills involve? Four elements spring to mind. Firstly, the mayor's role is a political one. It is the mayor's job to shape and support the political agreements that underwrite local action. Central government and local government collaboration ought to be the *sine qua non* of social development. Dialogue between the mayor and the minister ought to be a powerful tool. But money and power intervene. Many cities around the world have this city-versus-nation tension.[14] Petty politics don't forge a lasting legacy. The promise of the supercity has always lain in getting political leaders to agree about priorities. The 2013 Auckland Housing Accord, however imperfect, is an example of the genre. There is nothing of the kind for education yet.

Secondly, the mayoral office delivers power and cachet. Reciprocity is an important element to how this works in practice. In the normal course of events, an invitation from the mayoral office to participate in deliberately constructed 'leadership encounters' creates opportunities for information-sharing and negotiation. Variations on advisory groups, expert forums, think tanks, and project governance bodies describe the ways in which the movers and shakers of cities work together. I've visited several of these (overseas) where the mayor's commissioner for education, chief advisor or delegated equivalent (titles vary) is a powerful aide to this process.

Thirdly, the work of community and educational transformation happens at the grass-roots, inside the centres, schools and institutions of learning, and with and alongside business and community leaders. The mayor could advocate in powerful places for barriers to be lifted, edges to be shifted, deals to be sealed and achievements to be rewarded.

Finally, more neighbourhood influence is possible through local boards and Auckland Council's community outreach systems than through many central government operations. Mayoral leadership for education involves creating the space for communities to commit to learning and be empowered for action.

This potential in the mayoral role is yet to be realised. Even the Auckland Council's social flagship effort, the Southern Initiative, initially failed to fire.

The Southern Initiative is one of two 'place-based priorities' in the Auckland Plan. It set out to 'facilitate change and improve quality of life through innovative, strategic action and investment'.[15] Many local school principals and teachers could reasonably claim to have never heard of the Southern Initiative. The council's local board members privately admitted in 2014 that the project 'steering group' was struggling to maintain their ongoing interest. The simple targets—remarkably congruent with the Better Public Services targets—perhaps seemed too passé to government agencies ('we're already doing that') to put through another process, and early claimed runs on the board might have been delivered anyway.[16] The resources to deal to the targets remained exactly where they were—inside government agencies or dispersed across the many services operating in the area. The council's chief executive publicly noted the absence of government commitment to 'partnership'.[17] The general manager of the Southern Initiative, highly placed within the council team but essentially operating solo, suddenly resigned mid-2014. Local board members complained about the miserly annual budget, but in May 2014 the council's governing body rejected a bid for more money. Quite why the work fell into the doldrums is not publicly available. Although it had impetus from the mayor, who set out publicly to be 'bold' in his thinking over the first years of its existence, the Southern Initiative approaches Harvard University professor Kotter's famous analysis of why transformation efforts fall over: no understood urgency over priorities; invisible leadership; confusing communications; slow empowerment; spray-and-hope planning and project-driven action with no uniting vision; and political back-slapping when victory is still a long way off.[18]

What is the theory of change behind the work of the Southern Initiative? There doesn't seem to be one that connects to ordinary people: only a succession of 'projects' that, like Eiseley's starfish, will make some difference—but probably not a transformative one. Social policy and social action is obviously more difficult for the council than building railway lines, motorways and bridges. To use a cliché, it's a learning journey. With any future shift in city leadership the temptation might be to eventually hand the whole idea over to central government agencies, as though the Southern Initiative's measurable failure to transform might be proof that local government involvement in social change is a waste of time and money, or to fold it inside the council's work to 'empower communities'. This is all about politics.

Moving the mountain

System reformers well-known to educators in this country and with international reputations, like Michael Fullan, emphasise 'guiding coalitions' as an important element in change. Their advice is usually directed at education system leaders.

However, there is a growing body of international research underpinning the work of social shift in cities that suggests the connection between education and community is important to the transformational task. It comes in two forms: the work of the 'collective impact' movement out of America and on 'public sector innovation' in the UK and Europe.

In a stimulating piece of writing I found many years ago called 'Moving the Mountain: A whole city approach to basic skills development',[19] Geoff Bateson describes the process that the UK city of Birmingham (about the size of Auckland, population 1 million) went through to address serious educational underperformance. The traditional approach the city had been using is familiar to us in Auckland: lots of pilot activity unconnected to mainstream funding; projects all over the place; low levels of reporting or accountability on overall outcomes; different agencies doing things in parallel; and so on. Key heads of service in the city were invited to sign up to a partnership approach. As previous chapters have explored, partnership comes in many forms. In this instance they established a governing body using a company structure. I asked Bateson why. Like the debates in Auckland about setting up 'hands-off' organisations for things like transport or water, in Birmingham the idea of a stand-alone company to oversee education and skills was initially viewed with public suspicion. While community-based project boards have all the air of inclusive community governance, meetings with large and fluctuating membership, however representative, have limited powers to draw out resources from the agencies that hold them or to make decisions about future directions that bind players to action. Like the deflated Auckland Social Policy Forum, the Birmingham experience included talk-fests where the most important item of business was receiving reports of matters done in the name of the leaders' group of the day. A joint venture board, however, held out the promise of a deeper level of agency commitment. To leverage resources takes subtlety. The 'ta-da' of a big building, big staff and big brand is overkill. A board is simply a key to a door. It must turn the key to release influence on how agencies do their core business—how they staff themselves; how they lead within their own organisation; how they create a culture of change within themselves; how they relate to each other; how they shape their own planning; how they implement; how they disburse their own resources to the joint task of transformation; and how they measure results.

The Birmingham Core Skills Development Partnership was a joint-venture board that could cut through the prescribed planning processes and the priorities and agendas of its council and constituent government agencies historically bogged down by partnership complexity. The evidence is that over a decade Birmingham successfully shifted its core skills profile.[20] The partnership's success included the standard ingredients in the recipe: competent communications and shared key messages, a shared vision and monitoring of agreed activities and their outcomes. There was an element of luck: a consistent group of people held key posts and built trust and cohesion as a group, and a change of government prioritised local relationships for education. The board had a crystal-clear decision-making structure—but even then it was not plain sailing. The eight-member board consisted largely of the local chief executives of the public sector agencies responsible for education, learning, skills and employment, with investment resources of over $30 million. Because the investments to be made were from 'shared or jointly owned money' and the focus was on 'core skills' as agreed in the memorandum and articles of association of the company, decision-making around an annual business plan was simpler—but still challenging. The board was accountable to the agencies that owned them and to the communities they served.

And there came a time in Birmingham when it was not so much job done, says Bateson, but 'secured at an adequate level where it is unlikely to slip back'. While educational performance in Birmingham improved considerably (as the metrics show), inequalities remain. The principle of equity is, of course, more than just data about school performance and league tables and percentages of adults with adequate literacy scores. Literacy, numeracy and language fluency are more than what you get from tests. The joint-venture board was a game-changer, but it eventually disbanded because the work moved away from making schools better, teachers better, working together better and sharing resources better. The work became much more about issues like child poverty, language and cultural inclusion, parent learning and system performance and service integration. The city needed a different kind of transformational mechanism.

Does the Birmingham experience teach us anything about game-changing in Auckland? It is one thing to want change; it is quite another to produce it.[21] Frothing up in our public service are coalitions of government agencies that operate as 'steering groups' to oversee joint action. The Social Sector Trials are one example; another is the Māori and Pasifika Trades Training support project, where the Ministry of Business, Innovation and Employment becomes the lead agency for a steering group whose job it is to let contracts to 'suppliers' of services, jointly communicate progress and reporting, and oversee evaluation. These governance bubbles float up as expressions of the government's commitment to joined-up service thinking. But cross-agency co-operation sits alongside top-down service design cascading from Wellington. A pejorative term of the UK Blair government's command-and-control approach to policy implementation was 'deliverology' via projects.[22] It describes moving from a tight vision via score-card accountabilities, stretch targets (and budgets to match), to progress reporting, collaborative reviews and carrots and sticks for performance. This kind of oversight doesn't deliver 'community governance' or empowerment as the Southern Initiative (perhaps naively) proposes.

There is a new global conversation, however, that moves us along the continuum from co-operation (via deliverology), to approaches that look for collectively shared outcomes and public sector innovation. These are complementary ideas, using a modus operandi with new words to describe apparently old ways of doing things:[23] 'looking for impact'; 'design thinking'; 'ideation'; 'generating value', 'empowerment'. Some of these are already being explored in Auckland.

The argument for 'collective impact', as it is being inquired into in the United States, rests on the total value of interconnected activities—the 'conditions for success', as defined by Stanford researchers Kania and Kramer:

- a *backbone organisation* responsible for leadership and making connections;
- a *common agenda*;
- *shared measurement* of the agreed outcomes;
- *mutually reinforcing activities*; and
- *continuous communication*.

There's a cynical view that these elements are no more than extensions of what already happens in lots of shared efforts. Isn't a 'backbone organisation' just a fancy name for a lead agency? Isn't a 'common agenda' just an expression of everyone wanting more or less the same thing? Might it be the simple equivalent of strategy that everyone already has to do anyway? Is 'shared measurement' no more than published league tables or general data compilations? Is 'continuous communication' merely the invitation to the AGM and a copy of the annual report?

Each of the conditions for success outlined in this research matters in ways deeper than surface words and traditional actions might suggest. This is not the place to explore the Kania and Kramer collective impact framework. But as South Auckland has already discovered with co-operatives, partnerships and collaborations of many hues, *how* matters as much as *what* and *why*. Collective impact is a disciplined effort built on the ecosystems of communities. Kania and Kramer's research showed that 'backbone organisations' are the critical pivot that weave the work of others together; the relationships they facilitate underpin the flowering of shared visions; their leadership becomes a catalyst for shift.

How might education and the Southern Initiative profit from the collective impact model, then? Both structures and processes matter. As the South Auckland experience has already shown, schools and kura have few signals to remind them that they are part of a wider educational, geographical and economic community. The collective contributions of schools matter. They contribute to 'pipelines' of learning for young people. But schools can comfortably operate as isolated islands, and the pipeline can spill out into a labour market that wants a different set of skills than those offered by schools. The guiding document of a school— the charter—can send it in a direction that undermines other parts of the system or runs counter to community priorities. The system of schooling misses a key structural element: a mechanism for collective and inclusive endeavours—a local 'backbone', if you like. We already know that top-performing education systems operate an intermediary layer. The education act that set up self-managing schools missed the importance of the connection between central and local, and now it is showing its age. It is not just South Auckland that needs a local mission-in-the-middle. More than a system tweak, having an intermediary is a significant structural response that makes community engagement in learning possible.

The mission-in-the-middle needs to have a defined mandate, defined role and independent governance. Should it have its own governance board, the appointees would need to be representative of the interests of all stakeholders. It should be nimble, flexible and lightly resourced. Its explicit task would be to consider government directions alongside evidence about local needs. Its work could include the mission of creating an equitable system that provides opportunities for all children to succeed. It could set priorities for charters that allow schools to become meaningfully 'collective' in their goals and targets. It could operate as a commission of inquiry on local matters, gathering data and evidence that supports action to address issues (like student attendance, or the redesign of networks). It could use the principles of co-design and shared problem-solving to take genuinely innovative approaches to community issues. It could certainly become a catalyst for innovation.

By consciously and deliberately adopting a community empowerment approach, Auckland's city-makers are now setting themselves up as a welder of community action—community governance, in other words. The approach is designed to deliver communities that are 'confident, inclusive, organised, co-operative, and influential.[24] The 2015 reorganisation of the council's community development team was designed to 'get out of the way' of communities' aspirations for themselves, perhaps facilitating action of the very kind that Kania and Kramer champion.

The council's approach doesn't appear to have explicit government endorsement. Instead, the government-sponsored way forward arises from

European initiatives—and maybe it's a competition of approaches. A unit using a Danish 'design-led approach' is currently exploring this second idea in South Auckland. It, too, focuses on leading a shared problem-solving process and rigorously measures the outcomes in order to determine value-for-money and effectiveness. The Danes have taken the concept of co-construction—familiar to many educators—and applied it to public policy. The theory is that raising children, caring for older people and transferring language and culture are much more efficiently done *without* a market, but a non-market economy is more efficient when all of a community's assets are engaged in making society work better. Police know that communities are safer when residents look out for each other. Teachers teach best when the learners are actively involved. Co-construction is another way of thinking about community governance.

Whatever their provenance, these initiatives will all have a combined, possibly even transformative effect when there are structures and processes that allow them to 'talk together'. Aucklanders were warned that it was going to take 10 years for the Supercity to find its feet. There's a niggling suspicion in some parts that Auckland has been captured by the property-owning classes and the waterfront, by downtown thinking and political inertia. One of the most challenging aspects to a colossus such as the Auckland Council is how to build internal capacity to function efficiently as one body and how to present oneself externally. How do education stakeholders engage with the spaghetti-plate of complexity that is the council—its Economic Development Strategy and the priority to grow local workforce skills; its community development arm and the projects and programmes related to children and young people; its local boards; its arm's-length council-controlled organisations; and the ambitious Southern Initiative? Are educators even aware of this sideways interest in their work? Do schools even recognise that the council has a legitimate interest them?

Education policymakers regard community engagement as an expression of the role of the board of trustees, as a requirement to 'consult' on a school's long-term strategy; but few communities would regard individual boards of trustees as contributors to community decision-making. Policymakers within local government, on the other hand, see 'learning' as embedded in an approach whose core purpose is to increase the level of power and influence that community and local people have over things they care about; a co-operative, networked way of working together, challenging inequalities, delivering social justice and human rights. Education policymakers and city policymakers have never before been required to engage with each other, except over property.

And that's a problem for South Auckland. Unrealised educational potential in our poorest suburbs becomes visible only as an aberration in the way the whole system works. Solutions simply rejig current transactional arrangements between the chartered (schools) or contracted (providers for-profit and not-for-profit) agents and the state, working to government priorities and Better Public Services measures.

In sum, educational institutions are not governed for or measured against their interrelated contributions to the economic, social and cultural wealth of their communities. They don't work within an ecosystem for transformation but as individual entities with their own immediate priorities.

Partnership confusion and collaboration shock

Partnerships are catch-as-catch-can, like dreams. They become anything you want them to be. In theory, as we have seen, collaboration is a shimmering spectrum. From simple contact and networking and standing side by side, to friendly co-operation and, as the relationship builds and trust grows, to effective working together, partnership grows value—but it is challenging. In reality, partnership with and across education-sector silos is mostly hollow promise. In the work of schooling improvement in South Auckland in the 1990s, 'partnership' narrowed to mean initiatives and projects. The projects crumbled when the money ran out. Schooling improvement work subsequently morphed into an optional extra, especially if your school did not come to the attention of the Education Review Office as ripe for 'failure', whatever that might mean. And now many schools treat the government's Community of Schools initiative as a Trojan horse—the implication being, what more could there be to learn here?

As for the high-profile charter school initiatives ('Partnership Schools/Kura Hourua'), the central partnership between the minister and the 'sponsor' who governs the school is barely more than a contractual relationship with only minor variances from the charters of regular public schools. In reality, such schools are no more than another competitor in the market. South Auckland's educational potential will never be released by new versions of the same model.

Is partnership the answer? In chapter six, on school decile, partnership surfaced as an idea for extracting better value from the additional funding schools receive, but it is highly unlikely that schools would voluntarily or could sustainably contribute their decile funding to underwrite collaborations or partnerships that set out to 'fix' broader social and home disadvantages. Similarly, in addressing school attendance, the mission to get every child in school all day, every day, demands a collaborative approach—but partnership that empowers communities is undermined by public sector contracting arrangements. As for the 'jagged edge' between schooling, higher education and work, partnerships have as many meanings as they have relationships. Schools partner with businesses or tertiary institutions in ceaseless exploration of what might be a comfortable trigger for praise from the Education Review Office or the media.

It seems that partnerships are mostly passé; proven trouble, even. Partnerships are part of the myth-making that sits alongside trickle-down theory and classlessness as cornerstones of democratic practice. In the 'community development' mainstream, social justice and education seem poles apart. And this is scary: community development radicalises actors as they look for new solutions to wicked problems. Partnership doesn't sit comfortably here.

The Auckland Council's engagement with education will depend on two things: *how* it steps into the partnership space and the willingness of the sector to respond to council efforts in return. Similarly, the government's success in driving social transformation will depend on its ability—via its emerging social laboratory approach—to connect the dots to fit the council's new community empowerment approach. These two approaches are not mutually exclusive, but there does seem to be an element of competition between them.

Collaboration and partnership are buzzwords, and initiatives spring forth as new shoots. The constraints for working together are often hidden in the DNA of how non-governmental organisations and public services work in this country. The landscape is unhelpful. Organisations and the people within them are stimulated by reward. Funders commonly select 'winner' organisations in a competitive contracting environment; organisations work in their own interests because it is easier to do it that way, even if they overlap with each other, because the contracts require them to. Government measures return on investment one programme at a time. Scale is sought from a single programme, organisation or approach. Organisations are forced into isolating behaviour because the next contract depends on the delivery of outcomes. Even with growing awareness that public contracts for services ought to be focused on 'outcomes', the incentives to collaborate are weak.[25]

We haven't shifted Auckland's social disparities this way. Shifting from top-down governance to devolution ought to work—yet somehow the education sector has shown that it hasn't. Giving individual schools powers over budgets, people and resources has empowered some and disempowered others. The educational disparities of Auckland, clear 30 years ago, are still with us today; national policy-making hasn't shifted them.

Anyone following education policy debates in this country would understand that they are very oppositional. From one point of view, those pushing market-based reforms are 'innovators' and nay-sayers are 'defenders of the status quo'. Others argue that the reforms so far only intensify the inequalities within the status quo or tinker at the edges of change. Policy change creates an illusion of movement, a bit like sitting in a train at the Britomart station when the next-door train moves out. There is no acknowledgement in the policy agenda that the complex lives of some students who arrive in schools are a stationary fixture in the education context of South Auckland. The policy for charters, the National Standards policy, the Investing in Educational Success policy, the Youth Guarantee policy, the early childhood education plans–however worthy their purpose, there's no data to show that any of them have materially raised the prospects of the most disadvantaged except in the most random of cases. The evidence is mounting that the segregations within Auckland and the increasing inequalities of our communities can be at least partly explained by the contribution of education policy-making to disadvantage. The enigma of devolution has been that it has not empowered communities. This is because, at its core, education policy assumes that competition, not collaboration, is the lever for change.

A pivot to a different future boils down, inevitably, to the intersection between four things: national education policy, school-based decision-making, local government and network leadership, and community effort to create a new ecosystem for action.

Conclusion

A constellation of approaches

Ma whero ma pango ka oti ai te mahi
—With the red and black threads together, the work becomes complete.

In digital gaming, an epic win is an outcome that is so extraordinarily positive you almost don't believe you can achieve it. By this standard, the metamorphosis of caterpillar to butterfly is an epic shift. But it is an uncomfortable one. When the caterpillar spins its cocoon and retreats inside, it releases enzymes that turn its present form into mush. The primordial soup then deliberately re-orders itself into its butterfly form. The creature's itch, ditch and switch is one of nature's wonders. An epic shift for learning in South Auckland will involve equal discomforts.

But it's important to recognise, as Aristotle did, that the whole is greater than the sum of the parts. As the OECD's Andreas Schleicher points out, in countries with high-performing school systems, self-management is but one element in a 'constellation of approaches'[1] to drive student achievement. To predict a new future for South Auckland, there needs to be synergy of movement, like the stars in your sign.

Therefore, in a seven-star constellation of approaches, policymakers ought to begin with the mothers and aunties of South Auckland; their aspirations for themselves and the children they care for. Empowered adults have skills that put them in control of their lives and their destinies, and they pass that power on to their children. Intergenerational approaches have proven potential, but public policy lags significantly behind. Multiple layers of outcomes are possible: lower spending on benefits; improved employment prospects for parents; positive parenting relationships focused on learning; and personal and family aspirations that soar. Who would not want that? It doesn't have to take years.

But it does have to focus on the key decision-makers in households: women.

A second star in the constellation sits closely beside the first. This star would boldly shine on the specific urban need for cultural and social regeneration—with a focus on Māori and Pasifika learning. The notion of public–private partnership, already a feature in the early learning sector, could leverage iwi and government resources through a social investment bond to create something more significant than sector-based programming. The point is to fundamentally reshape the kinds of services being delivered to the market, not just add numbers to a tally of child places in the early childhood sector or more-of-the-same adult education programmes paid for by the Tertiary Education Commission. Early learning services are the excuse, if ever you need one, for rethinking how families learn and earn, innovate and own.

The third star redefines relationships within the education sector, shaping a new understanding of how and why people connect. The suggestion of this book is for a next-generation version of governance to move schooling away from the market model; to establish missions-in-the-middle or network education commissions within communities that deliberately set out to build network cohesion and purpose. Legislation might mandate them, for example, to conduct a 'community inquiry' on matters of network interest (for example, school attendance, achievement in maths or bilingual learning opportunities; as well as community commissions related to school network reorganisation or whole-of-network matters like attracting quality teachers). We might be surprised by the results of well-conducted inquiries which treat citizens like adults, giving them respect and responsibility. Such inquiries would provide them with the opportunity to tell their stories, present them with all the information and choices at their disposal, and offer a sense of political legitimacy and genuine opportunities to shape *place-based* action.[2] In the very places where central policies look least likely to be able to deliver (South Auckland), place-based solutions ought to be crafted alongside and with communities. An intermediary is critical as a catalyst for partnership and problem-solving.

Fourth, South Auckland's contribution to city-making rests on its pride and ownership in its own transformation. Decile gets in the way of that. New forms of investment are needed for institutions that work with the most disadvantaged students from the day they arrive in the compulsory system to the day they graduate. This is a call, therefore, for a shift in the way schools are funded and resourced to meet government targets; implying a shift away, however gradual, from the market to a network approach for educational delivery.

The fifth star spotlights government settings for dealing with the most complex and intractable issues such as non-attendance at school and disengagement from learning. There can be no blueprint for ideal community governance, say community governance experts Bowles and Gintis.[3] But what we do know is that well-governed communities with social capital own the fruits of their success and failures and the assets with which they work. Their actions are visible and punishable, motivated by public spirit and modified by the shame of 'selfishness' and self-interest. School attendance provides an illustration of false steps already taken. Transformation involves both a clearer assessment of the purpose of schooling in an increasingly diverse world and amidst global forces for change, and a shift towards more holistic policy-making on issues that have a very local expression. In other words, a *place-based* approach to governance and governance quality, rather than a school-based one, nests the self-managing school model inside a collaborative frame that allows communities to flower from their own potential.

Sixth, I've argued here that the transfer from compulsory to post-compulsory education requires a purpose-designed oversight mechanism. An 85% achievement rate at NCEA Level 2 will not, of itself, deliver the city the economic transformation it is seeking. 'Working together' on school-to-work transitions makes some sense. But in business, as in education, collaboration works best when there's an overarching mission. It must be mandated, have a single governing body *overseeing the outcome* (not necessarily controlling all the inputs), and follow simple processes, and the metrics should promote inclusion and social and economic mobility as well as academic achievement. We need more subtle measures of outcome to understand whether young people are making good transitions. Auckland, in particular, needs its own outcomes oversight.

Finally, universal drivers for change are family wellbeing, spiritual health and inclusion in the social mainstream. When policymakers emphasise that education in South Auckland has transformational potential, they barely touch on the values-based arguments for better learning in that place. There are emotionally loaded and positive messages that South Auckland needs to hear about itself in order to engage in its own self-improvement. Inclusion in policy-making and local network leadership are essential prerequisites for tapping into local resources.

In summary, for education to play its part in creating well-ordered, economically and environmentally sustainable communities, it has to be much more deeply embedded within them; and so also in the social development and economic development ambitions for the whole of Auckland. Education can't continue to be characterised as a series of competing public service islands. Educational transformation begins with those big ideas—community development and economic development. They are not incidental to education, but fundamentally impact upon it.

Acknowledgements

To Alan Burton and Ann Dunphy, who added insights with every conversation. To professor Gary Hawke, whose critique and endorsement gave me incentive to complete this work. To Susan Warren, Alison Sutton, Shirley Johnson and Orly Jacobsen, my former colleagues at COMET who gave me the confidence to let go and write. To Chris Eichbaum, who supervised my original thesis, from which this book emerged. To Robin Houlker, whose expertise in the fields of early learning and family learning informed my understanding of the chains of disadvantage that shackle learning in communities. To Barry Curtis, Colin Dale and the team at Manukau City Council who welcomed me to the city, and Tipi Arthur and the people of Ōtara who connected my work to the flax roots. To others whose enthusiasms and reflections over the last few years have influenced my thinking and writing: among them, Bill Gavin, Papa Ku Tirikatene and Sonny Rauwhero, Charmaine Pountney, Phil Palfrey, Sharon Alderson, Colleen Brown, the women of the Akoteu Kato Kakala, the late Allen Chang, Colleen Young, Nicola Meek, Ngaire Ashmore and the Counties Manukau Grow Our Own Workforce project team, Moana Whaanga, Martin Cooney, Nancy McConnell, James McCarthy, Damon Salesa, Stuart Middleton, Chris France, Deborah George and Shaun Sutton, Barbara Rackham, Graham Bodman. To my brother Frank Stynman, who took time out from flying his aircraft to read my entire draft and provide comments. To my late father, Frank, the formative influence in my life; and my late mother Aath (*c'est la vie*!), who never understood what I could write about but applauded me nevertheless. And to Allan Vester, whose love and forbearance has allowed me to write this book.

Notes

Preface

1 Australian Public Service Commission, 2007. See also Clarke and Stewart, 1997
2 Chile, 2006
3 The Royal Commission on Auckland Governance devoted a whole chapter of its final report to the issue of social development in Auckland. Royal Commission on Auckland Governance, 2009

Chapter 1: Results that matter

1 Manukau City Council, 1998
2 Delors, 1996
3 Ibid.
4 John Hattie at the Knowledge Wave conference, hosted by the prime minister at the University of Auckland, 2003: *Hattie, New Zealand education snapshot, with specific reference to the Years 1 to 13*, 2003
5 Ripley, 2011
6 For example the Intermediary Network and New Ways to Work http://www.intermediarynetwork.org/brokerfunctions.html; and http://www.newwaystowork.org/
7 For example, Giloth, 2003; Conway, Giloth, and eds, 2014
8 There are many extant examples, such as http://data.gov.uk/sib_knowledge_box/intermediaries
9 Sherman, 2002; see also http://www.intermediarynetwork.org
10 Openshaw, 2009
11 Dawkins, 2009
12 Roberts and Gardiner, 2005
13 Porter and Kramer, 2011
14 Recent references to this include Peter Senge's contributions to the leadership conversation in the *Stanford Social Innovation Review*, http://www.ssireview.org/articles/entry/the_dawn_of_system_leadership
15 Daszko and Sheinberg, 2013
16 Epstein, Coates, Wray and Swain, 2005
17 Pillora and McKinlay, 2011

Chapter 2: Learning is intergenerational

1 Collins, 'Gangster kids keep time for church', 2009
2 Lashlie, 2010
3 Crichton, Templeton, and Tumen, 2015
4 Sutton and Vester, 2010
5 OECD, 2011
6 Perry, 2012
7 Hart and Risley, 2004
8 Gordon, 2013
9 Statistics New Zealand, 2012
10 Ibid.
11 Morrison, Bachman and Connor, 2005
12 COMET, 2007
13 Woulfe, 'The Best Start', 2014
14 Education and Science Select Committee, 2014
15 PriceWaterhouseCoopers, 2006
16 Wasik, 2004
17 Names have been changed out of respect for privacy.
18 Figures quoted by Unicef New Zealand from a 2010 report prepared by the Innocenti Institute in Italy. http://www.unicef.org.nzarticle/610nzscores6outof10inoecdearlychildcareeducationleaguetable.html
19 Johnston G., 2005
20 Johnston G., 2005
21 Obama, 2008, p. 249
22 Gluckman, 2011
23 Newberger, J. J., 1997
24 Heckman and Masterov, 2007
25 Dalli, et al., 2011
26 Wills, 2015
27 Crichton, Templeton and Tumen, 2015

Chapter 3: Early learning and market failure

1 The plan in reference is *Pathways to the Future, Ngā Huarahi Arataki: a ten-year strategic plan for early childhood educatio*n.
2 Ministry of Education, 2012
3 Counties Manukau District Health Board, 2010
4 COMET, 2007
5 Biddulph, 2007
6 In 2004, the Education Review Office noted that 'of the 28 [Pasifika] centres reviewed in 2003/4, ERO will be returning to 15 to carry out supplementary reviews'.
7 COMET, 2008
8 The New Zealand Treasury, 2009
9 Attributed to St Francis Xavier, a founder of the Jesuit order
10 Ministry of Education, 2012
11 Smith, et al., 2000
12 The standard reference for New Zealand policymakers is the Best Evidence Synthesis series. Farquhar, 1990
13 Wylie and Hogben, 2007
14 Robertson, 2007

15 PriceWaterhouseCoopers, 2006
16 Dorothy Pau'uvale's doctoral thesis illustrates these dilemmas beautifully. Pau'uvale, 2011
17 Veblen, 1899 [1973]
18 'Paul Levinson on cellphone bling'. Video accessed 19 September 2016. http://www.youtube.com/watch?v=kogyVFT86dw.
19 Chua, 2011
20 Biddulph, 2007
21 Dixon, et al., 2007; Ministry of Education, 2005a
22 Ritchie and Rau, 2009
23 This is an example of the many resource dilemmas for low-decile schools; high-decile schools do not expect to spend money, time and effort on preschool preparedness.
24 Widdowson and Dixon, 2011
25 Podmore and Te One, 2008
26 Auckland Rugby League website. Accessed 19 September 2016. http://www.aucklandleague.co.nz/about-us/mission-statement/
27 An initiative in West Auckland, evaluated for the Auckland Council, showed positive benefits. However, the project was too small to show significant impact on the larger goal of improving participation. Conway, 2012
28 It's ironic that this process may have to be renegotiated with the new Auckland Council. Loss of institutional memory may be a contributing factor. None of the other legacy councils had matching responses.
29 Hueber, 2012
30 Auckland Regional Public Health Service, 2012
31 Ministry of Education, 2012
32 Bennett, 2009
33 Ibid.
34 Auckland Kindergarten Association, 2011
35 Community activism resulted in a decision by the Ministry of Education late in 2014 to purchase a site nearby for a new early childhood service, thus freeing up land for the school to expand.
36 Winter, 2010
37 Education Counts: Number of licensed ECE services, by Territorial Authority with Auckland boards, service type and year. www.educationcounts.govt.nz/early-childhood-education/services. Accessed 12 August 2015.
38 From papers released under the OIA in 2013.
39 'Home-based sector review by the Ministry of Education 2012–13', 2012.
40 ELI: Early Learning Information System. Accessed 19 September 2014. http://eli.education.govt.nz/
41 www.lead.ece.govt.nz/~/media/Educate/Files/Reference%20Downloads/Lead/Files/RecentAnnouncements/EdRptSupportingHomeBasedECE.pdf
42 Key and English, 2014
43 Statistics New Zealand, 2014
44 Tamihere, 2011
45 Luafutu-Simpson, 2006
46 http://www.everychildcounts.org.nz/_w/wp-content/uploads/2011/09/Every-Child-Counts-Sep-2011-MH.pdf
47 Significant agitation among the Pacific community resulted in a 2012 Parliamentary Select Committee Inquiry into Pacific languages in early childhood education: Education and Science Select Committee, 2013 http://www.ririki.org.nz/wp-content/uploads/2015/04/He-Ara-Hou-Report-20112.pdf
48 http://www.lead.ece.govt.nz/ProgrammesAndInitiatives/ECEParticipationProgramme/TargetedAssistanceForParticipation.aspx

49 Ritchie and Rau, 2009
50 Reynolds, 2013
51 Mitchell, 2014
52 Louisa Wall, MP for Manurewa, has proposed a bill about this option; Johnston, 2012
53 Board of Inquiry: Wiri Men's Prison Proposal, 2011
54 Ibid.
55 Education Counts. Number of enrolments in licensed ECE services by Territorial Authority with Auckland Local Boards: http://www.educationcounts.govt.nz/statistics/early-childhood-education/enrolments; see also Ministry of Education, 2011
56 English and Tolley, 2012
57 Hunter, 28 August, 2014; Hunter, 30 November, 2014
58 'Improvement together stories', http://improvementmethodology.govt.nz/improving-together-stories; 'Building stronger foundations: improving early childhood outcomes', http://www.countiesmanukau.health.nz/blogs/building-strong-foundations-improving-early-childhood-outcomes/
59 Māori Economic Development Panel, 2012
60 Heckman and Masterov, 2004; The most-quoted New Zealand longitudinal study is the 'Competent Children, Competent Learners' study. Wylie, Hodgen, Hipkins and Vaughan, 2008
61 The Young Foundation in the UK has developed a particular interest and expertise in Social Impact Bonds (http://www.youngfoundation.org). Work in New Zealand can be found on the website of the Office for the Community and Voluntary Sector (http://www.ocvs.govt.nz).

Chapter 4: Broken partnerships

1 Quoted by Dr Jack MacDonald at the launch of the Manukau Education Strategy, September 30, 1998.
2 Herbert, 1988
3 The whānau philosophy is an organising principle for schools, similar to the traditional school house; it groups students together for curricular as well as extracurricular activities.
4 Hattie, 2009
5 Caldwell and Spinks, 2013
6 PISA – Programme for International Student Assessments; PIRLS - Progress in International Reading Literacy Study; TiMMS – Trends in International Maths and Science Study. Chamberlain and Caygill, 2012.
7 Ramsay, 1993; see also Snook, et al., 1999
8 Strike, 2003
9 Beeby, 1939
10 As expressed, for example, in the work of Russell Bishop and the Te Kotahitanga programme, http://www.tekotahitanga.tki.org.nz
11 Hawk and Hill, 2002
12 Education Review Office, 1994
13 Francis, 2011
14 Ibid, p. 182
15 Heifetz, 1994
16 *Manukau Courier*, 1994
17 Heal, 1994
18 Radio New Zealand, 1994
19 Hawk, 2012
20 Misa, 2012

21 Smelt, 2007
22 Pountney, 2000
23 Heal, 1994
24 Cathy Wylie reports that an NZCER national survey in 1993 found that the major initiatives of primary schools were related to property, not teaching and learning. Wylie, 2012
25 Fiske and Ladd, 2000
26 This story is recorded in a report to the Ministry of Education in November 2000. Robinson, Timperley and Bullard, 2000
27 Chapple, 1995
28 Robinson, Temperley and Ballard, 2000
29 The conclusions of the Smithfield Project, a major series of studies designed to analyse the progress of New Zealand's school choice/market reforms, were controversial. The first report suggested that the ability to realise choice is dependent on social class, gender and ethnicity; rather than raising educational standards, markets simply polarised them, leading to disadvantage for some students. Lauder, 1992; Lauder, et al., 1994; Lauder and Hughes, 1990; Lauder and Hughers, 1999.
30 Denny, 1996
31 Email communication from Susan Cave-Baragwanath, January 2013.
32 The health issues of secondary students received some attention as part of the AIMHI initiative, and eventually resulted in school nurses being funded into the schools by the relevant District Health Boards.
33 Hawk, 2012
34 Education Review Office, 1996
35 The *National Business Review* named her their New Zealander of the Year 1999 for being 'the best thing in New Zealand education'.
36 Education Review Office, 1996
37 Ibid.
38 Laxon, 1996
39 McCauley and Roddick, 2001
40 Ibid.
41 A research programme was put in place to evaluate progress. This section is based on conversations with principals and others involved in the project; and on the work of Kay Hawk and Jan Hill, the researchers.
42 Hill and Hawk, 1998
43 Only a later survey taken in 2000 could quantify the extent of health needs. Ministry of Health, 2009
44 Sinclair, 2006
45 Phillips, McNaughton and MacDonald, 2002
46 Education Policy Group, Massey University, 2003
47 The Cognition Institute commissioned some work on teacher attitudes and expectations; the work of Russell Bishop et al on the Te Kotahitanga project addresses the student–teacher relationship and its impact on learning.
48 Assessment and Use of Student Achievement Data (AUSAD) started from a discussion of the evidence of where kids were at and what use schools made of it.
49 McNaughton, et al., 2006
50 Limbrick, et al., 2005
51 Annan, 1999
52 From the Interim Report of the evaluation by Uniservices (a research arm of the University of Auckland). Timperley, Robinson and Bullard, 1999
53 Robinson, Timperley and Bullard, 2000, p. 90–92
54 Bates, 2009

55 Knight, Kirton and McCaulay, 2008
56 Hawke, 2002
57 Robinson and Timperley, 2004
58 Ibid.
59 Hargreaves and Fullan, 2012
60 Caldwell and Spinks, 2013
61 Bryk, Gomez, Grunow and LeMahieu, 2015
62 Kingdon provides the classic text about how issues arrive on to the policy agenda.

Chapter 5: Governance and power

1 The Public Education Network was a federation of Local Education Funds in high-poverty urban centres of the United States. Since January 2013, its work has been archived at http://publiceducation.issuelab.org/home
2 Section 61 of the Education Act 1989
3 Kelly, 1998; Smelt, 1998; Smelt, 2007
4 Wylie, 2007
5 New Zealand School Trustees Association, 2008
6 Robinson, Ward and Timperley, 2003
7 Online readability tests of samples of board training materials deliver scores that exceed those normally required for public materials.
8 Education Review Office, 2007
9 Vester, 2009
10 Collins, J., 2009
11 Hunt, 2006
12 Chisholm, 2011
13 *Metro*, June 2006
14 Chen, 2015, http://www.superdiversity.org/
15 The latest census data shows that there are more Samoan and Hindi speakers than Māori speakers in the Auckland region. http://www.stats.govt.nz/Census/2013-census/data-tables/regional-summary-tables-part-1.aspx
16 *Immersion schooling* is when all instruction takes place in the target language, so that a second language can be acquired. *Bilingual schooling* is when instruction takes place in two languages, so that both languages assume equal importance for development.
17 See Krashen, Steven. (1997). Why bilingual education? ERIC digest. http://files.eric.ed.gov/fulltext/ED403101.pdf
18 Lohr, 2012
19 'National Standards Shock', *New Zealand Herald*, http://www.nzherald.co.nz/nz/news/article.cfm?c_id=1andobjectid=10835909
20 'School Report', *stuff.co.nz*, https://www.stuff.co.nz/interactives/schoolreport/
21 Māngere Principals' Association, 2013
22 Ngatiwai speech, Partnership Schools Te Kura Hourua interview panel. Available on Official Information Act request.
23 Ministry of Education, 2011e.
24 Ministry of Education, 2011; See also the Property Tool Box on the Ministry of Education website.
25 OECD, 2009
26 Mourshed, Chijioke and Barber, 2010
27 See also Smelt, 2007
28 Wylie, 2012, p. 248
29 Wylie, pp. 236–243
30 Winter et al., 2012

31 'New Zealand Education: PISA 2012', *New Zealand Education Gazette,* 9 September 2013, Accessed 26 September 2016 http://www.edgazette.govt.nz/Articles/Article.aspx?ArticleId=8882
32 Wylie, 2012, p. 248
33 Hinchco, 2011
34 Robinson, Hohepa and Lloyd, 2009
35 See http://www.educationalleaders.govt.nz/
36 Annan, 2016
37 Smelt, 2007
38 O'Neill, 2015
39 'TeachNZ Scholarships', http://www.teachnz.govt.nz/scholarships/ Accessed 22 July 2014.
40 New Zealand Council for Educational Research, 2014
41 'Get It Right and Everyone Will Benefit', *New Zealand Herald*, 24 January 2014, http://www.nzherald.co.nz/nz/news/article.cfm?c_id=1andobjectid=11191117
42 *NZSTA News*, No 245, July 2014.
43 Mourshed, Chijioke and Barber, 2010

Chapter 6: The lost decile point

1 Boyer, 1996
2 Hirsch, 1976
3 Bourdieu, 1987
4 Brash, 2004
5 *New Zealand Herald*, 2004
6 This question was asked in various media, for example: http://www.converge.org.nz/pma/pr210204.doc
7 Thomson A., 2004
8 Chen, 2015
9 Ministry of Education, 2011
10 Ibid.
11 Sutton and Airini, 2011
12 Gary Orfield of UCLA wrote compellingly about the relationship between housing and schooling in Boston (Orfield and McArdle, 2006). He is co-director for the Civil Rights Project at UCLA and contributed to Carter and Welner, 2013.
13 Harker, 2000
14 Statistics New Zealand, n.d.
15 Ministry of Health, 2007
16 Ministry of Education, 2012f. Calculated from tables provided.
17 Bourdieu, 1987
18 From Ministry of Education school resourcing tables, retrieved 30 July 2015. http://www.educationcounts.govt.nz/statistics/schooling/resourcing/47696
19 Although decile isn't taken into account in staffing for schools, all principals in low-decile schools get a small incentive payment to work there; and some teachers do too.
20 Ramsay, 1981
21 *New Zealand Herald*, 2011
22 Carson, 2012; PPTA, 2012; Blaikie, 2012
23 Lubienski, 2011
24 Trevett, 2012
25 Auckland Now, 2012
26 'Development Trust', Remuera Primary School, http://www.rps.school.nz/contacts/development-trust.aspx
27 Paul, 2013

28 Putnam, 2000
29 There are exceptions, like the Tāmaki Transformation initiative's Manaiakalani project.
30 Minister of Education, 2012
31 International Students in New Zealand, Education Counts website https://www.educationcounts.govt.nz/statistics/international-education/international-students-in-new-zealand Accessed 10 October 2016.
32 Presentation from Macleans College to Auckland Council Economic Forum, August 6 2013
33 Ministry of Education, 2012e
34 Ibid.
35 '8 Tribes', http://www.8tribes.co.nz/tribe-summary.php
36 *Metro* (2016), Best schools in Auckland 2016,http://www.metromag.co.nz/city-life/education/best-schools-auckland-2016/ Accessed 10 October 2016.
37 Blackstock, 2013
38 Education Minister Hekia Parata on decile system, *Nine to Noon*, Radio New Zealand, 17 November 2014.
39 Wilson, 2013
40 This section is based on the work of Ruth Jonathon.
41 Jack Jennings, of the Centre on Educational Policy, a Washington think tank, reports that 'only 17% of charter schools produced higher test scores than comparable public schools, according to a comprehensive national review of such schools. Moreover, 37% of charters produced lower scores than public schools, and the remainder showed no difference from regular public schools'. Jennings, 2012
42 Adnett and Davies point to studies about school choice that show that social frames of reference are important to parents as they choose a school for their children, especially socio-economic status of the class cohort. Parents use cultural capital to 'decode' schools and interpret information to match their child to their preferred school. Adnett and Davies, 2002
43 Jonathan, 1989
44 Lubienski, 2011; Radio New Zealand, 2012
45 Radio New Zealand, 2012; See also the admission of a former principal (Haque, 2014) in his book *Changing our Secondary Schools*.
46 Dann, 1997; Patterson, 'School trims its zone', 2002
47 Patterson, 'Bribes offered to principals', 2002
48 Patterson, 'Schools unmoved by ruse', 2002
49 Jones, 2014
50 Harper and Shuttleworth, 2012
51 Thrupp, 2008
52 Haque, 2014
53 Thrupp, 2007
54 Education Review Office, 2010b
55 Children's Commissioner's Expert Advisory Group on Child Poverty, 2012
56 Productivity Commission, 2012
57 Dougherty et al., 2009
58 Ibid; Lubienski and Dougherty, 2009
59 Eaton, 2011
60 Dunphy, 2012
61 Productivity Commission, 2012
62 Ramsay, 1981
63 'Better Public Services', http://www.beehive.govt.nz/feature/better-public-services
64 Rogers and Mako, 2015

65 PPTA, Waikato Region, 2013)
66 Crichton, Templeton and Tumen, 2015
67 'Funding for children from welfare families revealed to schools', Radio New Zealand, http://www.radionz.co.nz/news/national/312753/funding-for-kids-from-welfare-families-revealed-to-schools
68 Figlio and Getzler, 2002
69 Atlanta Public Schools, for example, where the superintendent was accused (June 2013) of colluding with her staff to raise test scores. http://www.wsbtv.com/news/news/local/former-aps-superintendent-beverly-hall-arrives-arr/nXf43/
70 'Report details PAS catchment home price increase', *West Philly Local*, http://www.westphillylocal.com/2011/05/02/report-details-pas-catchment-home-price-increase/

Chapter 7: Who's not here? It's a community issue

1 Probability of achieving literacy and numeracy credits based on attendance and lateness in Year 8. Slide from Ministry of Education presentation, COMET Auckland, August 2015. http://bit.ly/1Q4qs77
2 This figure comes from the Ministry of Education's call for proposals for delivery of attendance services (Ministry of Education, 2012). The ministry later reported in its biannual survey of attendance that in 2012, approximately 62,000 students were absent from school for all or part of a day during the survey *week*. Of these, 15,000 students were unjustifiably absent from school. Mallari and Loader, 2013.
3 Chua, 2011
4 The Ministry of Education's guidelines provide some examples. Ministry of Education, 2011a.
5 Durham and McCurdie, *Extent of truancy in Manurewa: a keyhole report*, 2001
6 Colquhoun, 2010
7 The *Manukau Courier* reports: 'Any student who arrives back at school after the first week of term will face a special enrolment process with [Principal Robin Staples of Southern Cross Campus] and they'll have to explain why they're late getting there.' Colquhoun, 2010.
8 Ryan and Loader, *Attendance in New Zealand schools 2011*, 2011
9 Ministry of Education, 2012
10 Watson, 2008
11 Donn et al., 1993
12 Education and Science Committee, 1995
13 Fleming, 2006
14 Ibid.
15 Ibid.
16 Attendance and Absence in New Zealand Schools. Education Counts website, 2015. https://www.educationcounts.govt.nz/publications/series/2503 Accessed 11 October 2016.
17 Ministry of Education, 2015
18 Data compiled by COMET Auckland, 2015. Snapshot available on: http://www.cometauckland.org.nz/webfiles/CometNZ/files/SNAP_Manurewa.pdf
19 Durham and McCurdie, 2001
20 Ibid.
21 MartinJenkins, 2009
22 Data here from the Manurewa Enhancement Initiative 2005 Strategic Work Plan, September 2004.
23 See also Wynd, 2014
24 See *Attendance Matters* (Ministry of Education, 2011)
25 Ibid.
26 Meares and Osborne, 2012

27 See also Wylie, C., 2012
28 Neale, 2009
29 MartinJenkins, 2009
30 Cunningham, 2011
31 Two services providers shared this contract: the Solomon Group, based in Manurewa; and Strive Community Services, based in Māngere.
32 Jones, 14 March 2014
33 Carson, 2013
34 Townend, 2013
35 Youth Law Office Tino Rangatiratanga Taitamariki, 2012
36 Education Review Office, 2010a
37 Sutherland, 2011
38 McBride, 2012
39 Presentation to 2012 New Zealand School Trustees Association Conference, 'Skools In, Year Right'. As reported also in the *New Zealand Herald* (Garrett-Walker, 2012); and in other national media.
40 Blissett et al., 2009
41 Becroft, 2009
42 Data about stand-downs, suspensions, exclusions and expulsions is available on the Ministry of Education's Education Counts website: http://www.educationcounts.govt.nz/indicators/main/student-engagement-participation/80346. Ministry of Education, 2012a.
43 Crichton, Templeton and Tumen, 2015
44 Ministry of Justice, 2010
45 Ministry of Justice, 2012
46 Ministry of Justice, 2015
47 Becroft, 2013
48 Lashlie, 2010

Chapter 8: Of talent and potential, pathways and pipelines

1 Fred Dust, IDEO, http://www.youtube.com/watch?v=PJiOcpUUea4
2 Australian Public Service Commission, 2007, http://www.apsc.gov.au/__data/assets/pdf_file/0005/6386/wickedproblems.pdf
3 Stone, 1989
4 Robins, 1996
5 Ernst and Young, 1998
6 Crooks et al., 1996
7 Scarpetta, Sonnet and Manfredi, 2010
8 Allpress, 2013
9 Department of Labour, 2012; See also Department of Labour, 2009.
10 Pawson, 2004
11 Hynes, 2006
12 Fletcher Challenge was once the largest business/multinational in New Zealand. Its successor, Fletcher Building, remains one of New Zealand's largest listed companies.
13 Cox, 2006
14 More information about the trust can be found on the Youth Mentoring Network website: www.youthmentoring.org.nz
15 For example, bringing together 26 studies of youth mentoring programmes in New Zealand to identify associations between cultural appropriateness and programme effectiveness. Farruggia et al., 2011.
16 See, for example, Mentoring and Tutoring Education Scheme (MATES) Senior, Annual Report of the Great Potentials Foundation, 2011–12, p. 20, http://youthmentoring.org.nz/

content/docs/caps/Mentee%20to%20Mentor%20Mates%20programme17052013.pdf

17 A list of programmes is available on the youth mentoring website, www.youthmentoring.org.nz.

18 I first came across David Lewis's book *We, the Navigators*, when I was living in the Cook Islands in the early 1980s. In 2007 an exhibition and series of lectures at the Auckland Museum, *Vaka Moana*, reminded me of my earlier fascination. Both David Lewis's book and the book accompanying the exhibition (Howe, 2006) describe the voyaging techniques of navigators in some detail. A dead-reckoning system for the location of islands, for example, is known as the 'etak' system. Ben Finney (2006) writes: 'As he sails from his home island toward the target island the navigator envisages that the bearing from canoe to reference island shifts from one star point to another along the horizon in the background. This process divides the voyage into segments (*etak*) and tracks the canoe's progress by its completion of one *etak* after another by envisioning the reference island's opposite movement from one star point to another along the horizon.' This conceives the world in a totally different way to the navigators of James Cook's day.

19 The government's media release can be found at http://www.scoop.co.nz/stories/PA0308/S00055.htm

20 COMET, 2006

21 http://www.youthservice.govt.nz/

22 Collins, S., 2014

23 Tertiary Education Commission, 2011

24 See 'Faculty of Education and Social Work', University of Auckland, http://www.education.auckland.ac.nz/en/about/research/starpath-home/starpath-research.html

25 Johnston, K., 2015

26 Ibid.

27 Education Counts, http://www.educationcounts.govt.nz/home, Accessed October 21, 2015

28 The requirements, which can be reached in various ways, are outlined on the NZQA website, http://www.nzqa.govt.nz/about-us/news/quals-review-guidelines-update-2/.

29 'Breaking the Cycle of Education Underachievement', http://www.ihaveadream.org.nz/doc/Breaking%20the%20Cycle%20of%20Educational%20Underachievement.pdf

30 Rubie-Davies, 2005

31 Woulfe, NCEA: All shall pass, 2013; *New Zealand Listener*, 2015

32 'Currency' is a term used by Andreas Schleicher to describe why skills are so important.

33 Robertson, S. L., 2015

34 Chief Scientist, 2014

35 Pope, 2001

36 Education Review Office, 2011

37 Another 940 Trades Academy places from 2016. Youth Guarantee website. http://www.youthguarantee.net.nz/news-container/another-940-trades-academy-places-from-2016/ Accessed 11 October.

38 From the CEO's blog, 22 June 2012, www.countiesmanukau.health.nz/blogs/

39 Clark, 2011

40 Ibid.

41 From a benchmark study completed for the Māori in Tertiary Education (MITE) Project, a collaborative initiative among Auckland tertiary institutions. Reported in *Ka Miharo*, a publication of Te Wananga o Aotearoa, http://issuu.com/tewananaaotearoa/docs/kamiharo6

42 From the media release from the Tindall Foundation on 4 January 2010: 'Jobs Summit Projects Exceed Tindall Pledge'.

43 Middleton, et al., 2013

44 Conley, 2007

45 Science, Technology, Engineering, Maths

46 Capper, 1992
47 Blackstock, 2014
48 'Vocational Pathways', Youth Guarantee, http://youthguarantee.net.nz/vocational-pathways/
49 Stern, Dayton and Raby, 2010
50 Earle, 2013
51 It apparently goes back to an analogy first used in the 1970s; possibly Cohen, M. et al, 'A Garbage Can Model of Organizational Choice', *Administrative Science Quarterly*, Vol. 17, No. 1, March 1972, pp. 1–25
52 Auckland Council Economic Development Committee resolution, February 2014

Chapter 9: Have faith

1 Reference to Pompallier's request is available on the Treaty2U website, http://www.treaty2u.govt.nz; the primary source is William Colenso's *The Authentic and Genuine History of the Signing of the Treaty of Waitangi*, published by the Government Printer in Wellington, 1890.
2 See Moon, 2014
3 In 2006, 55.6% of those who answered the question on religious affiliation were connected to a Christian religion, compared with 60.6% five years earlier. http://www.stats.govt.nz/Census/2006CensusHomePage/QuickStats/quickstats-about-a-subject/culture-and-identity/religious-affiliation.aspx . In the 2013 census, 41.9% of New Zealanders who answered the question on religion claimed no religious affiliation. Statistics New Zealand, 2014.
4 'Auckland bucks downward trend in religion', Statistics New Zealand, http://www.stats.govt.nz/Census/2013-census/data-tables/reg-sum-tables-pt2-mr.aspx
5 MacLauchlan, 2012
6 Shallcrass, 1992
7 Jones, B., 2012
8 Thomson, G. V., 2006
9 Heenan, 2009
10 The New Zealand Treasury also acknowledges the inadequacy of GDP as a measure of our living standards. It has proposed a 'framework' to guide policy decisions and choices. The framework encompasses five key aspects important for improving living standards: economic growth, sustainability, increasing equity, managing risk and social infrastructure. Gleisner, Llewellyn-Fowler and McAlister, 2011.
11 Sen, 1999. 'In *Development as Freedom* Amartya Sen explains how in a world of unprecedented increase in overall opulence millions of people living in the Third World are still unfree. Even if they are not technically slaves, they are denied elementary freedoms and remain imprisoned in one way or another by economic poverty, social deprivation, political tyranny or cultural authoritarianism. The main purpose of development is to spread freedom and its 'thousand charms' to the unfree citizens. Freedom, Sen persuasively argues, is at once the ultimate goal of social and economic arrangements and the most efficient means of realising general welfare. Social institutions like markets, political parties, legislatures, the judiciary, and the media contribute to development by enhancing individual freedom and are in turn sustained by social values. Values, institutions, development and freedom are all closely interrelated, and Sen links them together in an elegant analytical framework. By asking 'What is the relation between our collective economic wealth and our individual ability to live as we would like?' and by incorporating individual freedom as a social commitment into his analysis, Sen allows economics once again, as it did in the time of Adam Smith, to address the social basis of individual wellbeing and freedom'.
12 Nussbaum, 2011
13 Stiglitz, Sen and Fitoussi, 2009

14 Ministry of Social Development, 2016
15 Henare et al., 2011
16 NZ Families Commission, 2014
17 Gleisner, Llewellyn-Fowler and McAlister, 2011
18 Henare, 2011
19 Veisinia Ha'unga, 2013, 'Student Voice' in *Learning Auckland,* Education Today, Wellington.
20 Ministry of Education, 2007
21 Ibid.
22 Data in this section reported by Solomon, 2008.
23 Given its success rate, the decision for closure seemed odd. Scott Esplin: 'It is the *policy* and *practice* of the Church,' observed the *Church News*, 'to discontinue operation of such [Church] schools when local school systems are able to provide quality education.' (Scott C. Esplin, 2008).
24 Wilson, 2013
25 Snook, 'Social class and educational achievement: beyond ideology', 2009
26 Woods, 1979.
27 Bishop, et al., 2009
28 Education Review Office, 2014
29 Manaia and Hona, n.d.
30 'Character Counts', KIPP, http://www.kipp.org/our-approach/character
31 The KIPP schools reference the work of eminent behavioural psychologists Martin Seligman, Chris Peterson and Angela Duckworth. See http://www.authentichappiness.sas.upenn.edu/Default.aspx.
32 Ministry of Education, 2007
33 Ministry of Education, 2002
34 'History of Curriculum Development', The New Zealand Curriculum Online, http://nzcurriculum.tki.org.nz/Archives/Curriculum-project-archives/Developing-the-draft/History-of-curriculum-development
35 Sandel, 2012

Chapter 10: Local leadership

1 Kotter, 2007; Kania and Kramer, 2011
2 The empowering communities approach is a community development theory of practice being adopted by cities globally, and adapted and adopted by Auckland Council in 2015.
3 Clark, 2013.
4 Hartwich, 2013
5 Orsman, 2014
6 Collins, S., 2013
7 Orsman, 2012
8 Royal Commission on Auckland Governance, 2009
9 Bennett, 2012
10 Centre for Social Research and Evaluation, 2013
11 McKinlay, 2013
12 Fukuyama, 1995; Bowles and Gintis, 2002; Putnam, 2000
13 Originally a term used by the Catholic Church, it is embedded in the constitution of the European Union, and widely discussed in the relationship between federated states (as in the US). See http://europa.eu/legislation_summaries/glossary/subsidiarity_en.htm; and Fleming and Levy, 2014.
14 Clark, 2016
15 Auckland Council, 2015

16 Anecdotal feedback from council officials and local social service managers
17 'Correspondent', Radio New Zealand, 3 June 2014, http://www.radionz.co.nz/news/on-the-inside/246211/correspondent-todd-niall
18 Kotter, 2007
19 Bateson, 2003
20 'The Word's the Thing', http://thewordsthething.org.uk/?m=201310
21 Harwood, 2014
22 Barber, Kihn and Mofitt, 2011
23 Kania and Kramer, 2011
24 Community Development Exchange, 2008
25 See Treasury scan of contracting for social services: http://www.treasury.govt.nz/publications/informationreleases/socialservices/pdfs/cossm-2789883.pdf

Conclusion

1 Caldwell and Spinks, 2013
2 Nabatchi and Leighninger, 2015
3 Bowles and Gintis, 2002

Bibliography

Adnett, N. and Davies, P. (2002, June). Education as a positional good: implications for market-based reforms of state schooling. *British Journal of Educational Studies*, 50(2), pp. 189–205.

Adult education and community learning working party. (2001). Koia! Koia! Towards a learning society. The Role of Adult and Community Education. Tertiary Education Commission.

Allpress, J. A. (2013). *The labour market and skills in Auckland*. Technical Report 2013/005. Auckland: Auckland Council.

Anderson, C. (2009). *The New Zealand Principals' Experience of the school board as an employer*. Survey Report to the New Zealand Principals' Federation and the New Zealand. Auckland: School Governance Solutions.

Annan, B. (1999). *Strengthening Education in Mangere and Ōtara*. Annual Report September 1997–June 1999. Manukau: Ministry of Education.

Annan, B. (2016). Future Education and Technology Conference, Auckland.

Armstrong, H. (2012). Does higher social diversity affect people's contributions to local schools? Evidence from New Zealand. New Zealand Association of Economists Annual Conference 2012.

Auckland Council. (2011). *Rugby World Cup 2011: Evaluation Report*. Auckland: Auckland Council.

Auckland Council. (2015). Update on the Southern Initiative. Agenda of Community Development and Safety Committee 18 February 2015. Auckland: Auckland Council.

Auckland Kindergarten Association. (2011, August 9). Auckland kindergarten to be bulldozed for car park. Press Release. Auckland.

Auckland Now. (2012, February 26). Parents paying millions in school donations. Retrieved August 20, 2012, from Auckland Now: http://www.stuff.co.nz/auckland/local-news/6481519/Parents-paying-millions-in-school-donations

Auckland Regional Public Health Service. (2012). Position Statements. Retrieved 24 May 2012, from Auckland Regional Public Health Service: http://arphsdnn.dev.netpotential.co.nz/about-us/position-statements

Auckland Rugby League. (n.d.). Mission Statement. Retrieved 5 August 2012, from http://www.aucklandleague.co.nz/about-us/mission-statement/

Australian Public Service Commission. (2007). *Tackling wicked problems: a public policy perspective*. Canberra: Commonwealth of Australia.

Ayres, S. (2013). America's 10 Million Unemployed Youth Spell Danger for Future Economic

Growth. Washington: Centre for American Progress.

Badkar, J. (2009). The Future Demand for Paid caregivers in a Rapidly Ageing Society. Wellington: Department of Labour.

Barber, M., Kihn, P. and Mofitt, A. (2011). *Deliverology: From idea to implementation.* London: McKinsey.

Bardach, E. (2000). A Practical Guide for Policy Analysis: The Eightfold Path to More Effective Problem Solving. London: Chatham House.

Barwick, H. (2006). *Youth work today: A review of the issues and challenges.* Wellington: Ministry of Youth Development.

Bates, T. (2009). National mission or mission improbable? In J. Langley (ed.), *Tomorrow's Schools 20 years on.* Auckland: Cognition Institute.

Bateson, G. (2003). *Moving the Mountain: a whole city approach to basic skills development.* Birmingham: Core Skills Partnership.

Bauman, Z. (2011). Migration and identities in the globalized world. Philsophy and Social Criticism.

Becroft, A. (2009). How to turn a child offender into an adult criminal—in ten easy steps. Children and the Law International Conference. Tuscany, Italy.

Becroft, A. (2013, October 18). Child and Youth Offending: Eisenhower Fellowships Greg King Memorial Lecture. Auckland: Principal Youth Court Judge.

Beeby, C. E. (1993). *The biography of an idea: Beeby on education.* Wellingon: NZCER. p. 124

Bennett, P. (2009, December 18). Air quality debacle threatens ECE centres. Wellington: Press Release, National Party Associate Education Spokeswoman. Retrieved from http://www.paulabennett.co.nz/index.php?/archives/12-Press-Release-Air-quality-debacle-threatens-ECE-centres.html

Bennett, P. (2012, September 11). Social obligations mean better outcomes for children. Retrieved 11 September 2012, from Beehive: http://www.beehive.govt.nz/release/social-obligations-mean-better-outcomes-children

Berger, A., et al. (2013). *Early college, early success: Early college high school initiative impact study.* Washington: American Institutes for Research (AIR).

Berl Economics. (2012). Giving New Zealand: Philanthropic funding 2011. Wellington: Philanthropy New Zealand .

Biddulph, F., Biddulph, J., and Biddulph, C. (2003). The Complexity of Community and Family Influences on Children's Achievement in New Zealand: Best Evidence Synthesis Iteration. Wellington: Ministry of Education.

Biddulph, P. (2007). *Early childhood education in Manukau: A stocktake.* Manukau: COMET.

Binning, E. (2010, May 18). Message sinking in: switching schools is bad for kids. *New Zealand Herald.*

Bishop, R., Berryman, M., Cavanagh, T., and Teddy, L. (2009). Te Kotakitanga: Addressing educational disparities facing Māori students in New Zealand. *Teaching and Teacher Education*, 1(9).

Bishop, R., Sullivan, D., and Berryman, M. (2010). Scaling up education reform: addressing the politics of disparity. Wellington: NZCER.

Blackstock, R. (2013, February 24). Special Report: Zone fights hit primary schools. Schooled in the dark arts. *Herald on Sunday*, pp. 1, 3; 22, 23.

Blackstock, R. (2013, June 23). Sunday Insight: Rich school, poor school: parents' decile dilemma. *New Zealand Herald.*

Blackstock, R. (2014, March 30). Corporates provide schools with new operating system. *New Zealand Herald.*

Blaikie, J. (2012). Rich kids still get more. *Education Aotearoa*, spring.

Blank, M. J., Melaville, A. and Shah, B. P. (2003). Making the difference: research and practice in community schools. Washington, DC: Coalition for Community Schools.

Blissett, W., et al. (2009). *Conduct problems: Best practice report.* Report by the advisory group on conduct problems. Wellington: Ministry of Social Development.

Board of Inquiry: Wiri Men's Prison Proposal. (2011). *Final Report and Decision of the Board of Inquiry into the Proposed Men's Correctional Facility at Wiri.* Wellington: Environmental Protection Authority.

Bourdieu, P. (1987). *Distinction: A social critique of the judgement of taste.* Harvard University Press.

Bowers, N., Sonnet, A., and Bardone., L. (1999). Giving young people a good start: the experience of OECD countries. In OECD, *Preparing youth for the 21st century: The transition from education to the labour market,* (pp. 7–86). Paris: OECD.

Bowles, S., and Gintis, H. (2001). Social capital and community governance. Working Paper 01-01-003. University of Massachusetts, and Santa Fe Institute, Massachusetts.

Bowles, S. and Gintis, H. (2002). Social capital and community governance. *The Economic Journal,* 112(483), pp. 419–436.

Boyd, B., Pyle, R. M., and Nabokov, D. (2000). In *Nabokov's butterflies: unpublished and uncollected writings* (p. 472). London: Allen Lane. The Penguin Press.

Boyer, Ernest L. (1996). The Scholarship of Engagement. *Journal of Public Service and Outreach.* 1:1, pp. 11–20.

Brash, D. D. (2004, March 26). Nationhood. Retrieved 19 August 2012, from National: http://www.national.org.nz/article.aspx?articleid=1614

Bruner, J. (1996). *The culture of education.* Boston: Harvard University Press.

Bryk, A. S., Gomez, L., Grunow, A., and LeMahieu, P. (2015). *Learning to improve: How American's schools can get better at getting better.* Boston: Harvard Education Publishing Group.

Bull, A., and Gilbert, J. (2006). Educational issues for schools affected by transience and residential mobility. Wellington: NZCER.

Bull, A., and Gilbert, J. (2007). Student movement and schools— what are the issues? Wellington: NZCER.

Bull, A., and Gilbert, J. (2012). *Swimming out of our depth? Leading learning in 21st century schools.* Wellington: NZCER.

Caldwell, B. J., and Spinks, J. M. (2013). *The self-transforming school.* London and New York: Routledge.

Callister, P. (2012, June). 'White flight': how data can spoil a good story. Callister and Associates. http://callister.co.nz/white-flight-how-data-can-spoil-a-good-story.pdf

Calman, L. J. and Tarr-Whelan, L. (2005). *Early childhood education for all: a wise investment.* New York: Legal Momentum.

Capper, P. (1992). Jagged edge revisited: Part the first—the secondary–tertiary boundary. Internal PPTA Circular HX92/032, 27/12/1, 4 February 1992.

Carson, J. (2012, September 5). Covert plan for user-pays education, claims report. Retrieved 5 September 2012, from stuff.co.nz: http://www.stuff.co.nz/national/education/7613842/Covert-plan-for-user-pays-education-claims-report

Carter, C. (2008, September 1). $9.3M boost for early childhood services. Retrieved 29 May 2012, from: http://www.beehive.govt.nz/release/93m-boost-early-childhood-services

Carter, P. L., and Welner, K. E. (eds.)(2013). *Closing the opportunity gap: What American must do to give every child an even chance.* New York: Oxford University Press.

Centre for Social Research and Evaluation. (2013). *Final evaluation: Social sector trials. Trialling new approaches to social sector change.* Wellington: Ministry of Social Development.

Chamberlain, Megan, and Caygill, Robyn. (2012). *TIMSS 2010/11 and PIRLS 2010/11 Key Findings: New Zealand's Participation in PIRLS and TIMSS.* Wellington: Ministry of Education.

Chapple, G. (1995, October 14). Schools for scandal. *New Zealand Listener,* pp. 36–38.

Chen, M. (2015). *Superdiversity stocktake: Implications for business, government and New Zealand. Auckland*: Super Diversity Centre.

Chief Scientist. (2014). *Tackling the school-industry mathematics divide*. Canberra: Commonwealth of Australia.

Children's Commissioner's Expert Advisory Group on Child Poverty. (2012). *Solutions to child poverty in New Zealand: evidence for action*. Wellington: Children's Commissioner.

Chile, L. M. (2006). The historical context of community development in Aotearoa New Zealand. *Community Development Journal* 4(4), pp. 407–425.

Chisholm, D. (2011, July-August). Saving Selwyn. *Metro*, pp. 58–62.

Chua, A. (2011). *Battle hymn of the tiger mother*. London: Bloomsbury.

City of Manukau Education Trust. (2002). Business and schools in Manukau. Manukau: City of Manukau Education Trust.

City of Manukau Education Trust. (2007). Governance and complex urban campus schools. Manukau: City of Manukau Education Trust.

Claridge, M. (2001). Geography and the inclusive economy: A regional perspective (WP 01/17). Wellington: New Zealand Treasury.

Clark, G. (2013). Livable and Business Friendly Cities: What is Auckland doing? How should the competition respond? Presentation for the Auckland City Council.

Clark, G. (2016, June 24). The sun still rises: London after Brexit. Washington, DC: The Brookings Institution.

Clark, J. (2011). *Workforce diversity literature review: How strong is the evidence to support the CMDHB business case to grow and employ a health workforce that reflects the population it serves?* Auckland: Counties Manukau District Health Board.

Clarke, M., and Stewart, J. (1997). *Community governance, community leadership and the new local government*. York: Joseph Rowntree Foundation.

Collins, J. (2009, October). Social reproduction in classrooms and schools. *Annual Review of Anthropology*, 38, pp. 33–48.

Collins, S. (2009, November 4). Gangster kids keep time for church. *New Zealand Herald*.

Collins, S. (2013, March 7). Minister vows to smash Auckland city limits. *New Zealand Herald*.

Collins, S. (2013, April 11). Special report: State of our children. NZ report card; Must do better. The *New Zealand Herald*, pp. A20, A21.

Collins, S. (2013, August 22). Suicide rates drop for youth, rise for elderly. *New Zealand Herald*.

Collins, S. (2014, April 9). Mayor's plea: Give youth a chance. *New Zealand Herald*.

Colquhoun, J. (2010, February 02). Late starters warned. *Manukau Courier*.

COMET (2006). Youth Transitions Services through Schools. Discussion paper 06/3. Manukau: City of Manukau Education Trust.

COMET (2008). Manukau today is New Zealand tomorrow: Report on proceedings of the Manukau Early Childhood Education Summit. Manukau: City of Manukau Education Trust.

COMET, Tomorrow's Manukau. (2007). Early Childhood Education in Manukau City. Manukau: City of Manukau Education Trust.

Committee for Auckland. (2008). Growing Auckland, Growing New Zealand. Auckland: Committee for Auckland.

Community Development Exchange (2008), materials available through http://www.iacdglobal.org/

Conley, D. T. (2007). *Redefining college readiness*. Eugene: Educational Policy Improvement Centre.

Consumer. (2010, June 1). Schools and the law: school fees. Retrieved 20 August 2012, from Consumer: http://www.consumer.org.nz/reports/schools-and-the-law/school-fees

Conway, K. (2012). *West Harbour PlayDays project*. Auckland: Auckland Council.

Conway, M., Giloth, R. P., and (eds). (2014). Connecting people to work: Workforce intermediaries and sector strategies. The Aspen Institute.

Corcoran, A., et al. (2013). Rethinking leadership: The changing role of principal supervisors.

The Wallace Foundation and Council of the Great City Schools.

Counties Manukau District Health Board. (2010). *External review of maternity care in Counties Manukau District*. Auckland: Counties Manukau District Health Board.

Cox, R. (2006). *Promoting the spirit of mentoring in New Zealand*. Winston Churchill Report. North Shore: Youth Empowerment Seminars.

Craig, E., et al. (2011). *The Health Status of Children and Young People in the Northern District Health Boards*. Dunedin: New Zealand Child and Youth Epidemiology Service.

Crichton, S., Templeton, R. and Tumen, S. (2015). *Using Integrated Administrative Data to Understand Children at Risk of Poor Outcomes as Young Adults*. Wellington: New Zealand Treasury.

Crooks, M. L., Webb, M. and Forster, J. (1996). *The Price We Pay: Young People, Poverty and Long-term Unemployment in Australia*. A report to the National Youth Affairs Research Scheme.

Cunningham, S. (2011). *Formative Evaluation of Neighbourhood Policing Teams in Counties Manukau District* . Wellington: New Zealand Police.

Dalli, C., et al. (2011). *Quality early childhood education for under-two-year-olds: What should it look like? A literature review*. Wellington: Ministry of Education.

Dann, L. (1997, October 22). Students miss out. *East & Bays Courier*, p. 1.

Daszko, M. and Sheinberg, S. (2013). Survival is optional: Only leaders with new knowledge can lead the transformation. Retrieved June 2013, from Marcia Daszko and Associates: http://www.mdaszko.com/ArticlesNewsletters.html

Dawkins, R. (2009). *The greatest show on earth: the evidence for evolution*. London: Transworld Publishers.

Delors, J. (1996). Education: the necessary utopia. International Commission on Education for the 21st Century. *Learning: the treasure within*. Paris: UNESCO.

Denny, G. (1996). Indicative Survey of Students At-Risk in New Zealand Secondary Schools. Porirua: Porirua College.

Department of Labour. (2009). *Youth in the New Zealand Labour Market*. National Monitoring Series. Wellington: Department of Labour.

Department of Labour. (2012). *Youth Labour Market Factsheet: June 2012*. Wellington: Ministry of business, Innovation and Employment.

Department of Labour. (2013). Labour Supply Forecasting by age, gender and qualification. Wellington: Department of Labour.

Dickison, M. (2013, February 4). Kickbacks costing parents. *New Zealand Herald*, p. A5.

Dixon, R., Meagher-Lundberg, D. W., Airini, and McMurchy-Pilkington, C. (2007). *Evaluation of Promoting Early Childhood Education (ECE) Participation Project*. Wellington: Ministry of Education.

Donn, M., Bennie, N. and Kerslake, J. (2013). *Who's Not Here? Working towards keeping 'absentee students' at school*. Wellington: Ministry of Education.

Dougherty, J., et al. (2009, August). School Choices in Suburbia: Test Scores, Race, and Housing Markets. *American Journal of Education*, 115(4), pp. 523–548.

Drucker, P. (1994, November). The Age of Social Transformation. *The Atlantic Monthly*, 274(5), pp. 53–80.

Duncan, A. (2009, November 10). The Promise of Promise Neighborhoods: Beyond Good Intentions. Retrieved September 5, 2012, from Department of Education: http://www.ed.gov/news/speeches/promise-promise-neighborhoods-beyond-good-intentions

Dunphy, A. (2012, October 11). Some uncomfortable truths. *Uninews*, 42(17), p. 8.

Durham, J. and McCurdie, C. (2001). *The extent of truancy in Manurewa: Keyhole Report*. Manukau: Manukau City Council.

Earle, D. (2013). Monitoring the Youth Guarantee policy 2010–2012. Wellington: Ministry of Education.

Eaton, J. (2011). An ethical dilemma. *Te Kuaka*, 5.

Eaton, J., Dunphy, A., Gargiulo, S., Gall, P., Ala'alatoa, B., and McNaughton, S. (2011). The

Great Decile Debate. *Te Kuaka* 3, 4–8.

Edmondson, J., Mohan, K., and Stewart, S. (2015, August 31). Ecosystem investing: Achieving impact at scale. Six lessons from a large-scale, cross-sector initiative to improve education. *Stanford Social Innovation Review.*

Edmunds, S. (2011, October 11). Rugby world cup work a bonus for many. *New Zealand Herald.*

Education and Science Select Committee. (1995). Inquiry into children in education at risk through truancy and behavioural problems. Wellington: House of Representatives.

Education and Science Select Committee (2013). Inquiry into pacific languages in early childhood education. Wellington: House of Representatives.

Education and Science Select Committee. (2014). Inquiry into engaging parents in the education of their children. Wellington: Education and Science Select Committee, New Zealand Parliament.

Education Policy Group, Massey University. (2003, September 29). *Literacy research in South Auckland: A critique.* Retrieved 12 December 2012, from Scoop: http://www.scoop.co.nz/stories/print.html?path=ED0309/S00129.htm.

Education Review. (2013, July). The dollar sign above every international student.

Education Review Office. (1994). *Confirmed Assurance Audit Report: Ngā Tapuwae College.* Wellington.

Education Review Office. (1996). *Schooling in Mangere and Ōtara.* Wellington: Education Review Office.

Education Review Office. (2007). *School governance: an overview.* Wellington: Education Review Office.

Education Review Office. (2009). EarlyChildhood Monograph Series: The quality of education and care in home-based early childhood services (January 2009) and care. Wellington: Education Review Office.

Education Review Office. (2010a). Good practice in alternative education September 2010: National report. Wellington: Education Review Office.

Education Review Office. (2010b). Including students with high needs. Wellington: Education Review Office.

Education Review Office. (2011). *An evaluation of service academies October 2011.* Wellington: Education Review Office.

Education Review Office. (2012). *Sir Edmund Hillary Collegiate Senior School Review.* Wellington: Education Review Office.

Education Review Office. (2012, August 29). The three most pressing issues for New Zealand's education system, revealed in latest ERO report. Retrieved November 19, 2013, from Education Review Office: http://www.ero.govt.nz/About-Us/News-Media-Releases2/The-three-most-pressing-issues-for-New-Zealand-s-education-system-revealed-in-latest-ERO-report

Education Review Office. (2014). *Towards equitable outcomes in secondary schools: Good practice.* Wellington: Education Review Office.

Education Review Office. (2015). School evaluation indicators. Effective practice for improvement and learner success. Trial document. Wellington: Education Review Office.

Eggers, W. D. and Goldsmith, S. (2004). Governing by network: the new shape of the public sector. Washington: Brookings Institution Press.

English, B. and Tolley, A. (2012, March 8). Next steps for new public-private prison at Wiri. Retrieved May 28, 2012, from: http://www.beehive.govt.nz/release/next-steps-new-public-private-prison-wiri

Epstein, P. D., Coates, P. M., Wray, L. D. and Swain, D. (2005). *Results That Matter: Improving Communities by Engaging Citizens, Measuring Performance, and Getting Things Done.* Jossey-Bass/ A Wiley.

Esplih, S.C. (2008). Closing the Church College of New Zealand: A Case Study in International Church Education Policy. In Neilson, R.L., Harper, S.C., Manscill, C.K. and Woodger, M.J. (eds). *Regional Studies in Latter-Day Saint Church History: The Pacific*

Isles. Provo, UT: Religious Studies Centre, Brighton Young University, pp. 161–180.

Ernst and Young. (1998). Costs of Youth Unemployment in Manukau. Unpublished paper.

Farquhar, S. (1990). Quality in early education and care: What do we mean? *Early Child Development and Care*, 64, pp. 71–73.

Farquhar, S.E. (2003). Quality teaching early foundations: Best evidence synthesis. Wellington: Ministry of Education.

Farruggia, S. P., Bullen, P., Solomon, F., Collins, E., and Dunphy, A. (2011). Examining the cultural context of youth mentoring: A systematic review. *Journal of Primary Prevention*, 32, pp. 237–251.

Finney, B. (2006). Traditional navigation. In K. R. Howe, *Vaka moana: Voyages of the ancestors*. Auckland: David Bateman Limited, pp. 156–185.

Fisher, D. and Shepherd, N. (2009, April 26). Child pollution fright. *New Zealand Herald*.

Fiske, E. B., and Ladd, H. (2000). *When schools compete: a cautionary tale*. Washington: The Brookings Institution Press.

Fleming, J. E., and Levy, J. T. (eds) (2014). *Federalism and Subsidiarity: NOMOS LV*. New York: NYU Press.

Fleming, T. (2006). *Who Counts? Young people out of systems in Counties Manukau*. Manukau: Counties Manukau District Health Board.

Francis, B. (2011). *Sir John Graham: Sportsman, master, mentor*. Wellington: Trio books.

Frey, R., and Powell, L. A. (2009). Protestant work ethic endorsement and social values in developing and developed societies: comparing Jamaica and New Zealand. Psychology and Developing Societies , 1, pp. 51–77.

Fukuyama, F. (1995). *Trust: The social virtues and the creation of prosperity*. London: Hamish Hamilton.

Fullan, M. (2004). Systems thinkers in action. Nottingham: Department for Education and Skills.

Garrett-Walker. (2012, July 16). Don't expel, keep troubled kids in schools – Judge. *New Zealand Herald*.

Gilbert, J. (2005). Catching the knowledge wave? The knowledge society and the future of education. Wellington: NZCER Press.

Gilbert, J. (2009). Catching the knowledge wave? The knowledge society and the future of education. Wellington: NZCER Press.

Giloth (ed), R. P. (2003). *Workforce intermediaries for the twenty-first century*. New York: Columbia, The American Assembly.

Gleisner, B., Llewellyn-Fowler, M. and McAlister, F. (2011). *Working towards higher living standards for New Zealanders*. New Zealand Treasury.

Gluckman, S. P. (2011). Towards better use of evidence in policy formation: a discussion paper. Wellington: Office of the Prime Minister's Science Advisory Committee.

Gordon, L. (2013). *Who achieves what in secondary schooling? A conceptual and empirical analysis*. Christchurch: Pukeko Research Limited.

Gulson, K. N. (2011). Education policy, space, and the city: Markets and the (in)visibility of race. New York: Routledge.

Haque, B. (2014). *Changing our secondary schools*. Wellington: NZCER Press.

Hargreaves, A., and Fullan, M. (2012). Professional capital: Transforming teaching in every school. London: Routledge.

Harker, R. (2000). Roll change and the removal of zoning, 1991–1998. *Set* 2, pp. 4–6.

Harper, P., and Shuttleworth, K. (2012, June 25). Claim Auckland schools skew zones. *New Zealand Herald*, p. A3.

Hart, B., and Risley, T. R. (1995). Meaningful differences in the everyday experience of young American children. Baltimore, MD: Paul H Brookes Publishing.

Hart, B., and Risley, T. R. (2004). The early catastrophe. *Education Review*, 77(1), pp. 100-118.

Hart, S. (2007, February 12). The art of business success. The *New Zealand Herald*.

Hartwich, O. (2013). *A global perspective on localism*. Wellington: The New Zealand Initiative and Local Government New Zealand.

Harwood, R. C. (2014). Putting community in collective impact. *Stanford Social Innovation Review*.

Hattie, J. (2003). New Zealand education snapshot, with specific reference to the Years 1 to 13. Knowledge Wave 2003: the leadership forum. Auckland.

Hattie, J. (2009). Tomorrow's Schools – yesterday's news: a quest for a new metaphor. In J. Langley (ed.), *Tomorrow's Schools 20 years on . . .* Auckland: Cognition Institute, pp. 121–132.

Hawk, K. (2012, May). School decline and failure. Retrieved November 5, 2012, from: http://www.educationgroup.co.nz/index.php?page=reflections

Hawk, K., and Hill, J. (2002). *Achieving is cool; what we learnt from the AIMHI Project to help schools more effectively meet the needs of their students*. Albany, Auckland: Massey University IDPER.

Hawke, G. (2002). *Education reform: the New Zealand experience*. Wellington: New Zealand Trade Consortium in association with NZ Institute of Economic Research.

Heal, A. (1994). Mr Fixit. *Auckland Metro*, pp. 148–155.

Heckman, J. J. and Masterov, D. V. (2004). *The Productivity Argument for Investing in Young Children*. Chicago: University of Chicago.

Heckman, J. J. and Masterov, D. V. (2007). The productive argument for investing in young children. (Working Paper No 13016). Cambridge MA: National Bureau of Economic Research.

Heenan, J. (2009). *The Cornerstone Values Approach to Character Education in New Zealand Schools*. New Zealand Foundation for Character Education Inc.

Heifetz, R.A. (1994). *Leadership without easy answers*. Boston: Harvard University Press.

Heifetz, R. A., and Linsky, M. (2002). *Leadership on the line*. Cambridge: Harvard Business School Press.

Henare, M., et. al. (2011, September 8). *He Ara Hou: The Pathway Forward. Getting it right for Aotearoa New Zealand's Māori and Pasifika Children*. Wellington: Every Child Counts. Retrieved July 14, 2014, from Every Child Counts: http://www.ririki.org.nz/wp-content/uploads/2015/04/He-Ara-Hou-Report-20112.pdf

Herbert, C. M. (1988). *The Best of Charlie Herbert*. Wellington: Department of Education.

Hill, J. and Hawk, K. (1998). *Achieving is cooler than it was: Achievement in multi-cultural high schools*. Albany Campus: Educational Research and Development Centre (ERDC), Massey University.

Hill, M. (2012, July 27). Bibles in schools divide leaders. *New Zealand Herald*.

Hinchco, B. (2011). *So why are principals opposed to National Standards?* Paper to National Standards Sector Advisory Group. Wellington: Ministry of Education.

Hipkins, R. (2013). NCEA one decade on: Views and experiences from the 2012 NZCER National Survey of secondary schools. Wellington: NZCER.

Hirsch, F. (1976). *Social limits to growth*. London: Routledge and Kegan Paul.

Hood, D. (2015). *The rhetoric and the reality*. Wairarapa: Fraser Books.

Hopkins, D. (2007). *Every school a great school: Realizing the potential of system leadership*. London: McGraw-Hill.

Howe, K. (2006). *Vaka Moana: Voyages of the ancestors*. Auckland: David Bateman Limited.

Hueber, A. (2012, January 19). Outcry over preschool in St Helier. *The Aucklander*.

Hunt, Graeme (Ed). (2006). *Selwyn College: Inspiration and reflection*. Auckland: Selwyn College.

Hunter, T. (2014, August 28). Childcare to float. *Sunday Star Times*.

Hunter, T. (2014, November 30). Weighing up roll-up risk. *Sunday Star Times*.

Hutchinson, V. (2011, April). It's going to take community – some thoughts on economics as if people and the earth mattered. Retrieved October 23, 2012, from New Zealand Social Entrepreneur Fellowship vivian paper: http://www.nzsef.org.nz/vivianpapers

Hutchison, V. (1998, September 2). Walking for change: Some thoughts from the Hikoi of Hope. Retrieved January 28, 2014, from Jobs Letter: http://www.jobsletter.org.nz/vivian/hikoi98.htm

Hynes, K. (2006). *20 Years on: evaluation of the peer support programme in New Zealand schools.* Christchurch: Peer Support Trust, Rotary International.

I have a dream foundation. (2013, April Tuesday 9). Managing students into school rather than out. Retrieved August 2, 2013, from ihaveadream.org.nz: http://www.ihaveadream.org.nz/news/Managing_students_INTO_school_rather_than_OUT

International Division, Ministry of Education. (2013). International student enrolments 2006-2012. Wellington: Ministry of Education.

Jackson, N. (2011). The demographic forces shaping New Zealand's future. Hamilton: NIDEA, University of Waikato.

James, C. (n.d.). Retrieved from http://www.colinjames.co.nz/speeches_briefings/Manukau_CC_08Jul18.htm

Jennings, J. (2012, January). *Why have we fallen short and where do we go from here?* Retrieved 23 August 2012, from Centre on Education Policy: http://www.cep-dc.org/displayDocument.cfm?DocumentID=392.

Jobs for the Future and New Ways to Work. (2000). *The Intermediary Guidebook: Making and Managing Community Connections for Youth.* Jobs for the Future.

Johnson, A. (2002). *A study of transience in South Auckland primary schools.* Auckland: Child Poverty Action Group.

Johnston, G. (2005). Women's participation in the labour force: New Zealand Treasury Working Paper 05/06. Wellington: New Zealand Treasury.

Johnston, K. (2012, September 9). Push to lower school age to four to boost learning and save cash. *Sunday Star Times*, p. A1.

Johnston, K. (2015, April 9). Shining examples emerge from list. *New Zealand Herald.*

Jonathan, R. (1989, November). Choice and control in education: parental rights, individual liberties and social justice. *British Journal of Educational Studies*, 37(4), pp. 321-338.

Jones, B. (2012, February 12). Bearded blokes spouting load of hogwash. *New Zealand Herald.*

Jones, N. (2013, August 1). 4700 suspensions bring call for a new approach. *New Zealand Herald*, pp. A14–A15.

Jones, N. (2013, August 1). Law group wants change after claims of illegal expulsions. *New Zealand Herald*, p. A5.

Jones, N. (2014, March 14). Schools play catch up for lost kids. *New Zealand Herald.*

Jones, N. (2014, July 24). Schools rethink zones in backlash. *New Zealand Herald*, p. A5.

Juthika Badkar, P. C. (2009). Ageing New Zealand: The growing reliance on migrant caregivers. Wellington: Institute of Policy Studies, Victoria University of Wellington.

Kania, J., and Kramer, M. (2011, Winter). Collective Impact. *Stanford Social Innovation Review.*

Kaufmann, E. (2010). *Shall the religious inherit the earth? Demography and politics in the 21st century.* London: Profile Books.

Kelly, J. (1998, December). Review of today's schools: governance and quality, by Simon Smelt. *Social Policy Journal of New Zealand*, 11.

Key, J., and English, B. (2012, June 25). Better Public Services. Retrieved 4 July 2012, from http://www.beehive.govt.nz/feature/better-public-services

KEY2 Real Estate Ltd. (2012). Big House, Great Flat Land, High Decile School. Ararimu. Retrieved 20 August 2012, from http://www.realestate.co.nz/1844686

Kingdon, J. W. (1996). *Agendas, Alternatives and Public Policies.* HarperCollins College Publishers.

Klein, N. (2008). *The Shock Doctrine.* Sydney: Penguin Group.

Knight, N., Kirton, N., and McCaulay, S. (2008). Developing partnerships for improving student outcomes. International Congress for Schooling Effectiveness and Improvement

Conference. Auckland, 6–9 January.

Kotter, J. P. (2007). *Leading change: Why transformation efforts fail.* Cambridge, Massachussets: Harvard Business Reivew.

Krugman, P. (1994). *The age of diminishing expectations.* Cambridge, Massachussets: The MIT Press.

Lashlie, C. (2010). *The Power of Mothers.* HarperCollins Kindle.

Lauder, H. and D. Hughes (1990) 'Social inequalities and differences in school outcomes' *New Zealand Journal of Educational Studies*, 25(1):37–60.

Lauder, H. (1992) 'Notes towards a new agenda for policy making in Aotearoa New Zealand' *New Zealand Annual Review of Education*, 1:1–14.

Lauder. (1994, March). *The creation of market competition for education in New Zealand: An empirical analysis of a New Zealand secondary school market, 1990–1993.* The Smithfield Project Phase One: First Report to the Ministry of Education. Wellington: Ministry of Education.

Lauder, H. and D. Hughes (1999) *Trading in Futures: Why Markets in Education Don't Work*, Open University Press, Buckingham.

Laxon, A. (1996, November 1). The trustees write the school report: Poverty the hardest lesson. *New Zealand Herald*, p. A11.

Laxon, A. (2013, February 23). It just doesn't add up. *New Zealand Herald.*

Leadbeater, C., and Wong, A. (2010). Learning from the extremes. Cisco White Paper.

Lee, A. (2000). Transient children: perceptions of how often transient children come and go.

Levin, B. (2008). *How to change 500 schools: A practical and positive approach for leading change at every level.* Cambridge, Massachussets: Harvard Education Press.

Lewis, D. (1972). *We, the navigators.* Canberra: Australian National University Press.

Limbrick, L., Knight, N., McCaulay, S., Kirton, N., Funaki, A., and Evans, J. (2005). *Ōtara: The learning community. Teachers' reflections on professional development in writing.* NZARE 2005. Dunedin.

Luafutu-Simpson, P. (2006). *Choices offered, choices chosen in Pasifika early childhood education: a Christchurch experience.* Christchurch: University of Canterbury. http://ir.canterbury.ac.nz/handle/10092/987

Lubienski, C. (2011, July 1). The decile delusion. Retrieved 12 September 2012, from *Education Review*: http://www.educationreview.co.nz/pages/section/article.php?s=Leadership+%26+PDandidArticle=21460

Lubienski, C., and Dougherty, J. (2009, August). Mapping Educational Opportunity: Spatial analysis and school choice. *American Journal of Education*, pp. 285–491.

MacLauchlan, G. (2012). *The passionless people revisited.* Auckland: Bateman.

Madjar, I., McKinley, E., Deynzer, M., and van der Merwe, A. (2010). *Stumbling blocks or stepping stones? Students' experience of transition from low-mid decile schools to university.* Auckland: Starpath Project, University of Auckland.

Mahoney, P., Park, Z., and Smyth, R. (2013). *Moving on up: What young people earn after their tertiary graduation.* Wellington: Ministry of Education .

Mallari, M., and Loader, M. (2013). *Attendance in New Zealand schools 2012.* Wellington: Education Information and Analysis, Ministry of Education.

Manaia, W., and Hona, D. (n.d.). *The changing face of Māori development.* Retrieved 29 August 2013, from F.I.R.S.T. Foundation: http://www.firstfound.org/manaia%20and%20hona.htm

Mangere Principals' Association. (2013, December 20). Principals express concern about charter school. Retrieved 20 December 2013, from Scoop Education: http://www.scoop.co.nz/stories/ED1312/S00122/principals-express-concern-about-charter-school.htm

Manukau City Council. (1996). Manukau Economic Development Strategy. Manukau: Manukau City Council.

Manukau City Council. (1998). Draft Manukau Education Strategy: Report to Strategic Management Committee, 19 May 1998. Manukau: Manukau City Council.

Manukau City Council. (1998). Manukau Education Strategy. Manukau: Manukau City Council.

Manukau Courier. (2008, September 15). Truancy officers take a stand.

Manukau Courier. (1994, March 22). Principal sacked. p. 1.

Manukau Courier. (2008, August 11). Preschool plan under scrutiny.

Manukau Institute of Technology. (2013). Bridging the Divides Conference 2013. Retrieved 17 July 2013, from Centre for Studies in Multiple Pathways: http://www.manukau.ac.nz/csmp/events/conference-2013

Māori Economic Development Panel. (2012). *He kai kei aku ringa: The Crown-Māori Economic Development Partnership.* Wellington: Māori Economic Development Panel.

Marginson, S. (1997). *Markets in education.* St Leonard's, NSW: Allen and Unwin.

MartinJenkins. (2009). *Evaluation of the District Truancy Services: Final Report.* Wellington: Ministry of Education .

Mayer, S. E. (2002). *The influence of parental income on children's outcomes.* Wellington: Ministry of Social Development.

McAllister, J. (2013, August 10). Council feet-dragging happening everywhere. *New Zealand Herald.*

McBride, K. (2012, July 15). Teachers our 'firstline' crime fighters – Judge. *Dominion Post.*

McCauley, L., and Roddick, S. (2001). *An evaluation of schools support.* Wellington: Ministry of Education.

McKinlay, P. (2013). *Reflections on the role of local and central government in the delivery of social services.* A report for the New Zealand Treasury. Auckland: McKinlay Douglas Ltd.

McNaughton, S., MacDonald, S., Amituanai-Toloa, M., Lai, M., and Ferry., S. (2006). *Enhanced teaching and learning of comprehensive in years 4 to 9 in seven Māngere schools: Final report.* Wellington: Ministry of Education, Teaching and Learning Research Initiative. Woolf Fisher Research Centre, UniServices, University of Auckland.

Meares, C., and Osborne, B. (2012). *Manurewa Truancy Survey.* Auckland: Auckland Council, RIMU.

Meek, N., Vester, B., Lythe, T., Sutton, A., and Warren, S. (2010). How education can make a bigger difference to Auckland's future. Auckland: COMET.

Metge, J. (1995). *New growth from old: The whanau in the modern world.* Wellington: Victoria University Press.

Middleton, L., Tanuvasa, D. A., Pledger, M., Grace, N., Loto-Su'a, T. T., and Smiler, K. (2013). Health Science Academies Evaluation. Wellington: Health Services Research Centre, Victoria University of Wellington.

Middleton, S. (2010). Multiple Pathways: Occasional Paper 1. Auckland: Centre for Studies in Multiple Pathways.

Middleton, S. (2012, June 19). Talk-Ed: Thwarting the belief in freedom of information. Retrieved 20 August 2012, from EdTalkNZ: http://www.stuartmiddleton.co.nz/?tag=decile-ratings

Miller, P. (2010). *Smart Swarm: Using animal behaviour to change our world.* New York: Avery.

Milne, J. (2012, September 23). National standards shock: Better grades in bigger classes. *New Zealand Herald.*

Ministry of Education (2005a). *Ministerial review of targeted policies and programmes: Ministry of Education's Promoting Early Childhood Education Participation Project.* Wellington: Ministry of Education.

Ministry of Education (2005b). *Māori Education Strategy.* Wellington, Ministry of Education.

Minister of Education. (2012). *New Zealand Schools Nga kura o Aotearoa. A report on the compulsory schools sector in New Zealand.* Wellington: Ministry of Education.

Ministerial Action Group on Drugs. (2003). Methamphetamine Action Plan. Wellington:

New Zealand Government.

Ministry of Education. (2002). *Curriculum stocktake report to the Minister of Education.* Wellington: Ministry of Education.

Ministry of Education. (2007). *The New Zealand Curriculum.* Wellington: Ministry of Education.

Ministry of Education. (2011a). *Attendance Matters.* Wellington: Ministry of Education.

Ministry of Education. (2011b). Pasifika in ECE. Retrieved 13 June 2012, from Education Counts: http://www.educationcounts.govt.nz/statistics/ece2/pasifika-in-eces

Ministry of Education. (2011c). *Profiles and trends 2011: New Zealand's tertiary education sector.* Wellington: Ministry of Education.

Ministry of Education. (2011d). Student numbers. Retrieved 27 August 2012, from Education Counts: http://www.educationcounts.govt.nz/statistics/schooling/july_school_roll_returns/6028

Ministry of Education. (2011e). *The New Zealand School Property Strategy 2011–2021.* Wellington: Ministry of Education.

Ministry of Education. (2012a). *Statement of Intent 2012–2017.* Wellington: Ministry of Education.

Ministry of Education. (2012b). Air Quality and Early Childhood Education. Retrieved May 24, 2012, from: http://www.lead.ece.govt.nz/GeneralInformation/InFocus/EnvironmentalIssues/Air%20Quality%20and%20Early%20Childhood%20Education.aspx

Ministry of Education. (2012c). Early Childhood Education: Enrolments. Retrieved 5 September 2012, from Education Counts: http://www.educationcounts.govt.nz/statistics/ece2/participation

Ministry of Education. (2012d). *Export Education Levy Key Statistics (Full Year).* Wellington: Ministry of Education.

Ministry of Education. (2012e). *Key financial indicators for schools.* Wellington: Ministry of Education.

Ministry of Education. (2012f). *Student Numbers.* Wellington: Ministry of Education.

Ministry of Education. (2013). *July school roll returns 2013.* Wellington: Ministry of Education.

Ministry of Education. (2015). Attendance in New Zealand schools 2014. Wellington: Ministry of Education.

Ministry of Health. (2007). 2006 Index of Deprivation. Retrieved 12 August 2012, from: http://www.health.govt.nz/publication/nzdep2006-index-deprivation

Ministry of Health. (2009). *Evaluation of Healthy Community Schools initiative in AIMHI schools.* Wellington: Ministry of Health.

Ministry of Justice. (2010). *An Overview of Child and Youth Offending Statistics in New Zealand: 1992 to 2008.* Wellington: Ministry of Justice.

Ministry of Justice. (2012). *Trends in Child and Youth Prosecutions in New Zealand: 2002-2011.* Wellington: Ministry of Justice.

Ministry of Social Development (2016). *The Social Report 2016.* Wellington: Ministry of Social Development.

Misa, T. (2012, June 25). Market model leaves schools to die. *New Zealand Herald.*

Mitchell, L. (2014, December 2). Put children's education before shareholders. *New Zealand Herald.*

Moon, P. (2013, February 13). Bible in Schools battlers denying our heritage. *New Zealand Herald.*

Morgan, G. (1986.). *Images of Organization.* Newbury Park, CA: Sage Publications Inc.

Morgan, G. (2012, July 31). Sir Bob, Gareth Morgan clash over low decile schools. Retrieved from: http://garethsworld.com/sir-bob-gareth-morgan-clash-over-low-decile-schools

Morrison, F., Bachman, H., and Connor, C. (2005). *Improving literacy in America.* New Haven, CT: Yale University Press.

Mourshed, M., Chijioke, C., and Barber, M. (2010). How the world's most improved school systems keep getting better. McKinsey on Society.

Nabatchi, T., and Leighninger, M. (2015). *Public participation for 21st century democracy.* New Jersey: Jossey-Bass.

Neale, I. (2009, March 14). Stepping up to fight truancy. *Manukau Courier.*

New Zealand Council for Educational Research. (2014). *2014 Annual Evaluation Report for the Teach First NZ Programme.* Wellington: NZCER.

New Zealand Herald. (2004, February 17). Poll puts National ahead of Labour.

New Zealand Herald. (2011, January 27). Are you struggling with school uniform costs? Your views. Retrieved September 5, 2012, from nzherald.co.nz: http://www.nzherald.co.nz/nz/news/article.cfm?c_id=1andobjectid=10702320

New Zealand Herald. (2012, June 20). Concern over school deciles overstated. The *New Zealand Herald*, p. A12.

New Zealand Herald. (2012, August 22). Hiding deciles bad answer to a fair question. The *New Zealand Herald*, p. A12.

New Zealand Home-Based Early Childhood Education Association. (2012, August 24). Mandatory qualifications for home-based childcare workers. Retrieved from Scoop: http://www.scoop.co.nz/stories/ED1208/S00137/mandatory-qualifications-for-home-based-childcare-workers.htm

New Zealand Institute. (2012). *More ladders, fewer snakes: Two proposals to reduce youth disadvantage.* Auckland: New Zealand Institute.

New Zealand Listener. (2015, October 24). Quality not Quantity. Editorial, p. 5.

New Zealand School Trustees Association. (2008). *School governance: Board of Trustees stocktake.* Report of findings. Wellington: NZSTA.

Newburger, J.J. (1997). New Brain Development Research – A wonderful winfow of opportunity to build public support for early childhood education! *Young Children*, 52(4).

Nussbaum, M. C. (2011). *Creating capabilities: the human development approach.* New York: Harvard University Press.

NZ Families Commission. (2014). *Families and whanau status report 2014: Understanding wellbeing.* Wellington: Social Policy Evaluation and Research Unit, Families Commission.

New Zealand Treasury. (n.d.). Estimates 2012 Vote: Education. Retrieved 29 May 2012, from Treasury: http://www.treasury.govt.nz/budget/2012/estimates/est12educ.pdf

New Zealand Treasury (2009). *Challenges and Choices: New Zealand's Long-term Fiscal Statement.* Accessed 19 September 2016.

Obama, B. (2008). *Change We Can Believe In.* New York: Broadway Books.

OECD. (1999). Preparing youth for the 21st century: the transition from education to the labour market. Proceedings of the Washington DC Conference 23–24 February 1999. Paris: OECD.

OECD. (2009). PISA Database 2009. Paris: OECD.

OECD. (2011). Doing better for families. Paris: OECD.

O'Neill, J. (2015). How charities are shaping education policy in New Zealand. PPTA Conference 2015. Wellington: Post Primary Teachers' Association.

Openshaw, R. (2009). *Reforming New Zealand secondary education: The Picot Report and the road to radical reform.* Palgrave Macmillan.

Orfield, G., and McArdle, N. (2006). *The Vicious Cycle: Segregated housing, schools and intergenerational inequality.* Harvard University, Joint Centre for Housing Studies, Boston.

Orrell, D. (2010). *Economyths: Ten ways that economics gets it wrong.* London: Icon Books.

Orsman, B. (2012, March 21). Council keeps 'social' interests. *New Zealand Herald.*

Orsman, B. (2014, June 13). Adams seeks major changes to Unitary Plan. *New Zealand Herald.*

Otero, G., and West-Burnham, J. (2004, 29 November). Educational leadership and social capital. National College for School Leadership. Leading Practice Seminar.

Pacheco, G. (2013). Estimating the cost of youth disengagement in Auckland. Business and economy in Auckland 2013 , Research Investigations and Monitoring Unit, p. 30–32, Auckland: Auckland Council.

Pacifecon for New Zealand Building and Construction Productivity Partnership. (2013). National Construction Pipeline Report. Wellington: Ministry of Business, Innovation and Employment.

Patterson, A. (2002, June 12). Bribes offered to principals. *Central Leader*, p. 1.

Patterson, A. (2002, June 28). School trims its zone. *Central Leader*, p. 1.

Patterson, A. (2002, August 7). Schools unmoved by ruse. *Central Leader*, p. 1.

Pau'uvale, D. L. (2011). Laulōtaha; Tongan Perspectives of 'Quality' in Early Childhood'. Auckland: MEd thesis, Auckland University of Technology University.

Paul, G. (2013, July 29). Five schools spending $400,000 on 1st XVs. *New Zealand Herald*, pp. A20–A21.

Pawson, R. (2004). *Mentoring relationships: an explanatory review.* Leeds: ESRC UK Centre for Evidence Based Policy and Practice: Working Paper 21.

Perry, B. (2012). *Household incomes in New Zealand: Trends in indicators of inquality and hardship 1982 to 2011.* Wellington: Ministry of Social Development.

Phillips, G., McNaughton, S., and MacDonald, S. (2002). *Picking up the pace.* Manukau: Strengthening Education in Mangere and Ōtara (SEMO), Ministry of Education.

Picot, B. (1988). *Administering for excellence: Effective administration in education* (Picot Report). Wellington: Department of Education.

Pierre, J., and Peters, B. G. (2000). *Governance, politics and the state.* New York: St Martins Press.

Pihama, L. (1996, December). Policy Constructions: In Whose Interest? A Critical Analysis of Parents as First Teachers in Relation to Māori Education. *Social Policy Journal of New Zealand Te Puna Whakaaro* 7.

Pillora, S., and McKinlay, P. (2011). *Evolution in communithy governance: Building on what works.* Literature Review. Sydney: Australian Centre of Excellence for Local Government, University of Technology.

Pink, D. (2009). *Drive: the surprising truth about what motivates us.* New York: Riverhead Books.

Podmore, V., and Te One, S. (2008). *Nurturing a culture of care for infants and first-time parents: the SPACE programme at Te Marua/Mangaroa Playcentre.* Wellington: Ministry of Education.

Pont, B., Nusche, D., and Moorman, H. (2008). Improving school leadership: Policy and practice. Paris: OECD.

Pope, C. (2001). High School Sport Academies: Should we run with them? New Zealand Applied Business Education Conference 2001.

Porter, M. E., and Kramer, M. R. (2011, January–February). Creating Shared Value: How to reinvent capitalism—and unleash a wave of innovation and growth. *Harvard Business Review.*

Postrel, V. (2008, July–August). Inconspicuous consumption. *The Atlantic.* Boston, Massachussets.

Pountney, C. (2000). *Learning our living: a teaching autobiography.* Auckland: Cape Catley.

Post-Primary Teachers' Association, Waikato Region. (2012). A Level Playing Field? The Importance of Local Funding in Financing Secondary Schools to Meet Future Needs. PPTA Annual Conference 2012. Wellington: PPTA.

Post-Primary Teachers' Association, Waikato Region. (2013). A hierarchy of inequality – the decile divide. PPTA Annual Conference. Wellington: Post Primary Teachers' Association.

PriceWaterhouseCoopers. (2006). *Manukau Family Literacy Programme: Outcomes valuation project.* Manukau: City of Manukau Education Trust.

Prime Ministerial Task Force on Employment . (1994). *An education, training and employment policy for young people.* The interim report of the Prime Ministerial Task

Force on employment. Wellington.

Productivity Commission. (2012). *Housing Affordability Inquiry.* Wellington: New Zealand Productivity Commission.

Public Agenda. (2009). Americans are more likely to give higher marks to local schools than schools nationwide. Retrieved from http://70.47.17.70/charts/americans-are-more-likely-give-higher-marks-local-schools-schools-nationwide

Putnam, R. (2013, April 8). Crumbling American dreams. *New York Times*, p. SR9.

Putnam, R. D. (2000). *Bowling Alone: The collapse and revival of American community.* New York: Simon and Schuster.

Radio New Zealand. (1994, March 22). Education Funding – Tangaroa College. Ngā Taonga Sound and Vision ID20603.

Radio New Zealand. (2012, June 25). Skewed enrolment zones prompts calls for re-think. Retrieved 4 September 2012, from Radio New Zealand: http://www.radionz.co.nz/news/national/109079/skewed-enrolment-zones-prompts-calls-for-re-think

Ramsay, P. (1981). *Tomorrow may be too late. Report on schools with special needs in Māngere and Ōtara.* Department of Education, Wellington.

Ramsay, P. (1993). Picot: Vision and reality in New Zealand schools: An insider's view. In B. Lingard, J. Knight, and P. Porter (eds), *Schooling reform in hard times.* London: Falmer Press. pp. 261–283.

Rashbrooke, M. (2013). *Inequality: a New Zealand crisis.* Wellington: Bridget Williams Books.

Reid, A. (2012, August 21). Opposition to removal of decile ratings. Retrieved 26 August 2012, from Newstalk ZB: http://www.newstalkzb.co.nz/auckland/news/nbedu/385469046-opposition-to-removal-of-decile-ratings

Reynolds, P. (2013, April 4). ECE centre licensing practice 'wasteful and absurd'. *Eduvac Education Weekly.*

Ripley, A. (2011). 'The World's Schoolmaster'. *The Atlantic.* Boston: Massachusetts. http://www.theatlantic.com/magazine/archive/2011/07/the-worlds-schoolmaster/308532/

Ritchie, J., and Johnson, A. (2011). Chapter 15: Early childhood care and education. In M. C. Dale, M. O'Brien, and S. S. (eds), *Left further behind: how policies fail the poorest children in New Zealand* (pp. 15–174). Auckland: Child Poverty Action Group.

Ritchie, J., and Rau, C. (2009). Ma wai nga hua? 'Participation' in Early Childhood in Aotearoa/New Zealand. *International Critical Childhood Policy Studies*, 2(1).

Ritchie, J., Harvey, N., Kayes, M., and Smith, C. (2014). Early childhood care and education, and child poverty. Auckland: Child Poverty Action Group.

Roberts, J., and Gardiner, B. (2005). *Exploring possibilities: an evaluation of the short-term effectiveness of the Secondary Futures Project.* Wellington: NZCER.

Robertson, J. (2007). *Parental decision-making in relation to the use of the Early Childhood Education services.* Wellington: Ministry of Education.

Robertson, S. L. (2015). Piketty, Capital and Education: A solution to, or problem in, rising social inequalities? *British Journal of Sociology of Education.* Special issue on Piketty and Capital in the 21st Century.

Robins, A. (1996). Young people in New Zealand: Opportunity and choice? *Social Policy Journal*, 7.

Robinson, V., Hohepa, M., and Lloyd, C. (2009). *School Leadership and Student Outcomes: Identifying What Works and Why. Best Evidence Synthesis.* Wellington: Ministry of Education.

Robinson, V., Timperley, H., and Bullard, T. (2000). *Strengthening education in Māngere and Ōtara evaluation: Second evaluation report.* Wellington: Ministry of Education.

Robinson, V., and Timperley, H. (2004). *Strengthening Education in Mangere and Ōtara: Final evaluation report.* Wellington: Ministry of Education.

Robinson, V., Ward, L., and Timperley, H. (2003). The difficulties of school governance: a layperson's job? *Educational Management, Administration and Leadership*, 31, pp. 263–281.

Rogers, L. and Mako, C. (2015). *Investing in Achievement, Excellence and Equity.* Wellington: Ministry of Education.

Roper, T., and Thompson, A. (2006). Estimating the costs of crime in New Zealand 2003/2004. Treasury Working Paper 06/04. Wellington: New Zealand Treasury.

Royal Commission on Auckland Governance. (2009). *Report of the Royal Commission on Auckland Governance.* Auckland: Royal Commission on Auckland Governance.

Royal-Tangaere, A. (1997). Māori human development learning theory. In P. T. Whāiti, M. B. McCarthy, A. Durie, and (eds), *Mai i rangiatea* (pp. 46–59). Auckland: Auckland University Press.

Rubie-Davies, C. M. (2005). *Teacher expectations and student self-perceptions: Exploring relationships.* Auckland: University of Auckland.

Russell, A. (2015). Radical community development: We do talk politics here. *Whanake: The Pacific Journal of Community Development*, 1(1), pp. 58–64.

Ryan, T., and Loader, M. (2011). *Attendance in New Zealand schools 2011.* Wellington: Ministry of Education.

Ryan, T., and Loader, M. (2012, February). *Attendance in New Zealand schools 2011.* Wellington: Ministry of Education .

Sandel, M. J. (2012). *What money can't buy: the moral limits of markets.* New York: Farrar, Strauss and Giroux.

Scarpetta, S., Sonnet, A., and Manfredi, T. (2010). *Rising youth unemployment during the crisis: how to prevent long-term consequences on a generation?* OECD Social, Employment and Migration papers, No 106. Paris: OECD Directorate for Employment, Labour and Social Affairs.

Scott C. Esplin, (2008). Closing the Church College of New Zealand: A Case Study in International Church Education Policy. R. L. Neilsen, S. C. Harper, C. K. Manscill, and a. M. Woodger. (eds). *Regional Studies in Latter-day Saint Church History: The Pacific Isles*, pp. 161-80.

Sen, A. (1999). *Development as Freedom.* London: Oxford University Press.

Shallcrass, J. (1992). Becoming a humanist. In Humanist Society New Zealand, *Celebrating 25 Years of the Humanist Society in New Zealand.* HSNZ.

Sherman, A. L. (2002). *Empowering compassion: The strategic role of intermediary organizations in building capacity among and empowering the impact of community transformers.* Charlottesville, VA: Hudson Institute.

Shirky, C. (2008). *Here comes everybody.* New York: Penguin.

Sidorkin, A. M. (2010). Are schools improvable? A rumination on positionality. *Philosophy of Education*, pp. 278–285.

Silverton, D. (2012, July 24). Truant scheme rocks on. *Howick and Pakuranga Times.*

Sinclair, G. (2006). *Celebrating AIMHI's success.* Manukau: Counties Manukau Health.

Loren, A. (2012, August 7). Sisters giving back. Retrieved 20 August 2012, from stuff.co.nz: http://www.stuff.co.nz/auckland/local-news/manukau-courier/7422988/Sisters-giving-back

Smelt, S. (1998). *Today's Schools.* Wellington: Institute of Policy Studies, Victoria University of Wellington.

Smelt, S. (2007). Empowering schools: How to think about subsidiarity and delegation. http://www.simonsmelt.com

Smith, A. B., Grima, G., Gaffney, M., and Powell, K. (2000). *Early Childhood Education: Literature Review Report for the Ministry of Education.* Dunedin: Children's Issues Centre Manawa Rangahau Tamariki.

Smith, M., and Aitken, J. (2012). *Ministerial inquiry into the employment of a convicted sex offender in the education sector.* Report to Hon Hekia Parata, Minister of Education. . Wellington: Ministry of Education.

Snook, I. (2009, October). *Social class and educational achievement: beyond ideology.* Palmerston North: Massey University.

Snook, I., Adams, P., Adams, R., Clark, J., Codd, J., Collins, G., et al. (1999). Education reform in New Zealand 1989–1999; Is there any evidence of success? Education Policy Response Group Occasional Paper. Massey University.

Society of Local Government Managers (SOLGM). (2012, June). Submission of the Society of Local Government Managers on the Local Government Act 2002 Amendment Bill. Wellington: Society of Local Government Managers.

Solomon, T. (2007). Towards an educational analysis of Māori and Pacific Island student achievement at the Church College of New Zealand. *MAI Review 1.*

Springford, L. (2006). Tomorrow's primary schools: Time to evaluate governance alternatives? *Policy Quarterly*, 2(3), 32-39.

State Services Commission. (2011). Better Public Services: Draft issues paper – results. State Services Commission. Wellington: State Services Commission.

Statistics New Zealand. (2012). *Vulnerable children and families: Some findings from the New Zealand General Social Survey.* Wellington: Statistics New Zealand Tatauranga Aotearoa.

Statistics New Zealand. (2014). *2013 Census QuickStats about culture and identity.* Wellington: Statistics New Zealand.

Statistics New Zealand. (n.d.). Geographic hierarchy. Retrieved 12 August 2012, from Statistics New Zealand: http://www.stats.govt.nz/surveys_and_methods/methods/classifications-and-standards/geographic-hierarchy.aspx

Stern, D., Dayton, C., and Raby, M. (2010). *Career Academies: A proven strategy to prepare high school students for college and careers.* Berkeley: Career Academy Support Network, University of California at Berkeley.

Stewart, D. J., and Nolan, P. (1992). *The middle school: essential education for emerging adolescents.* Palmerston North: Educational Research and Development Centre, Massey University.

Stiglitz, J. (2013). *The price of inequality.* New York: Penguin.

Stiglitz, J. E., Sen, A., and Fitoussi, J. P. (2009). *Report by the Commission on the Measurement of Economic Performance and Social Progress.* Paris: Commission on the Measurement of Economic Performance and Social Progress.

Stone, D. A. (1989). Causal stories and the formation of policy agendas. *Political Science Quarterly*, 104(2 (Summer), pp. 281–300.

Stone, D. (2002). *Policy paradox: The art of political decision-making.* New York: Norton.

Strike, K. A. (2003). Liberty, democracy and community: Legitimacy in public education. In W. L. Boyd, and D. Miretsky (eds), *American educational governance on trial: Change and challenges.* Chicago: National Society for the Study of Education.

Sutherland, A. (2011). The relationship between school and youth offending. *Social Policy Journal of New Zealand* (37), pp. 51–69.

Sutton, A., and Airini, D. (2011). *Education in the City: A snapshot of Pasifika Education in Auckland 2011.* Auckland: COMET.

Sutton, A., and Vester, B. (2010). *Unlocking Auckland's potential: Adult literacy and numeracy skills in the new Auckland.* Manukau: City of Manukau Education Trust.

Swinney, C. (2003, October). Crystal meth—the methamphetamine problem. *Investigate* magazine.

Tamihere, J. (2011). *He Ara Whakamua. Building pathways for the future. Final Report.* Te Mahurehure Marae, Pt Chevalier, Auckland: Families Commission.

Taylor, R. (1992, March 14). The Missing 3000. *New Zealand Herald*, pp. S2, p.

Tertiary Education Commission. (2011). Poutamatia: Youth transitions between secondary and tertiary study in New Zealand. Wellington: Tertiary Education Commission.

Thomson, A. (2004, December 14). Race-based funding worth $6m says National. *New Zealand Herald.*

Thomson, G. V. (2006). *Values education in New Zealand schools.* Welllington: New Zealand Principals' Federation.

Thrupp, M. (2007). Education's 'Inconvenient Truth': Part One – Persistent Middle Class Advantage. *New Zealand Journal of Teachers' Work*, 4(2), pp. 77-88.

Thrupp, M. (2008). Education's 'Inconvenient Truth': Part Two – The middle classes have too many friends in education. *New Zealand Journal of Teachers' Work*, 5(1), pp. 54-62.

Thrupp, M. (2013, November 28). National Standards data fixation barrier to useful change. *New Zealand Herald*, p. A33.

Timperley, H. S., Robinson, V. M., and Bullard, T. (1999). *Innovation and the persistence of old solutions: intervention dilemmas for schools at risk*. Wellington: Ministry of Education.

Timperley, Helen; Parr, Judy; (eds). (2010). *Weaving evidence, inquiry and standards to build better schools*. Wellington: NZCER Press.

Townend, L. (2013, December 28). Big shoes, Sir. *Manawatu Standard*.

Trevett, C. (2012, September 10). School costs parents more. *New Zealand Herald*, p. A8.

Tunmer, W. E., Chapman, J. W., Greaney, K. T., Prochnow, J. E., and Arrow, A. W. (2013). *Why the New Zealand national literacy strategy has failed and what can be done about it*. Palmerston North: Massey University Institute of Education.

Twose, H. (2012, September 3). Success: Just the formula to bring up baby. The *New Zealand Herald*.

Unicef. (2002). *A league table of educational disadvantage in rich nations*. Innocenti Report Card No 4. Florence: Innocenti Research Centre.

University of Canterbury. (2013, August 12). Reading Recovery not responsible for underachievement. Retrieved 12 August 2013, from Scoop: http://www.scoop.co.nz/stories/ED1308/S00049/reading-recovery-not-responsible-for-underachievement.htm

Vaughan, K., Roberts, J., and Gardiner, B. (2006). Young people producing careers and identities: The first report from the Pathways and Prospects project. Welllington: NZCER.

Veblen, T. (1899 [1973]). *The Theory of the Leisure Class* with an introduction by John Kenneth Galbraith. Boston: Houghton Mifflin.

Vester, B. (2009). *The challenges of complex urban schools*. Manukau: City of Manukau Education Trust.

Waitangi Tribunal. (2012). *Matua Rautia. Report of the Kohanga Reo claim*. Waitangi Tribunal. Wellington: Waitangi Tribunal.

Wasik, B. H. (2004). *Handbook on family literacy*. Mahwah, NJ: Lawrence Earlbaum Associates.

Watson, B. (2008, October 22). Truancy warning. *North Shore Times*.

Welfare Working Group. (2011). *Reducing long-term benefit dependency: recommendations*. Wellington: Ministry of Social Development.

WestPhillylocal. (2011, May 02). Report details PAS catchment home price increase. Retrieved February 2, 2013, from WestPhillylocal: http://www.westphillylocal.com/2011/05/02/report-details-pas-catchment-home-price-increase/

Where are Auckland's best schools. (2010, July 5). Retrieved 20 August 2012, from news.msn.co.nz/haveyoursay/.../where-are-aucklands-best-schools

Whitehead, J. (2008). *Putting productivity first*. Wellington: New Zealand Treasury.

Widdowson, D., and Dixon, R. (2011). *Final Report for the Evaluation of the Parent Mentoring Project in Manukau*. Wellington: Ministry of Education .

Wiley, C. (2001). *Competent Children: Findings and issues from the first seven years*. Wellington: NZCER.

Wiley, C., and Hodgen, E. (2007). *The continuing contribution of early childhood education to young people's competency levels*. Wellington: Ministry of Education.

Wilkinson, R. G., and Pickett, K. (2009). *The Spirit Level: Why more equal societies almost always do better*. London: Allen Lane.

Wills, R. (2015). *State of Care 2015*. Wellington: Children's Commissioner.

Wilson, S. (2013, June-July). The best schools in Auckland 2013. *Metro*.

Winter, P. (2010). *Engaging families in the early childhood development story*. Victoria, New South Wales: Ministerial Council for Education, Early Childhood Development and

Youth Affairs.

Winter, P., Baker, R., Aitken, D., and Morris, J. (2012). *Review of the New Zealand Teachers Council: A teaching profession for the 21st century.* Report to Hon Hekia Parata, Minister of Education. Wellington: Ministry of Education.

Woods, P. (1979). *The divided school.* London: Routledge and Kegan Paul.

Working Group on Post Compulsory Education and Training. (1988). Report on postcompulsory education and training in New Zealand (Hawke Report). Wellington: Office of the Associate Minister of Education.

Woulfe, C. (2013, November 30). NCEA slammed by tertiary assessors. The Listener.

Woulfe, C. (2013, May 3). NCEA: All shall pass. *New Zealand Listener.*

Woulfe, C. (2014, July 12-18). The best start. *New Zealand Listener*, pp. 14-22.

Wylie, C. (2007). *School governance in New Zealand: how is it working?* Wellington: NZCER.

Wylie, C. (2012). *Vital connections: why we need more than self-managing schools.* Wellington: NZCER Press.

Wylie, C. (2013). Secondary schools in 2012: Main findings from the NZCER national survey. Wellington: NZCER.

Wylie, C., and Hogben, E. (2007). *The continuing contribution of early childhood education to young people's competency.* Wellington: New Zealand Council for Educational Research.

Wylie, C., Hodgen, E., Hipkins, R., and Vaughan, K. (2008). *On the Edge of Adulthood: Summary of Key Findings from the Competent Learners @ 16 project.* Wellington: Ministry of Education.

Wynd, D. (2014). *The revolving door: Student mobility in Auckland schools.* Auckland: Child Poverty Action Group.

Youth Law Office Tino Rangatiratanga Taitamariki. (2012). *Out of sight, out of mind: The need for an independent education review tribunal.* Youth Law Office.

Index

C

D

E

F

G

H

P

R

S

T